Copyright © 2014 CelebrityPress® LLC

All rights reserved. No part of this book may be used or reproduced in any manner whatsoever without prior written consent of the authors, except as provided by the United States of America copyright law.

Published by CelebrityPress®, Orlando, FL

CelebrityPress® is a registered trademark.

Printed in the United States of America.

ISBN: 978-0-9912143-6-5
LCCN: 2012950216

This publication is designed to provide accurate and authoritative information with regard to the subject matter covered. It is sold with the understanding that the publisher is not engaged in rendering legal, accounting, or other professional advice. If legal advice or other expert assistance is required, the services of a competent professional should be sought. The opinions expressed by the authors in this book are not endorsed by Celebrity Press® and are the sole responsibility of the authors rendering the opinion.

Most CelebrityPress® titles are available at special quantity discounts for bulk purchases for sales promotions, premiums, fundraising, and educational use. Special versions or book excerpts can also be created to fit specific needs.

For more information, please write:
CelebrityPress®
520 N. Orlando Ave, #2
Winter Park, FL 32789
or call 1.877.261.4930

Visit us online at: www.CelebrityPressPublishing.com

CONTENTS

CHAPTER 1
EQUITY AMBUSH! HOW TO AVOID THE #1 MISTAKE MOVE-UP (OR DOWN) BUYERS MAKE
By Jay Kinder 15

CHAPTER 2
TRAINING DAY: ACHIEVING THE INFORMATIONAL ADVANTAGE
By Michael Reese 21

CHAPTER 3
LUXURY
By Sally Scrimgeour 29

CHAPTER 4
NEGOTIATING FOR EVERYBODY
By Jim Keaty 37

CHAPTER 5
CHOOSE THE RIGHT AGENT... IT'S EASIER THAN YOU THINK
By Harley Dufek and Chris Pierard 45

CHAPTER 6
SELLING A HOME: THE *VALUE* OF HIRING AN EXPERT
By Andy Mulholland 55

CHAPTER 7
GETTING TO THE HEART OF THE MATTER
By Bill Morgner 63

CHAPTER 8
LOOKING GOOD: REPAIRS AND UPDATES TO MAKE BEFORE SELLING YOUR HOME
By Cyndie Gawain 71

CHAPTER 9
PRE-EMPTIVE NEGOTIATION: A STRATEGY FOR SELLERS
By Michael Swift 81

CHAPTER 10
HOW TO WIN THE UPSIDE-DOWN GAME
By Brian Pitcher 89

CHAPTER 11
"I'M NOT GOING TO GIVE IT AWAY"
By Andrew Gaydosh 97

CHAPTER 12
THE 30 DAY TEST DRIVE
By Al Stasek 107

CHAPTER 13
AN ANALYSIS OF SUCCESSFUL HOME SALES
By Tom Daves 113

CHAPTER 14
LESSONS LEARNED: A STEP-BY-STEP GUIDE THROUGH THE REAL ESTATE PROCESS
By Lucas Howard. 121

CHAPTER 15
HONESTY, THE BEST POLICY
By Beverly Herdman 129

CHAPTER 16
THE VILLAGE EXPERT ADVISOR
By Glenn Stein and Michael Veri 137

CHAPTER 17

CORE CULTURE: BUILD YOUR TEAM FROM THE INSIDE OUT TO PROVIDE THE BEST EXPERIENCE FOR CLIENTS

By Jason Irwin 145

CHAPTER 18

IN CONTROL: HOW TO PRICE YOUR HOME TO GET TOP DOLLAR

By Jason Jakus 153

CHAPTER 19

SELLING YOUR HOME THE RIGHT WAY: 3 "Ps" FOR GETTING TOP DOLLAR

By Jeremy Back 161

CHAPTER 20

8 SECRETS TO GETTING TOP DOLLAR IN ANY MARKET

By John Sellers 167

CHAPTER 21

CRACKING THE CODE ONLINE: GET THE UPPER HAND AND SAVE THOUSANDS WITH THE POWER OF THE WEB

By Carlos German 177

CHAPTER 22
NET WORKS: HOW REALTORS MUST USE TODAY'S NEW MEDIA AND TECHNOLOGY TO GET AHEAD

By Leo Albanes 185

CHAPTER 23
PRICE ISN'T EVERYTHING: BOOST YOUR ODDS OF GETTING YOUR DREAM HOME WITH THESE LITTLE-KNOWN STRATEGIES

By Marc Cormier and Tania Ivey 193

CHAPTER 24
YOUR START DOES NOT DETERMINE YOUR FINISH: HOW TO RETIRE EARLY WITH REAL ESTATE

By Tracie Tom 201

CHAPTER 25
MORE EXPOSURE AND BETTER RESOURCES = FASTER SALE AND MORE PROFITS

By Michael LaFido and Linda Feinstein 209

CHAPTER 26
SETTING THE SCENE WITH STAGING

By Paula Drake 219

CHAPTER 27
WHY A TEAM?
By Renee Butler 227

CHAPTER 28
THE NEW SELLER'S MARKET: THE TOP 3 CHALLENGES HOME BUYERS AND SELLERS FACE AND HOW TO OVERCOME THEM
By Tim Majka, Esq. 235

CHAPTER 29
WHEN YOU NEED MORE THAN JUST A REALTOR
By Jeremy Ganse 245

CHAPTER 30
PERFORMANCE OUTSELLS PROMISES: PERFECTING PRICING TO GET A HOME SOLD
By Denise Swick 253

CHAPTER 31
INVESTING IN REAL ESTATE: 6 POWER POINTS FOR SUCCESS
By George Paul Vlahakis 261

CHAPTER 32
REFRIGERATOR AND DOG CONVEY: ELEVATING NEGOTIATION TO AN ART FORM
By Justin Kiliszek 269

CHAPTER 33

SELLING WITHOUT STRESS: TAKING
THE ANXIETY OUT OF REAL ESTATE

By Ryan Smith 277

CHAPTER 34

**7 CRITICAL MARKETING FACTORS
FOR YOUR HOME SALE**

By Alex Saenger 285

CHAPTER 1

EQUITY AMBUSH! HOW TO AVOID THE #1 MISTAKE MOVE-UP (OR DOWN) BUYERS MAKE

BY JAY KINDER

After 15 years in real estate and being involved in well over 4,000 transactions, I've seen *many* devastating "equity milking" mistakes made by home sellers. But none are more challenging or as costly as the one I am about to share with you.

Once you read this chapter, you will have the knowledge and understanding of how to avoid the "landmines" you will inherently find when you sell your current home to move-up (or down) to your next home. This advice applies if you are an empty nester and want to sell your family home for something smaller, if you are relocating, or if your family is expanding and you need more space.

Without a doubt, the riskiest real estate transaction of all is the one that requires you to sell your home and potentially wind up homeless or buy your next home and end up owning two homes. This is commonly known as the "Real Estate Catch-22."

My goal in this chapter is to give you the advice you need to make the best decision possible and give you some options most sellers don't know about, as well as some negotiation tactics that can lower your risk and make this a very smooth transaction.

BUY FIRST OR SELL FIRST?

The first question you must answer is should you buy first or sell first? You are most likely facing one of the following situations, and we will go through each one in-depth.

This is an exciting opportunity! You've probably lived in your home for several years while making upgrades and family memories. Now, it's time to move up and get a larger home for yourself or your growing family, or downsize and get something more manageable. You probably have a pretty good idea of what neighborhoods interest you at this point and you are waiting for the right home to come on the market so you can pull the trigger, or maybe you have even discussed building a new home.

So now what? The idea of selling first probably doesn't seem very exciting. What would you do if your home sold too fast?

Although we have been successful on many occasions with timing the sale at the same time you find, or finish building, your new home, we also know that you are at a big disadvantage with this approach.

Let me explain. Let's say you found the perfect home and you decide to put in an offer on it. In most cases, this requires a contingency that you sell your current home first. Think about this from the sellers' perspective: how likely are you to negotiate with a buyer who has a home to sell. In most situations, you wouldn't be very excited because an escrow and potential closing is likely 90 to 120 days away. So, at what price would a seller be willing to pull their home from the market and hope your home sells so you can buy theirs? Full price. That's what!!

As a buyer with a home to sell, you have no negotiation leverage, and you are negotiating from a position of weakness instead of a position of strength. So when that perfect home comes on the market, even if you can get them to accept a contingency, sellers will likely counter with a clause in the contract that states the following. "Seller to keep their home on the market, should seller receive another offer, buyer has 72 hours to remove contingency or seller can negotiate with other offer and this contract shall become null and void." Ouch!!

Imagine the home of your dreams gets another offer. You now have two choices: Go to a local bank, preferably one you bank with and ask for what is called a bridge loan, or let your dream home go.

THE BRIDGE LOAN ROUTE

A bridge loan allows you to replace your current mortgage and buy the new home all in one transaction. So instead of having two mortgage payments, you just have one interest payment temporarily until your home is sold. Let's discuss the pros and cons of this loan.

Pros

- You can negotiate from a position of strength on your new home.
- You have walk-away leverage.
- You don't have to feel pressured to sell your home at a discount.
- You can move into your new home and get your home market ready.
- You don't miss out on the home of your dreams.

Cons

- The bridge loan, although temporary, will have a higher interest rate.
- Interest rates could rise in the interim until permanent financing is obtained.
- The additional cost of closing twice.
- What if your home doesn't sell?

This isn't for every situation, but it is a good option in many cases. Having a Certified Expert Advisor™ review your situation is strongly advised. You can find a CEA online at: www.NAEA.com. It is required training for every person in my company.

Back to our situation.

If you waited to prearrange this financing, you are "under the gun" with 72 hours to remove your contingency. This is stressful and very unlikely, especially given today's strict lending guidelines.

My suggestion is that you do this upfront and make your offer noncontingent using the bridge loan as your strategy if you are in an equity position in your current home.

I've seen too many sellers lose their dream home, pay too much for their dream home, or fire-sale their current home just to make the deal happen. Doing the work on the front end will save you money and remove stress when making that move to a larger or smaller home.

THE CONTINGENT SELLER ROUTE

Another option you have that most real estate agents don't tell you is being a contingent seller. This can work well in a hot real estate market. You prepare your home for the market and list it prior to your finding your dream home or prior to the completion of your new home. Hang in there with me on this. You list your home contingent upon you finding a home within seven days of the time you accept their offer.

With this strategy you have the ability to counter the closing date to match your needs and shop comfortably for what it is that you are looking for. If the perfect home isn't out there, you can cancel the offer or ask the buyer for more time. It takes the right buyer for your home, but if you have the right buyer, you are selling at the top of the market and you are in total control.

This also gives you the walk-away leverage. Not "having to sell" allows you to negotiate from a position of strength.

In every situation, it is best that you go over your strategy with a Certified Expert Advisor™ and member of the National Association of Expert Advisors®. This will assure that you have a skilled negotiator and contract specialist in your corner.

If you are reading this book, you will need to go online and download a copy of *The 7 Mistakes Most Homesellers Make When Selling Their Home* at: www.kinderreese.com. If you downloaded this chapter from the website, I have already included this report for your review.

If you would like to reach my office directly to go over your home buying and home selling strategy, you can reach us at (972) 625-7355.

About Jay and Michael

Jay Kinder

Michael Reese

More than 10 years ago, Jay Kinder and Michael Reese inadvertently caught up with each other one summer afternoon at Lake Texoma. Real estate was the discussion of the day as a young Jay Kinder shared how he sold 233 homes the previous year to a very open-minded Michael Reese. Who knew that a chance encounter would turn into the wildly successful partnership that is now Kinder Reese Real Estate Advisors?

Since that day, Michael, Jay and their teams have sold more than 4,250 homes combined. Together, they've brought in more than $18,000,000 in commissions for their real estate businesses, and haven't looked back since that fateful day.

Both Jay and Michael have been members of *Realtor Magazine's* prestigious "30 under 30" group. They have also both been ranked within the Top 100 of the 400 most successful real estate teams in North America by Real *Trends* of *The Wall Street Journal*.

Individually, Jay has established himself as one of the top agents in the world, selling more than 3,000 homes while capturing 14% market share in Lawton, Oklahoma. In 2007, Jay was named #2 in the World for Coldwell Banker, competing with over 120,000 realtors – being the youngest to ever obtain this achievement. The results don't stop there. In 2007, Jay was also ranked #1 in Oklahoma and #2 in the Southern Region including over 1,700 realtors from 14 states. He has been recognized with the honor of #1 Sales Associate in Oklahoma in 2002-2010 before opening his new company, Jay Kinder Real Estate Experts in 2011.

Michael has also enjoyed immense success as one of Keller Williams' top 50 agents worldwide. He is regularly ranked as one of the Top 5 teams in the Southwest Region for Keller Williams, and he and his team recently broke the record for buyer sales for the Keller Williams he worked out of in Frisco, Texas – before going independent as the Michael Reese Home Selling Team. Michael earned $1,000,000 in GCI after only his 6th year in the business and he's never made less since then.

In 2004, Jay and Michael started Kinder Reese Real Estate Partners with the aim of helping success-minded agents like themselves create the business and lifestyle that virtually every real estate agent dreams about. Kinder Reese currently serves more than 23,000 agents across North America with its revolutionary business model and innovative business systems.

In 2011, they co-founded the National Association of Expert Advisors® (NAEA), which offers the most prestigious designations that a real estate agent in today's market can have. The Certified Home Selling Advisor® designee has been recognized as an agent with a highly differentiated, proven, repeatable system to get sellers up to 18% more than the methods of average real estate agents. The NAEA's goal is to provide the highest level of education, training and business materials to agents who are truly serious about bringing the absolute best consumer experience to today's home sellers and buyers.

The Certified Home Selling Advisor® designation is a four-part certification process that helps today's real estate agents learn what they need to truly distinguish themselves from their competition and establish themselves as the true, number one choice for real estate consumers in their marketplace.

They are both best-selling authors on Amazon's top ten list of books for small businesses with their book Trendsetters and they can be seen on NBC, ABC, CBS, CNBC and other major networks as Expert Advisors™ on the television show, *The New Masters of Real Estate*.

Currently, Jay lives in Frisco, Texas with his wife, Amber, and has three sons, Brayden, Karsen and Riggs. Michael lives in Frisco, Texas with his wife Stacey and their two sons Cache and Crew.

www.kinderreese.com
Tel: (972) 625-7355

CHAPTER 2

TRAINING DAY: ACHIEVING THE INFORMATIONAL ADVANTAGE

BY MICHAEL REESE

Let's face it, the world is changing! What's more is that technology is driving changes and collapsing time so that it allows them to happen faster and faster. Information is everywhere, and we now have instant access to more information than we can ever assimilate, yet at the same time, information has become so important to our lives that we couldn't live without it.

In the midst of all that information you will find countless experts who have made themselves similarly indispensable. Doctors, lawyers, contractors, auto mechanics—they all enjoy an informational advantage. And they use it to help you in ways they never could before while also boosting their business in ways they had never thought of before!

As a real estate agent, coach, and co-founder of The National Association of Expert Advisors®, the changes happening today could not have come at a better time. The problem facing the real estate industry is that a majority of the population of real estate professionals have made their living on information that was once exclusive, and now that same information is readily available to the public.

If you surveyed hundreds of professional real estate agents on what documented strategy they use to help their clients maximize their real estate investment, many would instantly think you were up to some sort of shenanigans. All these professionals have a different process for selling a home, even when they work for the same company or the same broker. Ultimately, this leaves the consumer desperately confused about where to go or who to use.

Imagine if agents who helped the home buyer find a home had to compel them to pay the closing costs upfront and out of their own pocket. How many of the thousands, or hundreds of thousands, of agents would be able to present the value they provide in the transaction well enough to their clients to justify their fees?

Not many. Why, you ask?

Let's start by understanding how most traditional agents get into the business in the first place and what these agents do all day. Most of them get into the business by default. Many because of some life tragedy, such as the loss of job, a painful divorce, or, in some cases, just looking for something to do.

A traditional agent spends their time chasing new leads or prospects, trying to find someone to help with their home purchase or sale. Their success is based not on how well they know or do their job professionally, but on how many new clients they can catch, or call every day. Would you want your doctor to be good at chasing clients or performing the duties you hire them to do? Traditional agents spend time doing the wrong things and, in the end, it can cost both them and their clients "the deal."

The shocking fact is most agents go hungry. They lose sleep at night hoping someone else sells their listing, or a friend or family member sends them another referral. And, sadly, they never clearly understand what is happening to them and what to do about it. The Internet is stripping what I like to refer to as the AFA (Average Frustrated Agents) from their traditional tool and informational advantage, the MLS—which is, simply said, their inventory of homes.

It wasn't long ago that all the information on homes was printed in a book exclusively for agents. Consumers greatly valued any access to the information, because the AFA's controlled all the supply. This exclusivity gave them great job security and an ironclad competitive advantage.

Today, the internet has a way of commoditizing services that hide behind inflated economic value to the consumer. This has happened in one industry after another. From life insurance to used cars, the web has eliminated the expert's upper hand by giving once-exclusive information to the online masses. In many cases, the industries have adapted to the new paradigm, creating new opportunities for success in the process. But some industries have been slow to change—real estate among them.

Now don't get me wrong, and certainly don't feel bad for them. The industry is fighting! And the war is being fought in Washington. Agents are protected by The National Association of Realtors (NAR), which is the lobbying group listed at No. 4 on opensecrets.org's list of political heavy hitters. But lobbying for agents, while important, is an invisible process to the frustrated consumer.

As the consumer continues to find the home they eventually buy on their own, online, AFAs know that the only value they have left to offer the home buyer is the same as a taxicab. As buyers become more savvy and move into the driver's seat, more of them are realizing that making a good investment and buying a home is synonymous! And to make sure they get the best deal on such a huge transaction, a cab driver just doesn't fit the profile of a good decision partner.

So why do some make great real estate investments and others end up settling for the best of today's options? Why do most buyers end up doing business with the first agent they come in contact with? Buyers find a house first, then find the agent by the phone number advertised for more information on that specific property. Or even worse, they use a friend or family member to handle the transaction.

If you subscribe to this idea of a real estate transaction being an investment, then how do you make good investments? Would you pick your family's financial advisor based on their relationship to you? Who would you pick if one choice clearly had a better, proven financial strategy for families with your same goals? Would your decision take into consideration any of their skills and specialized knowledge derived from extensive continued training?

You see, picking an agent you like is important, but real estate investors work with the agents who have a system for finding the best deals. Whether they like you or not, the best real estate investors interview agents to find the one with the best training, knowledge, and system to support their goals. They don't work with someone unless they have demonstrated that they can help them get an acceptable return on investment.

To help an investor get a good deal, the agent must have the highest level of knowledge and be able to evaluate the property's true worth after taking into consideration all the factors, and detractors, that will allow them to purchase the property under value.

The art of being a "Certified Expert Advisor™" is understanding all the variables that go into, not just selling, but also buying a home. Because, frequently, the home seller needs to buy a home and vice versa. How do you manage this process if you are a seller whose time frame to buy is dictated by something that is out of your control: the sale of your current home.

Most agents call managing both the buy and sale of a home *The Real Estate Catch-22*. Cracking the real estate code is understanding every element of selling and buying and using both to the advantage of your client. You can buy a home under market value, but if you lack the skills to attract the top offer for the home they are selling within a short period of time, your client might not be able to realize the benefits of finding a home under market value.

Even if you have the money to invest, that does not translate into making a good investment. When a person has a home to sell and is in a position to take the profits of that sale to reinvest in another property, the one element that impacts this process more than any other variable is the sale price of the existing home.

So why does one home sell while others seem to remain on the market like potted plants? Well, first my observation has proved to me that no home seller wants to list their home, only to have it expire in six months with minimal activity. I understand that, ultimately, the homeowner will dictate what investment and repairs get made to the home. So you hold the keys to implementing the smart decisions that dictate if a home attracts the best offer in a timely manner and if the sale completes once an offer is made.

Why is it if you ask ten agents to determine the value of your home, do they all give you a different answer? Why do some agents recommend you stage a home while others advise to lower the price? Does carpet in the bedroom or an unstained fence help you attract a high or low offer? How does timing play into all of this if a deal of a lifetime comes on the market, but you need the proceeds from the sale of your home to buy the next one?

It would seem that after 100 of years of transactional data, someone would've put together a checklist of what exactly to do and in what scenario to enhance the value and marketability of a home. There actually has been market data that has proved the final appraised value of the home can be influenced by investing in the condition. Taking the right steps upfront will not only enhance the value of a home but also position it to sell more quickly—in any market. All the recommendations an agent makes, or fails to make, is a result of experience and training. Yet, as mentioned above, the average agent typically fails to acquire both in ways that effectively assist their clients.

Your agent should have several types of knowledge. The most important is market knowledge. They need to have a good understanding of not only the national market but also the local market. Specifically: the local market data pertaining to the price point at which you are buying or selling. They need to understand how the market affects your decisions that go into buying or selling your next home. A Certified Expert Advisor™ understands that consumers don't make bad decisions; they simply get poorly advised.

Cracking the Real Estate Code, said differently, is picking the right agent. There is nothing that you do that has a more significant impact on the home you buy or the outcome of listing your home for sale than the agent you hire. Agents have a choice to invest in themselves like doctors or lawyers, or any motivated professional. The right kind of training to empower them to effectively and accurately analyze, synthesize and communicate the key elements of real estate transactions to their clients, and ultimately, determine the client's ability to achieve their desired goal. It is this training, properly applied, that creates a new informational advantage for the truly professional agent!

The most respected certification and training investment a professional agent can make is in becoming a Certified Expert Advisor™. By completing both the Certified Home Buying Advisor® and Certified Home Selling Advisor® courses, they acquire a true informational advantage over the average agent. But more importantly, they become a highly effective resource that is capable of counseling and directing their clients to understand what it will take to achieve their goals and maximize their ability to accomplish them!

About Michael and Jay

Michael Reese

Jay Kinder

More than 10 years ago, Jay Kinder and Michael Reese inadvertently caught up with each other one summer afternoon at Lake Texoma. Real estate was the discussion of the day as a young Jay Kinder shared how he sold 233 homes the previous year to a very open-minded Michael Reese. Who knew that a chance encounter would turn into the wildly successful partnership that is now Kinder Reese Real Estate Advisors?

Since that day, Michael, Jay and their teams have sold more than 4,250 homes combined. Together, they've brought in more than $18,000,000 in commissions for their real estate businesses, and haven't looked back since that fateful day.

Both Jay and Michael have been members of *Realtor Magazine's* prestigious "30 under 30" group. They have also both been ranked within the Top 100 of the 400 most successful real estate teams in North America by Real *Trends* of *The Wall Street Journal*.

Individually, Jay has established himself as one of the top agents in the world, selling more than 3,000 homes while capturing 14% market share in Lawton, Oklahoma. In 2007, Jay was named #2 in the World for Coldwell Banker, competing with over 120,000 realtors – being the youngest to ever obtain this achievement. The results don't stop there. In 2007, Jay was also ranked #1 in Oklahoma and #2 in the Southern Region including over 1,700 realtors from 14 states. He has been recognized with the honor of #1 Sales Associate in Oklahoma in 2002-2010 before opening his new company, Jay Kinder Real Estate Experts in 2011.

Michael has also enjoyed immense success as one of Keller Williams' top 50 agents worldwide. He is regularly ranked as one of the Top 5 teams in the Southwest Region for Keller Williams, and he and his team recently broke the record for buyer sales for the Keller Williams he worked out of in Frisco, Texas – before going independent as the Michael Reese Home Selling Team. Michael earned $1,000,000 in GCI after only his 6th year in the business and he's never made less since then.

In 2004, Jay and Michael started Kinder Reese Real Estate Partners with the aim of helping success-minded agents like themselves create the business and lifestyle that virtually every real estate agent dreams about. Kinder Reese currently serves more than 23,000 agents across North America with its revolutionary business model and innovative business systems.

In 2011, they co-founded the National Association of Expert Advisors® (NAEA), which offers the most prestigious designations that a real estate agent in today's market can have. The Certified Home Selling Advisor® designee has been recognized as an agent with a highly differentiated, proven, repeatable system to get sellers up to 18% more than the methods of average real estate agents. The NAEA's goal is to provide the highest level of education, training and business materials to agents who are truly serious about bringing the absolute best consumer experience to today's home sellers and buyers.

The Certified Home Selling Advisor® designation is a four-part certification process that helps today's real estate agents learn what they need to truly distinguish themselves from their competition and establish themselves as the true, number one choice for real estate consumers in their marketplace.

They are both best-selling authors on Amazon's top ten list of books for small businesses with their book Trendsetters and they can be seen on NBC, ABC, CBS, CNBC and other major networks as Expert Advisors™ on the television show, *The New Masters of Real Estate*.

Currently, Jay lives in Frisco, Texas with his wife, Amber, and has three sons, Brayden, Karsen and Riggs. Michael lives in Frisco, Texas with his wife Stacey and their two sons Cache and Crew.

www.kinderreese.com
Tel: (972) 625-7355

CHAPTER 3

LUXURY

BY SALLY SCRIMGEOUR

Noun: the state of great comfort and extravagant living

Synonyms: <u>opulence</u>, luxuriousness, sumptuousness, <u>grandeur</u>, <u>magnificence</u>, <u>splendor</u>, lavishness, the lap of luxury, a bed of roses, (the land of) milk and honey

Great comfort and extravagant living. That is exactly what luxury homes mean to those in the market to buy or sell them. More than a "house," luxury homes represent a lifestyle. Luxury homebuyers expect to feel and to envision the life they will have in that home and luxury home sellers must be prepared to help the buyers experience that dream.

That's where I come in. As a Realtor for over 15 years, I have mastered the luxury home market and created a foolproof process to bring buyers and sellers together. Both sides in the luxury market desire the same things: opulence, sumptuousness and lavishness. The luxury market has changed slightly in recent years; buyers increasingly want not just the grandeur of a large home, but also, the amenities not before available.

Call me the luxury home matchmaker, but my role is to bring the parties together with a specific list of needs that each party wants fulfilled by the other. Knowing what each side in the negotiation needs, and figuring out how to get a win for both can be a challenge. But, if you begin with an understanding that certain "hard limits" are not negotiable, the rest will fall into place. What the seller offers and the buyer wants usually meet somewhere in the middle. To ensure that happens, it is necessary to understand the needs lists for both sides. Much of what homebuyers and sellers want is the same for any home sale, so if you are not currently in the market for luxury real estate, don't worry. You will still be able to utilize most of this valuable information. I'll begin with what luxury home sellers should do to entice buyers.

When listing a luxury home, you must familiarize yourself with what homebuyers want at your price point. Remember, luxury homebuyers are not looking only for ideal floorplan and a certain number of bedrooms and bathrooms. Luxury homebuyers desire a feeling they get from the home; they want a certain vibe. The seller's job is to help the home express the lifestyle it offers. The home will better express the lifestyle possible there if the seller pays careful attention to:

1. Staging:

Vacant homes can sell, but they usually will not sell as quickly or for as much money as they would if the seller stages the home. Think of staging a home as dressing it for success. When I bring a client to see a home, I am bringing them to a first interview with the home. The buyer here is looking for the home to fill a position for them. They have an idea in their head of what type of home they want to "hire" for the job, but the right candidate will have that something extra, that sparkle that the other candidates do not. An unstaged home arrives for the interview in a basic, navy blue suit. A staged home has polished shoes, the perfect tie and qualifications beyond that which the buyer was originally seeking. Suddenly, the home wows the prospective buyer.

Let's look at staging a master bedroom as an example. First, we remove all the personal touches from the room like family photos and anything that creates surface clutter. The buyer cannot see himself in this bedroom with the seller's possessions front and center. Next, we arrange the furniture in unconventional ways that draw attention to the possibilities of the master bedroom as an oasis. We might move some furniture away from walls, for example moving a small loveseat and chair grouping into a conversation group set off by an area rug. The move evokes the possibility of a quiet chat together after a long day at the office or chasing the children. We infuse the room with several levels of lighting, overhead lighting with a chandelier, a floor lamp next to the reading chair, and taller, bedside lamps with 3-way bulbs to create layers of lighting that set the appropriate mood.

Next, we head into the master bathroom for some lifestyle infusion. We might remove bath toys from the garden tub and add rolled spa towels and scented candles of varying heights so that a buyer can see themselves taking a relaxing soak that the seller may never actually have taken in that tub. If the tub has never provided a scented bubble bath or an hour-long soak, no worries. The jetted tub will not ever tell and the buyer will be none the wiser.

I usually employ professional home stagers to assist my clients when they list their homes. Professional stagers know current trends in color and style, and offer creative ways to repurpose existing furniture and accessories to maximize their impact in a space. The stager highlights the home's strengths while diminishing the home's weaknesses.

2. DeClutter:

Before a home stager can stage a home in its full grandeur, there must be open space with which to work. Clutter kills the mood, especially in a luxury home. Removing things from the floor, from countertops and from on top of furniture opens up the space. It (almost) goes without saying, but dog toys strewn about the floor and loose papers on countertops will detract from the travertine flooring and the granite countertops. Pack it up for the move and hide the boxes.

3. Deep Clean:

I call this a toothbrush cleaning. When you list a home, you need to clean more thoroughly than the cleaning you do for day-to-day living. Professionals will deep clean and reach surfaces that are often overlooked. When was the last time you cleaned that crystal chandlier in the foyer? This is the perfect time to determine if you can bleach the kitchen or bathroom grout back to snowy whiteness or if it needs to be removed and regrouted.

4. Lighting:

Lighting influences how a buyer will see the home, both its strengths and its flaws. Sellers can created the right ambiance in each room by increasing wattage of lightbulbs, adding floor lamps, placing additional decorative lamps in the kitchen or bathroom, or by opening blinds and curtains to allow natural light to penetrate. Conversely, bright sunshine coming through a window might over-heat a room or cast an uncomfortable, harsh light. Diffusing the light through a sheer curtain might soften the appearance and make the room more inviting.

5. Paint:
Neutral is not always better. While a comfortable neutral pallette might appeal to more people, buyers in the luxury market are not looking for boring. Luxury buyers want rooms that feel luxurious, right down to the paint on the walls. Be mindful of local color trends and use paint to create an element of excitement or coziness depending on the space.

6. Furniture:
Nice furniture groupings add to the value of the space. Worn pieces, while well loved by the sellers, could change the way a buyer sees the entire room. Renting high-end furniture might cost additional money in the short run, but they are a marketing expense that will yield long-term gain at close.

7. Artwork:
Nothing brings a room to life like the perfect piece of artwork. Many sellers make the mistake of hanging all their art on walls. The right picture perched elegantly on an easel or a table by the window adds life to the room and accentuates the location where it rests.

Buyers will notice all the details about the home that the seller has so painstakingly addressed from the list above. They might also be looking for things the seller may never have considered. Sometimes trends influence what buyers seek in their luxury home. In the past, luxury buyers' key concern was square footage. Today, those same buyers will often trade square footage for added bonus features that did not even exist a few years ago. Here are just a few buyer wish-list items trending now.

8. Smart Home Technology:
First, we wanted our cars and cellphones to be "smart," now we want our houses to be smart too. Smart technology makes day-to-day operations in a home more efficient. It can include the ability to adjust the home's heating and cooling settings remotely from anywhere. That may not seem like a necessity, unless you are traveling halfway around the world for business and hear about sub-zero arctic air headed toward your home. However, the ability to turn on faucets

or turn up the heat to keep pipes from freezing might become very important, very quickly. Innovative controls mean that while you are working, you could turn on your oven to preheat or begin cooking your dinner.

Smart features are not only for convenience. Induction cooktops, for example, double as a safety feature by heating only when the metal cookware makes contact with the element, thereby eliminating the risks associated with a conventional stove. Smart water features and faucets turn on and off with motion to save water and some faucets provide larger droplets to create the *feeling* of more water while actually using less.

9. Outdoor Spaces:

Buyers desire magnificent outdoors living spaces in which to relax and entertain. Firepits, professional-chef caliber outdoor kitchens complete with wine coolers and saunas by the swimming pool are just some of the add-ons attracting buyers to luxury homes. If the patio with Italian marble columns is buried under five feet of snow, buyers won't be able to picture themselves lounging next to the statue of Venus while drinking a martini in the evening. Sellers might want to pay for snow removal to uncover the beauty or, at the very least, provide pictures of the buried features.

10. High-End Features:

Buyers expect high-end features in a luxury home. An excellent Realtor is responsible for pointing out those features so the buyer can check them off his wish list. I generally call attention to the interesting but overlooked features such as steam-showers, surround-sound systems, media rooms, jetted tubs, in-floor heating systems, soft-close cabinets and drawers, and commercial grade appliances. Buyers love these features, so you don't want them to miss them.

11. Professional Landscaping:

Curb appeal is always worth the money spent on professional landscaping. The pros know how to highlight a home's best architectural features with landscaping and lighting. Buyers want a home that looks great during the day and at night. Don't forget the importance of outdoor lighting. A home should look inviting by day and by night.

After addressing both the things sellers should do to improve their home's ability to sell and the buyers' wish list, the Realtor's job kicks into high gear. Without the right marketing, buyers will never see the home. Some Realtors list houses, we market them and our Marketing makes the magic happen.

When we market a home, we begin with **professional photography** of the luxury home. Professional photos capture the subtle nuances of the home in ways that a homeowner's quick snapshots cannot hope to achieve. Professional photographs of features like the wine cellar, the gourmet kitchen and the outdoor entertaining spaces paint a picture of the lifestyle the buyer will have in the home. They convey the opulent and rewarding lifestyle the home offers.

Coldwell Banker luxury property specialists handle more than $100 million in upper bracket home sales every day. We market to the right buyers using resources like *Distinctive Homes* and *Previews Homes & Estates* magazines. We recognize that more than 90% of homebuyers today search for homes on the Internet. We achieve superior online marketing results by combining SEO (search engine optimization) efforts with a distribution of our home listings to over 600 real estate Web sites. We use our internal network of 1,800+ sales associates to help match buyers and sellers, facilitating transactions for those moving up, downsizing, and relocating. We never forget for a second that the ultimate goal is bringing buyers and sellers together. The more marketing opportunities we create, the more likely we'll have a successful transaction, and satisfied customers. With that in mind, we created: **www.MinneapolisHomeListings.com** – a dynamic Web site with a robust homebuyer search, and more exposure for our seller's homes.

"Luxury" encompasses more than fulfilling needs. Luxury homes provide a magnificent lifestyle where dreams become realities. Through the magical intervention of the right Realtor, sellers and buyers become part of the alchemy of dreams coming true.

About Sally

As a successful Realtor since 1999, Sally Scrimgeour utilizes her Fortune 500 training background to provide exceptional customer service for her clients. When she moved her family across country, Sally experienced firsthand what it's like to be on the client side of a real estate transaction and was determined to make a difference in the real estate industry. She obtained her real estate license and has been committed to providing her knowledge and expertise to her clients ever since.

Serving the Twin Cities metro area for more than 15 years as a Realtor with Coldwell Banker Burnet, she has earned a reputation for tackling big challenges and getting great results. Sally has been awarded the distinction of being part of Coldwell Banker Burnet's President Club for numerous years. *Mpls. St. Paul Magazine* and *Twin Cities Business Journal* have recognized her as a *Super Real Estate Agent,* while her clients have identified her as a real estate agent demonstrating exceptional ability and service. This honor represents fewer than 7% of all licensed real estate agents in Minnesota.

By offering clients her in-depth knowledge of the local housing market, expert negotiation skills and professional home staging assistance, she provides stellar service to both homebuyers and sellers. Sally has also become well known for her marketing strategies—which utilize traditional methods and advanced, innovative technology and tools.

Sally believes in honesty and spends one-on-one time with her clients by counseling and educating them about the market. When working with sellers, she discusses the importance of pre-emptive negotiations. She has a proven, repeatable system that works. When working with buyers, she listens to them and finds the right community and home that meets their needs.

Understanding the challenges faced when making an important real estate decision, Sally's approach is to facilitate and expertly negotiate real estate transactions with skill, knowledge and integrity. Her goal is to create a smooth, successful transaction that all clients deserve.

When not doing real estate, Sally and her husband, Jim, who is also her real estate partner, enjoy spending time with their four children and their families. The family can also be found hitting the ski slopes, hiking, golfing and enjoying boating on Lake Minnetonka and Lake Waconia.

Contact Sally at:
Sally Scrimgeour
11455 Viking Drive, Ste. 200
Eden Prairie, MN 55344
Tel: (952) 200-9461

CHAPTER 4

NEGOTIATING FOR EVERYBODY

BY JIM KEATY

"Let us never negotiate out of fear. But let us never fear to negotiate."
~John F. Kennedy

As a top real estate agent with one of the fastest-growing firms in Louisiana, I love my job, but it can be overwhelming for those who don't understand the basics of real estate, especially the nuances of negotiating.

Good negotiation is an art form. Its take time, skill and practice. However, at its core, negotiating is simply understanding people, making the connection to work through differences and figuring out how to close the gap with problems.

Every new agent that comes to work with me seems fearful to negotiate during their first deals. There is nothing to fear in working through the details of a deal, if you keep in mind a few basic steps.

BE PREPARED

The prepared person will always outsell someone who isn't. There has to be a strategy for achieving what you and your client want. Enter into each negotiation with the mentality that you have nothing to lose and if you don't get the property you want, then you will leave in the same place you were before. Keep emotion out of a property until negotiations are complete. This is a business transaction until the deal is done.

Remember, the negotiation process begins long before any official offer is made. Part of any strategy should be ascertaining as much information as possible on the property and the reason for the sale. Ask questions and then ask more questions. Knowing the motive for the sale will allow you to prepare to negotiate and get your client close to a price they are willing to pay that will be accepted by the seller.

> *"A negotiator should observe everything. You must be part Sherlock Holmes, part Sigmund Freud."* ~Victor Kiam

I have many new agents who are so excited to have a deal on the table that they forget to find out crucial elements: what is their client's bottom line, what is their timeline and what is most important to them. Once you have this information, then outline your opponent's agenda: what are their preferences, alternatives, timeline and bottom line?

While this is a business transaction, don't ever forget people often make big decisions based on emotion and feelings. Regardless of the reason for making a move, there will always be one of two emotional connections to the decision: pain or pleasure.

With pain, they are usually moving to reduce frustration. For example, the commute to work is too long, there is not enough space, there is too much space, the neighbors are a problem, or the most difficult, a relationship has ended. With pleasure, they want to be closer to work, closer to family, around better weather, or closer to a favorite pastime, or a relationship is dictating a new place.

Whatever the reason, get to the root of it and know the underlying reason for the move. Understanding the intent and the motive of a move will always allow you to present information in a manner that relates to what is most important and allow both parties to rethink and adjust the price to a place that is acceptable.

BE RESPECTFUL, LIKABLE AND POSITIVE

I can't tell you how many times I've been in negotiations on a piece of property and when the realtor representing the other party didn't get what they wanted, they became flat out rude. *Don't ever lose your cool in the room.* Stay calm, honestly communicate, and do everything possible to understand the other side's position. I say it again, no matter how bad it is, *don't ever lose your cool in the room.* No one benefits from it.

Good negotiators are constantly looking for opportunities to enhance the relationship and strengthen their position. Pay attention to your opponent. Sometimes don't talk, just sit back and listen to what they want. Often times, when you stop talking about your needs and focus on your opponent's, things can become clear for everyone, and a common point can be found.

And while we are on the commonality issue, remember "Mirror and Match." Always do your best to act, dress and sound like your opponent. If your opponent is dressed down, dress down. If your opponent is dressed up, suit up. Something as simple as wardrobe will make your opponent relate to you.

If the other side feels a connection, they are more likely to work toward a deal that is satisfactory for everyone. If no one is able to relate on a personal level and either side feels disrespected, it is highly unlikely either side will be motivated to close the deal.

INVENT OPTIONS FOR MUTUAL GAIN— NEGOTIATE EVERYTHING

Start the negotiation off with as many terms as possible. Appliances and items like the refrigerator, washer, dryer, yard furniture, yard art, home warranty, and others should all be in the deal. This gives you more terms to negotiate with and you want the list to feel expansive at first glance. The more you seem to want, the better. Let me explain.

Odds are that most of things on your initial list are not important to the big picture, but anything you give up in the counter-offer may put you in a better position. The more options that are not really deal-breakers, the better.

For example, I always ask the seller to pay for a $500 home warranty in every offer I make, whether the client really needs it or not. Some sellers counter, not willing to pay for the home warranty, but in their minds, my buyer is giving up something.

Each item or term you can negotiate is a battle, and sometimes it is smart strategy to let your opponent win a few battles if the end result is you win the war. The perception of wins and losses is important to some agents, and there are many agents who feel that if they won most of their term negotiations, it is a good deal for their client and will bring the deal to escrow and eventually closing.

PAY ATTENTION AND UNDERSTAND ANCHORS

Very few real estate agents truly understand the bargaining dynamic known as "anchoring and adjustment." What this involves is setting boundaries, mental and tangible, for negotiation.

Here's an example from a transaction I recently handled that explains anchoring and adjustment pretty clearly. A couple I was representing listed their house for $400,000. The first offer from a broker came in at $275,000. Obviously it was too low, and some realtors might have been offended, but for explanation's sake, if I had taken the offer seriously, the negotiation would now have high and low anchors set at $400,000 and $275,000.

In reality, I responded that the $275,000 was not a reasonable offer, and the buyers needed to increase their offer, substantially, to even warrant further discussion. The next offer from the buyer was $330,000. We countered at $395,000. The buyers countered with $340,000. At this point, the buyer's agent tried to argue that they had increased their offer $60,000. I very politely reminded the agent that the first very low offer was not taken into serious consideration and that $330,000 was what we considered their opening offer.

Using the anchor method, I argued that the seller had come down $5,000 and the buyer had come up only $10,000, and we were not obligated to come down $35,000 to meet in the middle. The buyer then began negotiating in a more realistic range and we were able to adjust and get our seller much closer to the $400,000 anchor they wanted.

POWER OF SILENCE: USING SILENCE AS A TACTIC

Any good reporter knows that the most powerful technique they can use to get an interview to talk is silence. It is not by accident that interviewers often let dead air stand in the room to make a subject feel uncomfortable and want to fill the silence with more information that should ever be given. The same rule applies when negotiating. Never feel obligated to respond quickly to any offer. The only thing a fast response ensures, unless it is a final offer, is that your client is desperate to get the deal done.

Never be afraid to slow down, be quiet or even suspend negotiations. It sends the message that there are other options and puts you in the position of control and power.

Silence can and will put pressure on the other side to act, often when they don't want to, and lets the other side know you are fully aware of what you are doing. As human beings, our natural habits teach us to respond to everything and to do it quickly. A confident negotiator appreciates what Simon and Garfunkel profoundly referred to as "The Sound of Silence."

> *"Never forget the power of silence, that massively disconcerting pause which goes on and on and may last induce an opponent to babble and backtrack nervously."*
> ~Lance Morrow

DON'T EVER LOSE YOUR COOL

> *"The most difficult thing in any negotiation, almost, is making sure that you strip it of the emotion and deal with the facts."*
> ~Howard Baker

If you didn't get it from earlier in this article, let me repeat myself: Losing your cool is *never* acceptable. Acting unprofessional, no matter how far south the deal is going, won't just lose you one piece of business; it can and will lose you plenty of future business as well. Losing your cool equals losing your reputation. Reputations are like matches. Once you blow out a match, you can't relight it. The same goes for your reputation. Once you ruin it, there is no going back and ever completely repairing the damage.

That being said...

> *"Anger can be an effective negotiating tool, but only as a calculated act, never as a reaction."*
> ~Mark McCormack

Negotiation is about knowing what you want, going after it, and respecting the other person in the process. In essence, it's all about compromise. This means looking out for yourself, but also being willing to bend to satisfy both parties.

Negotiating, done correctly, builds professional relationships. It does not burn bridges. There are many routes to a final destination, so make sure your road map has plenty of options to circumvent detours if you fail to reach an agreement at first.

BE WILLING TO WALK AWAY

As a buyer's agent, even if it's the house of your client's dreams, if the seller won't come down to the maximum price you have set for your budget, walk away. As difficult as it may be, you have to keep emotions out of the equation to avoid overpaying.

Taking a strong stand, more often than not, will get talks moving because no agent wants a potential buyer to walk away. And even if you do walk and no offer is made, just relax and be patient. More often than not, you will get a call a few days later looking to restart negotiations.

Stay hard to this rule—don't overpay for a property. It will put you and your client in an awkward situation. Real estate is a word of mouth industry, and if the word is you overpay, you might as well start looking for a new job.

DON'T EVER GLOAT, DON'T EVER BRAG

The deal is done. The papers are signed. Don't ever do the dance of joy in public or be foolish enough to say you would have done the deal for less. And yes, I have actually witnessed agents to do this.

As NFL great Jerry Rice once told Terrell Owens after an Owens' touchdown antic: "Act like you've been there before." In other words, be professional all the time—no matter what.

Gloating not only makes you look amateurish, but the other agent will get revenge in one way or the other —I promise. Realtors talk. You know that. I know that. And an "Owens-like" agent will be the subject of many an email and phone call. The fallout isn't pretty. Future offers for other homes will generate no response, and potential clients will be warned about your antics. Retribution isn't worth it.

Be a professional—first, last and always.

FINAL THOUGHTS

Any business, whether it's real estate or selling paper, for example, is about relationships. In the age of smartphones, we are quickly losing the ability to talk to one another and connect on a personal level. Maybe I am old fashioned, but I hope we return to a mentality where human contact is placed at an equal value as a text message or an email. Getting to really know people will not only make you a good negotiator, it will make you a good agent that clients will trust and refer to their friends and family. We work and thrive in a word of mouth business, so please, choose yours carefully.

About Jim Keaty

Jim Keaty is a Louisiana native, who knows his state and loves to make good deals for its homeowners. He is a graduate of the University of Colorado at Boulder, where he studied economics.

Jim is the owner and broker of Keaty Real Estate (www.keatyrealestate.com), one of Lafayette's fastest-growing real estate companies. Keaty Real Estate, opened in 2004, now includes more than 30 agents who are all experts in serving their clients, while forging deals that are beneficial for both the buyer and the seller.

Jim lives with his wife Danielle Chastant Keaty and his two young daughters, Mae and Josephine, affectionately nicknamed "Joey." Jim and his wife look forward to watching their kids grow up in one of the most unique and welcoming states in the country.

Before Jim started his own firm, he followed up his bachelor's degree in economics and minor in business from Colorado with a degree from American Real Estate College in 2003. He began his professional real estate career with Coldwell Banker.

Jim is dedicated to making the real estate industry in Louisiana transparent and respected, working with the local and state realtor associations. In 2006, he received the Realtor Association of Acadiana President's Award and was nominated and awarded as one of The Times of Acadiana's "Best" Realtors in Lafayette in 2010. In 2012, Jim was the recipient of the Exponential Growth Award from Kinder Reese and was recognized as one of the "Best" Realtors in Lafayette as well as having his agency named one of the "Best" real estate companies. He was also awarded "Best Realtor" in Lafayette in 2012-2013 by Locals Love Us.

Jim is actively involved in the community he serves, from 2005-2009, he participated with Rebuilding Together, providing repairs and maintenance for low-income homeowners. In 2007, he served as president of the Faith House women's shelter, and that same year was selected as a "Twenty under Forty" by *Daily Advertiser*, which recognizes outstanding young business leaders.

What does Jim love best about being an accomplished realtor? It is not the accolades and awards, but the unique challenges he faces every day, and creating deals where everyone walks away smiling.

CHAPTER 5

CHOOSE THE RIGHT AGENT...IT'S EASIER THAN YOU THINK

BY HARLEY DUFEK AND CHRIS PIERARD

When it comes to making promises and not getting results, Henry Ford put it best: "You can't build a reputation on what you are going to do."

Unfortunately, many real estate salespeople come to the table with what appears to be a great plan to sell your home—only to disappoint you with unfulfilled assurances—not getting you the results you were expecting the day they left your home with listing paperwork in hand. And oftentimes, the lack of results is accompanied by a myriad of excuses about the market, time of year, etc. as to why your home didn't sell. In fact, you get everything in the world except the one thing you wanted—results.

Many agents make large promises, underdeliver, and don't get within 100 miles of delivering the results they promised when you first meet with them. Expert agents, however, always deliver on their promises. Here's an example: Take Carrie from Washington. Carrie was looking for someone to help sell her mother's home and decided to meet with us to find out what she needed to do to maximize the equity she'd walk away with after the sale.

We grabbed our contractor and met Carrie at the home where we gave her a specific rundown of what needed to be repaired or updated before the home went on the market. At the time, we estimated that she'd get a return of $2 for every $1 she spent to make the home saleable. Carrie took our advice, made the necessary upgrades and repairs, put the home on the market, and the home sold in four days for $35,000 over asking price. There was a bidding war on the home when the offers came flying in as the result of more than 30 agents showing the home over that short, four-day period. The best part is that Carrie got $3 in return for every $1 she spent to get the home in shape to be sold.

Now those are the kinds of results people want when working with a real estate agent. And the good news for you is that you can find an agent who can do the same for you if you know what you're looking for. The better news is that after you read this short chapter, you'll know exactly what it takes to locate and secure the best agent for the job of selling your home.

ONE SIZE DOES NOT FIT ALL

The first thing you need to know is that one size definitely does not fit all when it comes to marketing and selling a home for all it's worth. Your needs as a home seller are vastly different than those of the other home sellers in your marketplace. In fact, to get the best results, you need a customized solution to get you the most money for the sale of your home within a time frame that works for you, and do all of this without driving you crazy in the process.

And yet, despite the fact that there are almost 1.2 million real estate agents in the United States, more than 96 percent of them would give you the EXACT same strategy to put your home on the market and sell it—if it sells at all. Think about that for a second, only 4 percent of the entire real estate population has a program and system to provide you with a turnkey strategy to help make the process of selling your home profitable, easy and fun. And yet, you can spot any one of these 4-percenters in your marketplace, with ease, once you know what to look for. The best part is that you'll never have to be in the situation where you feel like you're rolling the dice and gambling with your biggest asset, because picking the perfect agent will be easy after today.

THE 7 ELEMENTS OF THE RIGHT REAL ESTATE AGENT

There are 115 variables that must be managed properly when selling a home to get you, the seller, the best deal possible while providing you world-class service along the way. When you pick the right real estate agent, he/she will have mastered how to expertly manage every one of these variables to provide you with the ultimate real estate experience—every time.

Here are the seven elements you must look for when selecting the right real estate agent to help you with the sale of your home.

Element #1: They Must Be an Expert
When we say expert, we mean *expert*. *Webster's* dictionary defines the word "expert" as "having, involving, or displaying a special skill or knowledge derived from training or experience."

Unfortunately, the majority of real estate agents in the country only need to get somewhere between 90 and 120 hours of education and training to get their real estate license. Not only does this time requirement pale in comparison to that of hairdressers (450 to 1,000 hours to get licensed) but very little mandatory training is required of agents after they get their license.

Agents who are experts learn like they're going to live forever. They engage in ongoing training programs, and some of the true experts in the industry obtain the Certified Home Selling Advisor™ designation to provide unparalleled sales, marketing and customer service to every seller they meet with. In addition to that, real estate agents that are experts know *everything* there is to know about the national and local real estate markets, the current economic conditions and how they affect the price of home sales, and just about every other housing and economic indicator that can impact how your home gets sold.

Expert real estate agents in your market should spend a significant number of hours and dollars each month on research that allows them to give you the direction you need on pricing and positioning your home to get the most amount of money for your sale—no matter what the current conditions dictate.

Failing to pick an agent who is an expert to sell your home could cost you as much as 3 to 5 percent of your asking price. Make sure the next agent you choose to work with is an expert.

Element #2: They Must Understand Differentiation
Differences sell. The more different something is, the more money it sells for and the faster it sells, especially when it comes to your home.

The 96-percenters we mentioned earlier in this chapter usually subscribe to the same strategy when it comes to getting your home on the market: put a sign in your front lawn, your home on the MLS, and get it on the internet (maybe). That's usually it.

Unfortunately, it's hard for your home to stand out versus the competition's when your listing floats aimlessly in the sea of thousands of homes for sale on the MLS and internet. In fact, your home doesn't stand out at all.

The right real estate agent knows the strategies to differentiate your home from other similar homes in your marketplace. He/she understands how to and the importance of:

- Getting your home staged to net you up to 5.4 percent more for your home
- Evaluating your home to target the most likely buyer for it
- Getting your home preinspected to save you as much as $7 for every $1 in repairs needed
- Getting a home warranty in place the day your home is listed to get you up to 2.2 percent more

…plus a whole lot more.

The best fishermen on the planet know that you need the right bait to catch the fish you want. Selling your home works much the same way: You need to differentiate it from the others on the market so the buyer you want—the one who's willing to pay your price and close at a time acceptable to you—comes your way.

Element #3: They Must Understand Exposure
You could have the nicest home in the nicest neighborhood with the best upgrades on the premium lot in your neighborhood, but if a prospective buyer can't find it to look at it…then it doesn't matter. The right real estate agent —a true expert as we've discussed—understands the importance of exposure and knows how to get a maximum amount of it in getting your home sold.

Not surprisingly, one of the main requirements of getting your home maximum exposure is having a strong marketing budget. The right agent knows you need to have money to market a home properly in a large enough area to get the right buyer for your home.

Average agents— let's call them Average Frustrated Agents™ (AFA)— only sell about 6 to 10 homes per year and make roughly $37,500 over that time period. After business and living expenses, there's not much money left to help cast a wide enough net to find the right buyer for your home. Experts, sell 10 to 20 times the number of homes as the average agent does, meaning they have thousands of dollars to invest each month in:

- Targeting your property properly on the internet so the best buyers for your home find it
- Getting your home on the top five sites for real estate traffic
- Taking professional pictures of your home to improve the first impression buyers get of your home, which happens more than 90 percent of the time online
- Using professional copywriting strategies and tactics to get better responses to your property listing

…and other strategies that result in more of the right buyers seeing your home.

There's no magic to it…it's just what experts do.

Element #4: They Must Work Well With Others
In just about every market in the country, real estate agents control as much as 71 percent of the home sales through bringing ready, willing and able buyers to the table. Knowing this, experts have systems in place to target the right buyers and buyer agents to ensure that more buyers see your home than any other home in your marketplace.

When choosing the right agent, you must pick the agent who does the best job cooperating with other agents in the marketplace, one who has a strategy geared specifically toward building and maintaining strong relationships with other agents. Some of the strategies experts employ are hiring buyer specialists in the market area they work in to get them to bring their buyer prospects to your listing, providing incentives and bonuses to increase the appeal of your home to the population of buyer agents in the marketplace, and ensuring that the proper compensation is made available to all buyer agents so that your home gets considered every time it's a match for one of their buyers. By knowing how to keep buyer agents in your marketplace motivated and excited about their listings, the right agent will be sure to get them excited to show and sell your home first.

Element #5: They Must Generate Lots of Buyer Leads
If you've never sold anything before or if you've never owned a business, then you might not realize how important lead generation is to a real estate agent. Without generating an abundance of buyer leads on a consistent basis, no agent would be able to get your home sold. The right agent will employ strategies to acquire and then convert large numbers of buyer leads to ensure that your home gets sold fast and for the price you are looking for.

As part of this process, the right agent will have a team of highly trained real estate agents and technology in place to provide quick, professional responses to people calling in about your home. In the world of real estate, an agent has about 15 minutes to respond to a lead in order to turn that lead into a legitimate buyer or seller opportunity for a particular home. After 15 minutes, the agent is 21 times less likely to work with that lead in helping them buy a home.

Having the right people and tools in place to handle the leads you get on your home could easily mean the difference between your home selling or not selling. Experts will also have lead follow-up systems and buyer loyalty programs that help keep them top of mind with buyer prospects so that they choose them over the competition when it's time for them to buy.

Again, if an agent cannot generate a sufficient number of buyer leads and respond to them quickly while providing professional service, your home may not sell.

Element #6: They Must Be a Good Negotiator
Have you ever heard the saying: "That guy/girl is a great salesperson; he/she could sell ice to Eskimos"? It's a compliment and it means that this salesperson is obviously a great negotiator too, because almost every sale has an element of negotiation to it.

You'll know that you're picking the right agent to sell your home because he/she will be able to "sell ice to Eskimos." More specifically, the right agent will be an expert negotiator who uses proven negotiation strategies to benefit you.

Also, the right real estate agent won't need your home to sell worse than you do because he/she is so dependent on the income to pay the bills. The right real estate agent is unattached to the outcome on their own behalf and works exclusively for you to get you the best price, terms and conditions on the sale of your home.

Experts go through a tremendous amount of sales and negotiation training to get you the best results you want. Their goal is to create a win-win situation where you and the buyer are extremely happy with the outcome of your home sale. Their goal is to have everyone be ecstatic with the home that is sold and the real estate agents involved in the process.

As part of their negotiation expertise, experts look for pitfalls and issues that could derail the negotiation before they even get started. That way, they can save you from dealing with a tremendous amount of stress—and maybe from getting involved in a particular negotiation to begin with.

Element #7: They Must Be Able to Execute Their Plan
We've kind of come full circle at this point. We started the chapter talking about results, and we're going to wrap it up in much the same fashion. The right real estate agent has the best plan for you and your family and has the right systems, strategies and people in place to execute it.

The right agent is concerned with many things when it comes to helping you get your home sold, but his/her chief concern is your satisfaction with the results you get. To ensure that you are 100 percent happy with the results you get, you're going to want to pick an agent that has a:

- Market research team to help you target the best price for your home
- Prelisting team to help prepare and position your home for market
- Marketing team to ensure you get maximum exposure and profitability on the sale of your home
- Closing team to provide the highest level of service to you before, during and after you get to the closing table

...plus a whole lot more to help you with managing your listing through the entire process.

Saying you're going to do something and actually delivering on what you said you'd do are two things. The right real estate agent *always* executes the plan that he/she lays out for you when they sell your home.

About Harley

Harley Dufek is one of the industry's foremost real estate sales gurus and leadership mentors. He is best known for his ability to truthfully "call a spade a spade" when it comes to letting the general public know how to find standout, integrity-driven agents to help them manage the purchase or sale of their biggest investment. Harley's successful real estate career and visionary leadership legacy spans two decades.

Born and raised in Alaska with an independent "can do" attitude, Harley began his entrepreneurial sales career at age 16 with a successful residential window-washing business. Harley generously credits the influence of his parents in instilling the importance of honesty, integrity and a game-changing approach to client service. Harley helped his father build custom homes and watched his mom create and run a successful entrepreneurial endeavor that remains highly lucrative today.

Today, Harley's passion is to share his real estate trade secrets with others to help them achieve their goals. He does this by merging all aspects of his fulfilling real estate career, including the founding of his own company, Exclusive Home Realty, specializing in first-class service for every client. To find out more, go to www.ExclusiveHomeRealty.com.

Harley is the recipient of numerous real estate awards and designations. He is also the founder and president of "Help Stop NF2," a 501c3 public charity foundation dedicated to educating the world and curing the disease NF2, inspired by his wife Rebecca. Read more about Rebecca's story and the new film produced to help find a cure at www.HelpStopNF2.org.

About Chris

Chris Pierard is a real estate trailblazer and frontrunner and has a passion for the "art of the deal." Chris has invested in stellar real estate opportunities and helps other agents buy and sell properties using the same successful instincts, ethics and principles. Chris has over 15 years successful executive-level management and finance experience with companies he's founded and launched in the Seattle area, including real estate.

What ultimately motivates Chris Pierard? The inside-industry awareness that real estate agents might be undertrained and undermotivated. Chris is concerned that agents today lack the skill and savvy to guide their clients in the single, largest financial transaction of their lives. Chris's passion is to shake up the status-quo and provide the smartest blueprint possible for everyone to identify the best real estate agents out there.

Chris also excels in the art of negotiating. He shares these critical skills far and wide because he wants the best and brightest real estate agents to profit from his knowledge base.

In addition to Chris' passion for helping fellow agents and home sellers/buyers, he is active in his community, Rotary, St. Vincent De Paul Society, is a youth sports coach, husband, father to three kids under age 10, and loves golf and fishing. Currently, Chris is co-owner of Exclusive Home Realty, specializing in first-class service for every client. To find out more, go to www.ExclusiveHomeRealty.com.

CHAPTER 6

SELLING A HOME: THE *VALUE* OF HIRING AN EXPERT

BY ANDY MULHOLLAND

Only the man who crosses the river at night knows the value of the light of day. ~ Chinese Proverb

Real estate sales take place every day throughout the world. As a Realtor that has grown a successful team, I've been privileged to represent and negotiate on behalf of hundreds of buyers and sellers in these transactions. However, in my time in the business, I've seen far too many sellers leave thousands of dollars on the table by choosing poorly when they decide how and with whom they list their home. This chapter explains exactly what has cost them their equity, and how you as a seller can avoid making the same mistakes.

The world sees real estate agents as a commodity. But the reality is that not all agents are created equal. Did you know that the average agent in the United States sells only 8 to 12 homes a year? Did you know it only takes 90 hours of classroom time to get a real estate license in most states? Did you know that, according to the National Association of Expert Advisors, the average agent spends only $89 per month on advertising themselves and their listings?

So, the question becomes, how are these relatively unknown statistics affecting sellers? According to the National Association of Expert Advisors® (NAEA), **58.4%** of the homes in the United States **do not** sell before the listing expires or they are taken off the market for some reason. Over 80% of homes that do sell, end up selling below the asking price. These concerning realities are widespread issues in our industry and the average consumer is not aware of these unfortunate statistics.

As you probably know, there are numerous options available to today's seller when it comes to selling their home. Below I describe and briefly discuss five common options to anyone selling their home, and how each will affect the amount the seller walks away with at the end.

OPTION 1 - THE DISCOUNT AGENT: HIRING A FRIEND, FAMILY MEMBER, OR CO-WORKER

In today's world, it seems everyone knows someone who has a real estate license. The "friend, relative or co-worker" real estate agent often offers a discounted commission rate especially if working with a friend or family member.

That sounds good in theory, but let's take a closer look at how this will more often that not, cost a seller in the end. First, an agent willing to drop their commission to gain a listing is most likely not going to be very good at helping a seller get their home sold for top dollar. If the agent is willing to give their own money away that easily, how hard do you think they will they fight for the seller's money when it comes time to negotiate? Lets say they give the seller a 1% or 2% break in the commission. With the lack of marketing, resources, experience, and the obvious lack of skill in negotiating, they will not have what it takes to get top dollar, and it will end up costing the seller much more than they are "saving." Of course, that is if the home sells at all.

Another reason we see homes sell for less with a "discounted" agent is because that agent may then offer a lower commission to a cooperating agent for bringing a buyer. Many sellers are not aware that their agent will advertise a portion of their commission in the MLS to entice cooperative agents to bring buyers to the property. Imagine if your home was listed in the MLS paying out just 1% or 2% to the buyers agent, while the majority of listings are paying out 3% or more. The listing offering the lower payout will most likely see less activity and therefore lower offers, if they get one at all. I'm shocked by the number of sellers that have no idea what their agent is offering to cooperative agents on their behalf, when it is easily one of the most effective ways to increase interest in a property.

Looking at *price* rather than *value* is not the way to pick an agent.

OPTION 2 - FOR SALE BY OWNER (FSBO)

FSBO is an attractive and very well-intentioned option for a seller. It makes sense; no one wants to spend money when they don't need to. In a market like we are seeing today, where there is very low inventory and steady sales, finding a buyer is relatively easy. So who in their right mind would still choose to pay an agent to sell? Well, as easy as it might be to find a buyer, the hard part when selling is having the systems, skills and resources to get **top dollar**, **limit a seller's liability**, and then **managing the process so the deal doesn't fall apart**. When a seller lists as a FSBO they have decided to do take on those tasks themselves, and will statistically sell for less with much greater risk to themselves and the sale. According to the National Association of Realtors® (NAR) independent survey of buyers and sellers, the average FSBO sold for just $174,900 while the average agent-assisted sale sold for $215,000. They also found that FSBO sales accounted for just 9% of all sales in the U.S.

So, let's pretend a seller is lucky enough to be in that 9% that do make it to the closing table on their own. Are they really saving the 6-7% in the end? To find out, we need to break down the numbers. Did you know the overwhelming majority of FSBO's end up selling to a buyer that has representation from an agent, and end up paying that agent a 3% commission? So, in reality, at first glance the FSBO option looks like a 6-7% savings when it's usually at most a 3-4% savings in the end.

But does the FSBO option really even present a potential 3-4% savings? Or is it possible it's actually *costing* sellers money even after they pay a commission, because they are not listed with an agent? Well, of course that depends on what agent they choose to list with, but assuming they choose one with a proven, repeatable plan such as the one we use, they might re-consider the value of the FSBO option altogether.

What if you experienced problems with one or several of the 115 variables you will encounter when selling your home? How will you determine the correct asking price for the house? How will you know if you receive a fair offer? How should you negotiate that offer to get top dollar? What if there are problems with the appraisal? What does it mean if the offer is contingent upon the buyers financing? Who will manage the closing to make sure the appraisal is ordered? What if the appraisal comes back low? What is earnest money and how much is enough to deter a buyer from cancelling the contract? How long should an inspection contingency last? What if there is an issue with the buyer's loan on the day of closing?

When you consider these issues are only a few of the **realities** of the selling process that we as agents manage every single day, it becomes obvious the value a _great_ agent brings to the table is worth every penny they charge and more. The system I've created for my team has been specifically designed to _pre-emptively_ manage these potential risks so they rarely come up. We call it "bullet-proofing" the transaction, and it has saved our clients countless hours of time, loads of stress, and thousand of dollars by having the experience and systems to manage any potential issues.

Another very important consideration that can't be overlooked when choosing the FSBO option is the restricted marketing opportunity, specifically the MLS. I won't get into all the disadvantages of not being in the MLS, but I think it's obvious; the MLS can change your exposure drastically and immediately get your home in front of thousands of buyers, thereby producing a higher net offer. The property must be marketed correctly, and positioned well in the market; but if it is, the MLS becomes a tool that offers exponential returns.

OPTION 3 - MLS ENTRY COMPANY OR A FLAT FEE COMPANY

A "Flat Fee Company" will work with sellers and charge them a fixed amount up front to list their home in the MLS. The cost for this service will vary depending on the options, but the company may charge somewhere around $1,000 - $2,000 up front and it is paid whether the house sells or not. The company basically places an ad in the MLS that says something like, "Contact seller for all questions. Seller is representing themselves. This is an MLS entry only." However, in that entry, it also tells the buyer's agent they will be paid 3%. So, the seller has paid a $1,000 - $2,000 flat fee and is also committed to paying 3% to the buyer's agent.

From that point on, the seller is on their own to navigate through the 115 variables involved in selling a home. While it's a step up from the FSBO technique because they are listed in the MLS, the seller is still acting independently. They have no expert representation to help them determine the value of their home, no one to negotiate the contract terms of the purchase agreement, and no one managing the contract to close process. The market has proven that MLS entry companies bring very little value to the table, as the overwhelming majority of them are no longer in business.

OPTION 4 - THE TRADITIONAL AGENT OR THE "AFA" (AVERAGE FAILING AGENT)

We all know at least one of these – the "Average Failing Agent" or AFA. These are the agents that sell 6 to 8 homes a year, probably have a second job, and are barely making enough money to cover their real estate business expenses. These agents account for over 80% of those in the business, yet typically do only 20% of the business. The AFA is the biggest factor in sellers not receiving top dollar for their home.

An "AFA's" marketing technique is identified as:

The 3 P's :
- Place a sign,
- Put it in the MLS, and
- Pray that another agent brings a buyer

Most of the time a property listed by a traditional agent will expire before the house is sold. That's what happens to 58.4% of sellers nationally, according to the NAEA®. I hear these stories all the time in my area as well. One example was with a recent client who tried to sell their home for over 6 months before they finally cancelled the contract with their agent and called me to come list the home. When I spoke with them, they told me their previous agent said she was "very busy" and asked **them** to take some photos of the house and email them to her so she could use them for marketing. My jaw dropped to the floor! They agreed, they couldn't believe it either, but at that point they just wanted to get the house on the market. It didn't end up selling with that agent, so we put our system to work and sold it within 2 weeks. Since then, I've had several other sellers of homes that didn't sell tell me their agent asked them to take the photos as well! We have a professional photographer on staff to take all photos, it's one of the most important things we do to market our listings! Shame on those AFA's!!!

Another example happened very recently when I took over another expired listing. The seller tried to sell their home for several months with an agent they met at an open house. When I explained to them an AFA, they said, "Andy, that's exactly the type of agent we had." They said he was a very nice person, but that he didn't give them good advice, did very little marketing, and took pictures with his cell phone instead of using a professional photographer (I guess that is one step up from asking the seller to take them!). The only advice he had for them was the typical, "drop the price" approach. The result was that the home did not sell. I picked up the listing and put it through our proven, repeatable system. We listed it at the **exact same price** as the AFA, but our team sold the house in 4 days for $3,000 over the asking price.

The list I have of similar examples is endless, but the common lesson learned by the sellers is that the right agent makes ALL the difference.

OPTION 5 - THE EXPERT ADVISOR

Imagine you woke up tomorrow and found out you needed major surgery. Imagine it was the kind of surgery that would determine whether you lived or not. Would you consider hiring a friend, relative or co-worker who happened to also do surgeries on the side and was willing to give you a discount? Of course not! Would you decide to operate on yourself to save the money? No way! How about hire a surgeon that had only performed surgery a handful of times in the last year? Absolutely not! Instead, you would seek out the surgeon that was an expert in their field, an expert at the exact surgery you needed, and one that had performed it hundreds of times with a great track record of success!! You would focus on the *Value* that person brought to your life, rather than the cost.

Hiring a real estate agent is no different. Expert Advisors® with the National Association of Expert Advisors are the experts in their real estate industry.

As an Expert Advisor myself, I use a proven, repeatable system that is backed by market research to sell homes for up to 18% more than traditional real estate methods. My team of Expert Advisors has a track record of selling in the top 1% in our industry, and selling in half the time it takes a traditional agent in our market. The NAEA has identified 115 variables in the home selling process, and as Expert Advisors we follow 7 very specific laws to manage those variables effectively. Depending on how well or how poorly those variables are managed will directly effect how much or how little your home sells for, or if it sells at all.

CHOOSE WISELY – CHOOSE VALUE

What is a cynic? A man who knows the price of everything, but the value of nothing. ~ Oscar Wilde

Choosing the right representation when selling your home really comes down to a decision of price versus value. Sellers who opt for the first 4 options above are focused on price. Individuals who choose an Expert Advisor are focused on value. The reality is that focusing on price usually diminishes the value of your representation and will likely cost you literally thousands of dollars in the end. Many people step over dollars to pick up pennies. I encourage you not to be one of them. Choose wisely.

About Andy

Andy Mulholland is a native of Rochester, MN, where he has built a real estate business that is changing the way real estate is bought and sold in the US. In his first year in business, his local Realtor Association named him Rookie of the Year when he sold a record number of homes for a first year agent. Four short years later, Andy has built up Handy Andy Real Estate Experts, Inc. to become one of the highest producing real estate teams in all of MN. He was named a Top 10 RE/MAX agent in the entire state, out of hundreds of agents, while practicing in a market a third the size of most. His unique home selling system, and 59-Day Guaranteed Sale Program has resulted in his team selling more than seventeen times the number of homes the average agent sells in his area each year. At the age of just 29, and after only 3 years with RE/MAX, Andy was inducted to the RE/MAX Hall Of Fame, a level of business that takes most agents 10 or more years to reach.

Andy is a Certified Expert Advisor with the National Association of Expert Advisors® (NAEA). His training with the NAEA has earned him designations as a Certified Home Selling Advisor® (CHSA) and Certified Home Buying Advisor (CHBA).

In 2014, a three-time Emmy award-winning Producer selected Andy to be part of the upcoming documentary, Selling America, which will feature Andy and the unique system he uses to sell homes for up to 18% more, and in half the time of traditional real estate methods.

Andy currently resides in Rochester MN with his wife and two sons.

You can connect with Andy at:
andy@handyandyrealtorteam.com
www.HandyAndyRealtor.com
www.facebook.com/HandyAndyRealtor

CHAPTER 7

GETTING TO THE HEART OF THE MATTER

BY BILL MORGNER

In their quest for success, people often look for the newest bright shiny objects being propagated by the gurus of each business vertical. While I stay attuned to all the newest ideas, scripts and hooks in the real estate industry, I have found my road to success has been paved with some very basic principles that have transcended both time and sales-specific techniques. I would like to bring us back to some very basic standards that I have found to be highly effective in my business.

I don't want to be misunderstood. I strongly believe scripts are important and must be internalized. Shift points must be understood and executed accurately. However, beyond the technical aspects of your job, you must be present. Get to know your client as a human being, strike up a conversation, look for opportunities of commonality or differences, and above all, enjoy them. It's when people begin to relax and feel comfortable with you that trust begins to be established, and then you can take them where they need to go.

I hear coaches talk about listing appointments and how they get the listing within 20 minutes. They have it down to a science, like a machine. They get the listing and then move on to their next prospect. You may get the transaction, but the big question is, "Are you going to win a raving fan in that scenario?" That's really where the rubber meets the road.

WHAT IS MY JOB?

I have dealt with clients who have decided to sell their home because it was too small, or because of the death of a loved one, or to move to a retirement home, or to move closer to their children, or simply because they can't afford to live in the house any longer because of a downturn in their finances. I even had one client who decided to sell her house so she could use the equity to pay for an elaborate wedding she always wanted. The reasons may vary greatly, but the fact remains that each person in a real estate transaction is experiencing some sort of shift in their personal life.

As a result, I have functioned as a marriage counselor, employment counselor, grief counselor, life coach, and even errand boy. How do I feel about those inherited roles? I wouldn't change a thing. You see, for the first two years of my real estate career I wasn't the least bit concerned about what was going on in people's lives. I was in this business to make money, and I was determined to be the best and the highest volume real estate advisor in my region. However, during that time there was absolutely no pleasure or sense of fulfillment in what I was doing, no matter how many transactions I successfully negotiated.

After a great deal of introspection I quickly realized I was leaving out what may be the most important element of the real estate transaction: the human component. It was then that the proverbial "light bulb" came on. I realized there were service opportunities all around me where I could be instrumental in making a difference in the lives of people by genuinely helping them with their real estate needs, not just selling them a house. At that moment I immediately changed my focus, and my career has been on an upward trend ever since. A word of caution is in order here. While I wholeheartedly believe we need to involve the human element in our transactions, there is always the ever-present danger that you can get overinvested if you're not careful. My advice is to show genuine concern and empathy so you don't become part of the problem instead of part of the solution.

I'm reminded of what Theodore Roosevelt said, "People don't care how much you know until they know how much you care." When a client encounters an advisor who genuinely seems to care about them and doesn't view them as just another business transaction, the bond that is created can become very deep, profound and meaningful to that person. I have found it to be extremely important to understand that principle when engaging in business so that I can fully understand each client's specific needs and address them in a personally professional way. The term "personally professional" may seem dichotomous at first glance, but I believe we can maintain our professionalism, and do it in a personal way that makes it a meaningful experience for all involved.

HELP YOUR CLIENTS THROUGH DIFFICULT TRANSITIONS

One of my clients spent 26 years in a relationship and has never been single for any significant length of time. Her husband passed away suddenly and she found herself, for the first time in her life, trying to determine what to do as a suddenly single person. When I first met her she had scattered yet hopeful ideas about what the rest of her life would become at 73 years of age. You see, 25 years ago she and her husband toured a model home with which she fell in love. She also fell in love with a 15-foot artificial palm tree that adorned the entry of the model home. Her husband told the builder, "We will buy a house from you on one condition: You must include this palm tree my wife loves so much." The builder agreed, and that 1980's palm tree and ceramic base became a permanent fixture in their home. Now it stood (very tired and outdated) in the entry way of their home under the dramatic 25-foot ceiling, but it was a very sentimental piece of history that reminded her of the man she loved and with whom she shared her life. It became my job to help Beth understand the updates to her house that would be necessary to be able to sell it, including parting with the palm tree.

You can approach those responsibilities with a sense of dread or with a heart of service. Some of your efforts are going to be noticed, while some will be invisible. Some of them are going to be appreciated and some are going to be swept under the rug. However, it will be these little things that are going to make a difference in not only how you feel about the service you offer but also how your client navigates the change you are facilitating.

Since this client sold her house and moved into her new home, I have watched her actually bloom. She started dating again, and all of this change has enabled her to begin to let go of her past and become open to experience her life anew. For me, it was much more rewarding to watch her experience this new chapter in her life than it was to receive the commission for the transaction.

MAKE *ALL* YOUR CLIENTS FEEL IMPORTANT

We all have heard, "Know who the decision-maker is." I have found that sometimes the apparent decision-maker is not always the decision-maker. I went into the home of an older couple, Bill and Mabel, who wanted to sell their home, and it was very clear that the husband was the decision-maker. I was sitting on the corner of the sofa in the living room, and Bill was sitting in close proximity on the near corner of the love seat. Mabel conspicuously took a small childlike chair, placed it near his feet, and sat down almost in a subservient manner. Instead of taking the position on the love seat next to her husband, and out of all of the seating in the room, she chose to sit in this very small chair at her husband's feet. During the entire conversation I knew Bill wanted me to direct the conversation to him. But I purposefully turned my attention to Mabel and asked her directly, "What do you think?" That's when she timidly chimed in and said, "One of the things I never liked about the other agent was that she always seemed to talk down to me, and I really didn't appreciate that." Based on what I saw that day, I can see how that could easily happen. Her husband was such a strong personality that everybody would naturally turn their attention to him, and the wife would get pushed off to the side. I chose a different approach; I chose to include the wife, and it was noticed and appreciated.

EXERCISE THE GIFT OF SILENCE AND THE ABILITY TO PARAPHRASE AND RESTATE

Bill made it very clear that they don't need to sell and that they're not going to give the house away. In real estate, we get that kind of push-back all the time, so that was nothing unusual. So, in response to them, I paraphrased everything we talked about: "We've established that you folks want to move back to Arizona to be close to your son and that you have put a considerable amount of money into this house, and with the market today, we know that you're not going to get all of that investment back." They put about $300,000 of improvements into the house, but it was worth only about $100,000 more than they paid for it originally. We then discussed the option of putting a tenant in the property and holding onto the property. Bill immediately said no. At that point I looked at him, then I looked at Mabel, then I said, "Then why am I here?" I then sat back and waited in silence. They were waiting for me to say something else, and I wasn't going to do it. After a long pause, Bill looked at Mabel and said, "Is it OK? Can I tell him?" He began by saying, "We've never told anyone else this," and continued to share with me the real story. They had been in an estranged relationship with their son in Arizona for years, and they really never got to know their grandchildren. At that point, the whole dynamic of our meeting changed. It wasn't about the commission any longer; it was about helping them achieve their goal to be reunited with their family—their son and their grandchildren. It was great to get that kind of connection with this couple because I went through a similar situation with my own father. This became very personal to me and I related to them my own story. They lit up like candles as our connection deepened. I probably would have never heard the real reason they wanted to move if I had not waited in silence.

If you can get to a place of trust, you can get the real story, and you then have the opportunity to become a part of that story by helping to co-create a solution. It becomes important to you. To facilitate that shift, your attention must come in complete alignment with their intention. This dynamic takes the sales experience to an entirely different level.

The art of listening and the ability to paraphrase and restate are important skills. We often get caught up in the business transaction: What should the list price be? What has to be fixed? Can we find a buyer? How quickly can we sell the property? And the list goes on. Our mind is going 100 miles an hour, but in reality, the thing that will maximize our opportunity is to just be 100 percent present. Be present with that client and reiterate to them what you heard, asking for clarification when you don't quite understand.

ABOVE ALL, BE YOURSELF

There isn't a day that goes by that I don't get at least a couple of offers in my email from real estate gurus offering some new bright shiny object. The offer promises to absolutely revolutionize my business with guaranteed results. We're drawn to these coaching programs because we see individuals who have great success in their own market where they are able to be themselves. Once these coaches have been successful in their own business, they then create scripts and a process allowing others to follow their example. Agents will then take these ideas and scripts, memorize them and put them into action with some success, and sometimes great success. However, what I have found is that people need to know whether or not you can be trusted. They are more concerned about feeling heard and about feeling they are in the "right hands" when it comes to their home sale. After I discovered that for myself, I began to see a shift in my business. I have allowed my own personality, curiosity and quirkiness to be present and to be a part of the conversation. People don't want to be sold; they want to be heard and to establish a trust relationship.

I make it a conscious practice to be authentic, allowing people to be drawn to my message and to who I am. Being focused on bringing out my heart, my expertise and my passion to serve has transformed my business and the depth of the relationships I enjoy with my clients.

MY CHALLENGE TO YOU

Most clients are quite intuitive and can pick up on whether your concern for them is genuine or superficial. They will know if they are just another payday to you. I encourage you to demonstrate genuine care and compassion when helping them through this transition time in their life. I'm not talking about just putting on a good game face of compassion, but genuine, heartfelt caring to help them achieve their goals.

I don't expect this chapter to revolutionize the real estate world, but if one person will read this and have an "aha" moment, then I will have effectively communicated to someone. I would challenge you to try this approach to see if it doesn't revolutionize your business. Relate to your client and get to know them. Make the relationship more than just a cold business transaction. I'm confident you will find that genuine care and consideration will always transcend time and technique and will never become outdated.

About Bill

Bill Morgner was born and raised in San Antonio. Graduating from Dallas Christian College, he pursued his passion for being of service and inspiring others as a youth and music minister at Castle Hills Christian Church. Always desiring ways to expand himself, Bill went back to school and obtained his license to be an Adjuster in the State of Texas and went to work for USAA Insurance Company in 1992. After several promotions with increasing responsibility, Bill ultimately found himself working as an assistant vice president over the Pacific Division for AIG Personal Lines Insurance Companies, servicing claims for AIG Mass Marketing Inc. and AIG Agency Auto. Bill's job involved growing his division from a start of 33 staff in one office, expanding to over 380 staff in 12 locations across California, Oregon and Washington within two years. His ability to connect with people, coupled with his talents in leadership and strategic planning, helped him be successful in navigating the hyper growth his group experienced. Bill is characterized as a man who leads from his heart while working to achieve exceptional results. Bill is a Broker Associate for HomeSmart Professionals (The Morgner Group) in Palm Springs, California, and recently completed (2012) his MA in Spiritual Psychology from the University of Santa Monica.

CHAPTER 8

LOOKING GOOD: REPAIRS AND UPDATES TO MAKE BEFORE SELLING YOUR HOME

BY CYNDIE GAWAIN

The condition of your home is the number-one determining factor in the price you will get for the sale of your home and how long it will take to sell. No one would expect to get full Kelly Blue Book value for their car if they tried to sell it without a full detail in and out, repaired interior, a full set of working tires and a working engine. Why would you expect market value for your home if it is not in good condition?

TWO TYPES OF BUYERS

Things that were popular once go out of vogue and buyers change. Today's buyers usually fall in one of two categories. One type buyer wants a move-in ready home because they are too busy to select carpet and paint, much less other repairs. The other type of buyer wants a property in disrepair so they can make a low-ball offer and get a deal. These buyers typically overestimate the cost to repair and add something in for their time and trouble.

Sellers used to offer a carpet allowance. Today we cannot do that because lenders will not allow it. Additionally, if you try to do that, you will be appealing to buyer number two above and not buyer number one who will pay more to not have a hassle.

I often hear an objection from sellers that they do not want to make an update to the home because the buyer might not like it. If you do something neutral enough, buyers will still buy because they know they have time to personalize the home as time goes on. If the buyer wastes money remodeling again, that is not your concern so long as they buy.

I had a seller who had priced his 1950s unremodeled ranch home at the same price as an updated house in his neighborhood. His logic was that he saw the buyers of his neighbor's house come in and redo all the changes after the seller remodeled. When his did not sell for six months, he called me. I relisted and gradually educated him. Finally, instead of selling at $205,000 as he expected, the house sold at $175,000 with no repairs or updates. He was really lucky to get that much. Making the changes up front or realizing the true as-is value in the beginning would have saved him a lot of time and headache. By the way, it was a buyer number-two type who purchased the home!

COST/BENEFIT

In determining what to repair and what not to repair, it boils down to cost/benefit. If it will cost you $5,000 in negotiation to not replace the stained carpet upstairs, and it would cost $2,000 to replace, replace the carpet. If you can add granite to your kitchen for $5,000, but it will net you around $2,000 on your sales price because granite is not expected in your price point, then do not do it. Determining the value it will add to resale is an art and not a science. Your agent can help as well as analyze the sales price of recent sales in your area and what condition and amenities they had.

BEAUTY VS. FUNCTION

Who is your target market? Is it accountants, engineers and IT specialists? Then function is exceptionally important. All the big ticket items need to be not only working but not too old. Is it a married couple or a professional female? Then beauty and appearance is more important than an old air conditioner.

I recently made suggestions to a young couple getting ready to sell their entry-level home and move up. The husband was concerned because the air conditioner was old. I was concerned because the paint colors were not neutral enough and there was no granite in the kitchen and old gold fixtures in bathrooms. They elected to offer a home warranty in lieu of a new air conditioner and make the cosmetic changes. The house sold in two weeks for close to full price in a down market! The age of the air conditioner was never a negotiation point.

WHAT IS FUNCTIONAL?

Get a home preinspection to find out what is going to show up on the buyer's inspection report. If you do not want a written copy that you have to share, ask the inspector to give you a verbal report. However, you still need to address items on the seller's disclosure notice if you choose not to repair them.

The water heater, air conditioner, heater, foundation and roof are the biggest expenses a buyer will have if they have to be replaced soon. These items do not have to be new, but make sure they are working as intended. Replace missing shingles or check with your insurance to make sure you do not need a new roof. It is better to know up front than in the middle of a negotiation on repairs. Also, repair rotted wood on the exterior.

WHAT ARE GRANDFATHERED ITEMS?

Your inspector will address issues like GFCIs, panel boxes that have bad reputations, panel boxes in closets, bare bulbs in closets, wires outside that are not in conduit; and a myriad of other items. Code requirements change as the years progress. If you are building or remodeling, it needs to be brought up to current standards. If you are reselling, however, there is typically no law that says these items have to be brought up to today's standards. Ask your realtor which items that buyers in your area will baulk at and consider those to repair or be ready for a possible negotiation item. In my area, it is panel boxes. I suggest that the seller be prepared if we cannot negotiate it. Sometimes it never comes up.

LENDER-REQUIRED REPAIRS

FHA appraisers seem to have all taken classes in the last few years on how to be obstinate, unrealistic #@#'s. They are acting like VA appraisers used to act. I have had a home fail FHA appraisal because a light did not work in the garage when, in fact, it was just unplugged.

Knowing up front which items from your preinspection might be red flags to appraisers can save you money, time and headaches down the road.

WHAT IS OUT OF VOGUE?

We get used to how our home looks, and it feels good to us because it is home. If you do not watch home shows about redecorating or selling homes, you might not be aware of what is in vogue and what is not. Below is a list of items that can hurt the sale of your home:

- Wallpaper (unless you cannot tell it is wallpaper)
- Popcorn ceilings
- Gold fixtures in bathrooms and kitchens, and door knobs
- White appliances instead of black or stainless steel
- Overgrown bushes
- Moldy tiles in bathroom
- Dirty windows, carpets, etc.
- Non-neutral colors or colors that were popular years ago
- White, put-your-sunglasses-on interior wall paint (unless it is an ultra-contemporary home)
- Formica or butcher-block countertops
- Paneling
- Outdated light fixtures
- Mini-blinds
- Old worn or stained carpet or the old, inexpensive manufactured wood floors
- Vinyl flooring instead of tile
- Smoke, cooking and pet odors

The area you live in and price point of your home is going to make a big difference. A $60,000 starter home in a not-so-great neighborhood can have some of the items above if every other house sold in the area has them.

If every house that has sold in your area has had granite countertops, and you still have butch block, you could be in trouble.

NO MONEY FOR REPAIRS AND REMODELING?

The best plan is to plan in advance. I had a smart young man who had been in his home three years call me in for advice on how to spend his money over the next three years on his home. This way, when he was ready to sell it, it would be in condition to get top dollar. I did a walk-through and gave him pros and cons and a prioritized list.

If you don't have time to plan ahead, here are some things to consider:

- Painting yourself is not fun but is cheap and makes a big difference.
- Look at the little things that you can do that will make a difference.
- Ask your realtor for shortcuts that might help. For example, in the right price point, you might be able to resurface a bathtub or countertop instead of replacing it.
- Consider doing some trade with a handyman. Do you or someone in your family have a talent he would trade work for. One client's wife was a massage therapist and he found a handyman with a bad back who wanted to trade.
- There are companies that take payment at closing for new carpet and foundation repair.
- What can your insurance repair, such as broken windows or foundation repairs?
- Have a lender leave documentation on a FHA 203k Rehab Loan. The buyer can roll in repair and remodel costs into his loan. Some even cover foundation repair.
- As a last resort, have samples in-house and quotes, and offer the upgrade or repair at closing. I recently did this on a home whose main buyer objection had been that there were no granite countertops in the kitchen. The sellers could not afford to put them in, but they did still have $5,000 in negotiation room on the price of the house. So we got quotes on granite and samples, and left them in kitchen. I called every agent who had shown the house and offered the granite at closing. That

was the deciding factor for a buyer to purchase!

DO NOT OVERIMPROVE OR PERSONALIZE TOO MUCH

Sometimes sellers have the money to make the updates and start enjoying the process so much they overspend or overimprove. One client in a nice neighborhood went overboard on the quality of each item he installed. He also put in items that were not really necessary. He could not afford to price the house where it needed to be because of his expenses.

He also put in a bathtub-shower combination that had a telephone, CD player, Jacuzzi, steam shower, radio and many other gadgets. He did this because he had always wanted one. It was too personalized. The majority of women looked at it and thought it looked like a spaceship had landed in the master bath. They also had issue with that many electrical things in a shower.

This house never sold and is being rented by a man.

HOME WARRANTIES

Home warranties have changed over the last few years. You may have had one before, which always stated that what you wanted repaired was not included or was a "pre-existing" condition. Now there are extended plans that include pre-existing conditions.

Choose a realtor who has a good relationship with a home warranty company. I do a lot of business with one company. If my clients have any trouble, I call my marketing representative, and she bends over backwards to help my clients. This can help you during the time your home is listed if you choose to get coverage during the listing period. If something needs repair, it could be covered. Also, a good agent will sell the home warranty to the buyer or buyer's agent so they know if that old air conditioner goes out, they will have it covered during the warranty period. I have sold several homes with old air conditioners using this strategy!

STAGING

Staging includes not only the placement and amount of furniture and clutter you have but also some of the items listed above and below.

Here are the basics:

- Less is better. Too much furniture and "stuff" can make a house look smaller. Clean, clean, clean.

- Light and bright. Open drapes and blinds, replace light bulbs, remove old fashioned heavy drapes and wash windows.

- Do not overlook the power of drive-up. I have had buyers refuse to go into a house because they did not like the outside. Clean up landscaping and make sure your drive-up is appealing. Two of my clients complained when I suggested they cut back bushes because they liked the privacy the bushes gave them in front of their windows. Both houses sold soon after a bush-trimming overhaul.

- Power wash outside, especially around front door. While buyers are standing there waiting for the realtor to get the door open, they are looking at wasp nests, cobwebs, dirt, and old outdated door handles. Make sure your front door is easy to open. There is nothing worse than loosing a showing because the non-mechanically inclined realtor (me) could not get the door unlocked.

- If your home is vacant, stage with some furniture if you can. If you cannot, then at least do a minimum of decorative items on countertops and fireplace mantle. My favorite staging items are fluffy towels in bathroom and a nice shower curtain. I rented a house with a really ugly bathroom just because I had decorated the bathroom with palm tree towels, mats and shower curtain—all popular décor at the time. A $50 investment saved me another month of no tenant and no rent.

SUMMING UP

Be sure and select a realtor and/or stager who has a lot of experience with homes in your price point and in your area. Pick their brains. Ask to see other homes on the market, go to open houses, search online and ask to see pictures of sold homes. All of this will help you decide what is worth doing and what is not.

You want to avoid going through a rough negotiation and you are at your bottom line for what you will net on your home and then expensive items come up in the inspection. The deal falls apart because you cannot now afford to fix the items. It is better to know up front, even if you do not repair, because at least you can have those possible repair requests in mind when you are in negotiation.

The only thing worse might be having your home on the market for a year and having to make your bed, keep it clean, and leave for showings for a year. All because it is not updated to the standard that other homes in your neighborhood are at your price point.

How much money you make on the sale of your house is dependent on the market at the time, the negotiation power and creativity of your agent, the marketing of the house, the availability of the house to be shown, your pricing strategy, and in my opinion, the biggest factor is how the house looks and in what condition it is in. Take care of this big factor, so that even if all the other factors are not there, you will be smiling all the way to the bank!

About Cyndie

Cyndie Gawain is an independent realtor with Distinctive Realty, serving Dallas and Collin Counties in Texas for over 11 years. With an MBA and a special knack for creative marketing as well as the patience of a saint, Cyndie is the go-to person to get your home sold or help you find the perfect home. She has lived and worked and played all over the DFW metroplex for 30 years. That gives her the unique ability to perfectly match a buyer's lifestyle, pocketbook and preferences to the perfect neighborhood.

Smart buyers know that you must buy at the right time, the right place and the right price. Cyndie is an expert at helping you find the best deal in the best neighborhood for future growth of your investment.

Cyndie has been voted one of Dallas' Best Realtors by D Magazine and has won Best Customer Service Awards while at Ebby Halliday. An eternal student, Cyndie has numerous real estate designations and over 600 additional hours of real estate classroom training.

Cyndie's average days on market for her listings is 65. That is 31 days less than the Dallas average at the time these numbers were calculated. Her list price to sales price ratio is stunning 98 percent!

Call for a personal consultation: (214) 669-9920
www.DallasHomesExpert.com

CHAPTER 9

PRE-EMPTIVE NEGOTIATION: A STRATEGY FOR SELLERS

BY MICHAEL SWIFT

Everyone wants to have an advantage over the other side when they're negotiating for the best deal. There are many thoughts on how to best do this when you are on the side of a seller in a real estate transaction. As a real estate broker and expert advisor, I have tried many scenarios. After selling hundreds of homes over my 23 year career, I have come to realize the best way to get the most amount of money for my clients and save them from the many headaches that are possible from the sale of their home, is to front-load the sale with pre-emptive negotiation strategies.

There are 115 variables in the home selling process that must be properly managed to make sure that not only your clients sell their home for the highest price possible but also so that the process will not be a headache for them. I learned a long time ago that if your clients do not like the process, even if they achieved the highest price possible, they will not want to refer anyone to a process that they did not enjoy. As a real estate broker and a business owner, my main goal is to have as much repeat and referral business as possible. If you don't make the selling process as enjoyable and headache free as possible for your clients, you can kiss the repeat and referral business good bye. In order to give your clients the best headache-free experience as possible, you must employ pre-emptive negotiation strategies.

STACK THE DECK IN YOUR FAVOR

It would be wise, well before the negotiations even begin, to stack the deck in your favor. This is why it is very important to pick your real estate agent wisely. Your agent should be someone who has quite a few transactions under their belt and from every one of them learned what to do and what not to do. You pay your real estate agent for the experience he or she brings to the table so choose well. Even if your agent has great intentions and is someone you think you can trust and rely on (in the case of a friend or relative), it won't matter much if they don't have the experience and 'know how' needed to sell your home for top dollar... and at the same time make the transaction as seamless and enjoyable as possible.

THINKING AHEAD

Pre-emptive negotiation is when you look into the possible future to see what can and most likely will happen given certain scenarios in the home selling process. Kind of like a chess game when you have to think ahead many moves. There are quite a few things a buyer can do to get a better deal if they are given the right ammunition.

Knowing ahead of time what can be used by a buyer to place themselves in a position of strength in a negotiation is crucial. Taking away those possibilities before they even present themselves is paramount to not only protecting your sellers best interests, but also in providing them with a smooth transaction while selling their home for the highest and best price possible. The job of a real estate agent, in my opinion, is to protect your client. Protect your client not only from the legal aspect of getting sued, but also protect them from the headaches that can be avoided by thoroughly thinking out the home selling process and flawlessly implementing a systematic plan of attack.

DIFFERENTIATION

When selling a home you have to attract as many people to the front door as possible. You do this through the marketing of the home. But before you even start marketing the home you have to prepare it. The more people who look at your home and like it, the more the perceived value will be and thus the higher price you will receive from that home. You have to differentiate your home from the competition in a positive way. So when marketing a home, you have to make it as appealing as possible. The homes that have the most value are the homes with the least amount of hassles to a buyer. A "fixer-upper" will attract far less qualified buyers to the front door than a "turn-key-move-right-in" home will. A "turnkey" home will also fetch a much higher price than a "fixer upper."

If the most valuable and sought after homes are considered to be "turnkey," then it would be in the sellers best interest to make their home just that way—or at least get as close to "turnkey" as possible.

PRE-INSPECTIONS

You may think your home is move-in ready because you are, of course, already living in it. You may also think that there is nothing wrong with your home but you may be wrong. When was the last time you were underneath the home checking on the plumbing or on the roof looking at the shingles? If you were to purchase a home would you take the word of the seller that everything is perfect or would you have a professional home inspector take a look at it for you? If you're a smart homebuyer, you would have a qualified professional home inspector as well as termite and roof inspectors (amongst other possible inspectors) look over the home. So, if this is the case, why is it that most sellers don't do this ahead of time? That is my question exactly.

Once a buyer writes an offer on your home and you accept that offer, you have taken your home off the market for other prospective buyers. Now the buyer may have the upper hand. If you don't know what needs to be repaired ahead of time and needed repairs are found when the buyer does their inspections, there could be a bunch of problems heading your way.

When the buyers do their inspections and a bunch of expensive repair work is found, the buyers may now have the upper hand with their newfound negotiating position of strength. I will talk about the three most common scenarios that may now happen.

1) The buyer could say "heck no" and cancel the contract. If this happens, it could leave a perceived black mark on your home. Other buyers will question why the other buyer walked away? What is so wrong with that house that someone wrote an offer and then later backed out? This could put a negative thought in a potential buyers mind

that you want to avoid if at all possible. If a buyer is going to decide against buying your home, you want them to decide against it before they even write the offer and not after they are already under contract with you. If you can't repair the problems with the home, then you will need to disclose them up front before a buyer even thinks about writing a purchase contract.

2) Let's say the buyer still likes the home, but wants to have the work completed before they move in. Some lenders will not even fund their loan until certain repairs are completed. This could cause a serious problem that could extend the time to the closing, or even worse, kill the deal. In this scenario the buyer will write a request for you to repair the damage. Let's say that the work that was found has a bid of $10,000. Let's also say that the escrow period is 30 days and the inspection period is 17 days.

On the 17th day, the buyer sends you the request for repair – thus only giving you 13 days to repair the damage that was found before the scheduled day of closing. You are now under the gun and because time is of the essence, you may have to pay a premium to get the work done in the short amount of time left. This is a stressful situation to be in and should be avoided if at all possible. What if you knew about this needed work before you even put your home on the market? You may have been able to complete the repairs for a much lower cost because you could bid out the necessary work for the best deal. Not only could you possibly spend less money on the necessary repairs, but you would also take away the chance of a buyer walking away from the property and giving it a black mark that could turn away other potential buyers. Basically, at this point the negotiation strength is in the hands of the buyer and not in the hands of the seller.

3) Instead of requesting the repairs, (if not demanded from the lender), the buyer asks for a reduction in the price of the home or asks for a credit to reflect the $10,000 worth of repair work that needs to be completed. In some instances a buyer may even ask for more than the $10,000 because they now have to figure in the cost of their time to find and manage a contractor to do the work. In addition, if the work is severe enough that the buyer can't live in the home while the repairs are being completed, then there is another cost to them that will have to be recovered from the lowering of the price.

As you can see all three scenarios are not positive for a seller and can be easily avoided if inspections are done well before you even think of putting the home on the market. Yes there is a cost to having home inspections completed on your home, but the cost of these reports is an investment in planning for a smoother home sale process. In my experience, the cost of the inspections is small in comparison to the value and peace of mind you get from having them.

By finding out all of the potential problems that your home may have, you can then formulate a game plan of how you are going to take care of the problems ahead of time. Or, at the very least, disclose those problems/repairs to all prospective buyers well before they write an offer on your home and tie up your property, just to back out later.

What if we have the inspections but can't afford to pay for the repairs? Not a problem, price your home accordingly, taking into consideration the needed repairs and DISCLOSE everything you know. Therefore, if a buyer does write an offer on your home they will know ahead of time what they are getting themselves into. This will minimize the chance of the buyer backing out of the home purchase because of something they already knew existed; unlike the other scenario of once they have tied up your property and then back out because they found out of the problems after the fact.

Using the pre-inspection scenario means that you have to plan your "day to market" well ahead of time. Don't start thinking about having your inspections done a week or two before you want to have your home on the market. This may not give you enough time to plan for the time needed to repair any problems found. You need to have a strategy and time to implement it for the best possible outcome. By having your home inspections up front before you put your home on the market, you are taking away some of the potential negotiating power from the buyer.

HIRE A PROFESSIONAL STAGER

The next step in front loading your negotiations is to have a professional stager come to the home for a consultation. It has been proven over and over again that a professionally-staged home will sell for, on average, 6% to 8% more than the same home that is unstaged. Staging of course is not free, and the cost of staging can vary depending on if the home is already furnished with acceptable furniture or if it is vacant. Either way, more often than not, the cost of staging will be more than recouped and is well worth the investment. A whole book can be written and in fact many have been written on staging your home for sale, so I will only cover a tiny bit here.

So, besides making your home a "turnkey" home, the act of staging it just puts the cherry on top. Staging works. Have you ever been to a new home builder and saw any of their new homes without furniture? Of course not. They want to make sure that the home has a homey feel to it…which can't typically be found in a vacant home.

Besides just the furniture selection and placement, a professional stager can help you with many other things such as: color selections of interior and exterior paint that should be used to give the best pop, lighting techniques to make rooms look larger, suggestions on what needs to be cleaned or prepared better, pointers on what can be done to give the home the best curb appeal and what upgrades you may be able to do to get you a higher return than the money you have invested in those upgrades.

Again, timing is crucial. You have to plan well ahead and give yourself plenty of time to set the stage and set it well.

UTILIZE A PROFESSIONAL PHOTOGRAPHER

Once the stage is set, make sure you hire a professional photographer to take the absolute best pictures of your home inside and out. These days the majority of buyers will look at your home first online. You have to make your home look amazing online or you may never get those buyers to even come to the door. I can't tell you how many times I have seen pictures of homes online that look like the agent took the photos with their phone. Grainy, dark, blurry, out of focus and sometimes even upside down or turned 90 degrees. Unbelievable! A professional photographer does more than just take pictures from an expensive camera. They will know when is the best time of day to photograph the exterior of the home to capture the home without shadows. They will also know what angle lens should be used for different shots. Professional photographers are worth their weight in gold but they can only do a good job if what they are taking pictures of actually looks appealing.

Pre-emptive negotiation strategies work. They work so well that I have in the past turned down listings because the potential client didn't want to use them or didn't think it would matter if we did or didn't. Knowing how well pre-emptive negotiation strategies work and knowing that if they are not employed will not only make my job a lot harder but could make the selling process very stressful for my client. I would rather turn down a potential client now than let them down later. If the transaction is stressful and doesn't turn out the way the client thinks it will, they will ultimately, in most circumstances, blame you for it—even if they didn't do what you suggested. People talk and bad news travels fast. The bad news that you failed to sell their home and/or didn't give your clients a good experience could leave your reputation with a black mark in the community. It's much better to turn down a listing than have people talking about what you failed to do.

About Michael

Michael Swift is a California native and real estate broker with over 23 years of real estate counseling and sales experience. He lives in the beautiful San Francisco Bay Area with his wife Tara, daughter Aviana and son Alec, who are his BIG why in life and are at the root of his success over the years.

Receiving his real estate license at the young age of 19 back in 1991, Michael read every book on the subject of real estate and customer care that he could get his hands on. He also went to as many real estate seminars as he could in order to learn as much about the business of real estate as possible. Although real estate is a tough business to succeed in, especially for someone who was so young at the time, Michael flourished by focusing all of his time and efforts making sure that his clients were more than satisfied with their real estate experience. Flash forward 23 years...Michael currently attributes 93% of his business to the referrals of his past and current clients, which says a lot about what his clients feel about him and his business.

Michael focused primarily on helping people out of foreclosure through forbearance agreements and short sales for his first 4-5 years in the business during the real estate down cycle of 1991-1995. Due to his overwhelming success helping people negotiate these complicated scenarios, he was sought after by many real estate brokers in the community to help with their clients as well. He was recruited to Re/Max Executive in the San Francisco Bay Area in 1993 as an Associate Broker to help train all of the office agents on how to successfully negotiate forbearance agreements (the modifications of those days) and short sale transactions.

Currently, Michael is one of the top real estate brokers in the San Francisco Bay Area and is in the top 1% of real estate sales nationwide. In 2013, Michael exceeded the $40 million mark in real estate sales for the year. Michael attributes most of his business success to the systems he has in place to proactively manage every step in a real estate transaction. This ensures that no balls are dropped and client communication is constant so each client has a positive experience and an experience that they would want to refer others to.

Michael holds the prestigious designations of: Real Estate Broker, Master Certified Negotiation Expert® (MCNE) Certified Home Buying Advisor (CHBA), Certified Home Selling Advisor® (CHSA), Certified Distressed Property Expert® (CDPE), Accredited Staging professional (ASP), Home Retention Consultant (HRC), Certified Foreclosure Specialist (CFS), Short Sale Foreclosure Resource (SFR), Certified Short Sale Professional (CSP), and Certified Short Sale Agent (CSSA).

Michael can be reached at: michael@TheSwiftTeam.com

CHAPTER 10

HOW TO WIN THE UPSIDE-DOWN GAME

BY BRIAN PITCHER

Every week, I meet with multiple homeowners who want to sell their homes, but they have a problem. They don't have any equity in the home to sell it. In fact, they are sometimes upside down by $50,000 to $100,000 or more. What do you do when you need to sell, but you don't have enough equity and you don't have enough money to bring to the table to close? Or you don't want to bring money to the table and throw good money after bad? There are lots of variables when it comes to this type of situation. The good news is that there are options. There are many options and choices, but not all of them will ultimately work in your favor. In this chapter, I will tell you the story of one of my clients and the situation he was in and how he dealt with it. Many of you, I am sure, can relate.

THE BEGINNING OF THE END

My client bought his home in 2006. The economy was very robust and real estate was a safe and secure investment. The purchase price of his home was $630,000. It was a new home that was a former model home. He believed that it was going to be a good investment as home values were skyrocketing. He purchased the home with 100 percent financing using a common 80/20 loan. After a year went by, the home had jumped in value, up to $700,000. So he refinanced the second mortgage to pull out that equity. It was a great time to invest, and an extra $70,000 would go a long way toward some other investments. A $70,000 investment could get you a significant return to pay for the house itself. It seemed to be a no-brainer, and it appeared that the market was going to continue to go up. Investments were doing really well, and he had equity in multiple houses. What could go wrong?

February 2008 came and went, and it became the peak of the market in the Salt Lake City area, but the residential real estate market started to crash. Other investments that he had were failing, and it appeared that he might actually lose everything over it. However, he thought that if he could just wait it out long enough, the market would correct and he would be OK. In fact, he made it another year and a half until November 2009. At that time he was able to look at the real estate market and realize that the home that he owed $700,000 on was worth at best $500,000. The tenant in the home was not making payments and the other investments that he had invested in had fizzled out and had no chance of making any comeback. Things were not looking good. After he realized where the values were, some simple math told him that it was going to take him at least 15 years to pay the mortgage down to $500,000. That was also if he had a 30-year fixed loan. Unfortunately, he had an interest-only ARM, meaning it was going to take a lot longer then 15 years to break even.

SHORT SALE WAS THE ONLY CHOICE

What seemed to be a great investment had turned into a big ball and chain. He went through all the questions that everyone goes through. "If I let it go, will I get sued for the difference? Will I have a tax liability? What will this do to my credit? How will it affect my credit cards and other credit lines? What will everyone else think? Am I better off to file bankruptcy? Is it worth it just to rent it and hold onto it until the tenants pay it off?" "What am I going to do?" Everyone that he spoke with had different responses to these questions and a lot of opinions. He had people tell him that he was morally wrong to stop paying on the mortgage when he could still hold on. Others said that from an investment standpoint the best thing that he could do was bail. After researching and talking to a bankruptcy attorney and an accountant, he decided a short sale would be the best thing to do. There were tax strategies to not have to pay taxes on the cancelled debt, so as long as he could get the debt forgiveness on the mortgages, then that would be the best route. If the bank wouldn't forgive the debt, then it would be better for me to file bankruptcy. A plan was put into place to attempt to short sale and have the bankruptcy option as a last resort.

The property was listed, an offer was submitted, and the negotiations began. This was a Bank of America loan, and at that time they were really backed up. After three offers falling through because of the delay in the process, we were finally able to put the deal together. It took just over a year and a half to negotiate, and the final sales price ended up being $380,000. We were able to get Chase to forgive the second mortgage and Bank of America to forgive the debt as well. All fees, commissions, etc. were taken care of through the short sale so that he didn't have to bring any money to the table. This was a true success and a big relief.

THINGS WERE LOOKING UP

Once he decided to short sale the one home, he decided that there was another rental that he was upside down on by about $100K that needed to be shorted as well. The situation was a similar story on that one, but the ironic part is they both finished up in the same month. It was May 2011. After both closings were complete, there seemed to be a large weight lifted off of his shoulders. He was nicer to be around as a husband and father, and he didn't have as short of a fuse. He was generally happier to be around. The financial stress of the past three years was rough, but he was glad to have it behind him.

He was now looking to get back in the investment game again, but be able to buy at the new prices instead of the overinflated prices from the bubble. With the completed short sales behind him, his credit recovered within six months, meaning it jumped back up to a 680 credit score so that he could now buy a truck that he had his eye on as a goal. The Chevy dealership said that he had good credit, enough to qualify for the zero percent financing.

ALL'S WELL THAT ENDS WELL

So in summary with the short sales completed, he had about $450K of debt forgiven, and he now had a clean slate to build upon. He learned a lot about the bubbles and vowed never to get sucked into the hype of investing. It has to make sense before you count on market conditions or appreciation to invest. He learned to have to think about the worst-case scenario, because worst-case scenario happened for him a few times.

This client was very grateful to have been able to negotiate his way out of the debt, not have a tax liability, not have to file bankruptcy, and do it all without destroying his credit for years to come. This client now teaches short sale seminars in different parts of the country and consistently bails other people out of their tough situations also. You may be surprised to know that the client of whom I have been telling the story about is myself. One of the reasons that I know so much about the short sale industry and negotiating with the banks is because I had to go through it too. I know what it feels like to shed the burden of being several hundred thousand dollars in debt, with very little hope of coming out of it without filing bankruptcy. I do know what it feels like to go through financial stress and not knowing what the outcome will be. Doing a short sale is not fun, but it is better then the alternatives. The only regret I have is that I wish I had started sooner. If you need to do a short sale or even file bankruptcy, the sooner that you start, the sooner that you can recover.

IS A SHORT SALE FOR YOU?

As I stated before, I meet with multiple homeowners every week and help them figure out if they need to short sale or not. My rule of thumb, based on simple math, is that if you are upside down by 20 percent or more on your home after paying closing costs and commissions, that you are generally better off to short sale and shed the debt. After you complete the short sale, you can get into the home that you want with 20 percent down after two years or 3.5 percent down after three years with an FHA loan.

You'll be able to lock into a great rate and also buy when the prices are down instead of at the peak of the bubble. You will likely be at least five to 10 years closer to the goal of retirement by taking the strategy that I have spoken about. Most people will not retire until their home is paid for. If your basis in the home is less, then you are more likely to pay it off and pay it off sooner.

Now if you can afford your home and you don't plan on moving ever, then this conversation is obviously not for you. However if you plan on moving within the next 10 years, then you are more likely better off to short sale it.

MAKE SURE YOU GET AN EXPERT

If you are thinking that you need to do a short sale, then there are a lot of variables that need to be taken into consideration. In order to get the short sale approved, you need to be able to demonstrate a hardship. If cash flow is tight, then more than likely you have a hardship of some sort that will work. Then you need to pick a realtor who understands and is experienced with short sales. If you would like help with picking one for your area, send me an email and I would be happy to find you one who has a lot of experience. I already have networks in place to put short sale sellers with good short sale agents. Any agent can do a short sale, but the best short sale agents have a strategy for completing the short sale.

The short sale process is different for every bank, and you can find a lot of it on the internet. What most people have questions about is how does it apply to their specific situation? That is where we come in. If you feel like you need to get out from under the house and short sell it, then we can help you get out. If you want to stay in the home, then we will find a way to see if it is possible for you to stay.

ALTERNATIVES TO A SHORT SALE

What are the options for you if you are less than 20 percent upside down on your home? The idea here is that if you can hold on long enough that you will eventually be OK on your loan. If you have a good loan, good credit, and no intentions of moving, then there isn't a reason to put yourself through the pain and suffering of doing a short sale. You can turn the property into a rental property, do a lease option, or sell the property subject to seller financing.

The truth is that holding onto real estate properties and paying them off is how millionaires are made. However only about 10 percent of the population is able to withstand the stress and liability of being a landlord. So my advice is that if your payment on your home is close to what your rents are, then you will be OK. If you are negative on your rents by $500 or more, more then likely you will lose the property eventually and you are better off to short now rather than later. If you do a rent to own or lease option, then you can get higher than market rents because you are renting with the intent of selling the property to the new tenants. You do need to be careful on this one, though, and make sure that your end-selling price is less than where you believe the values will be when the lease term is up.

Seller financing is a way to sell the property to someone who is basically willing to take over your payments and the negative position in the property. This is usually a longer term of five to seven years before the new buyers are required to refinance you as the seller out of the deal. This strategy relies on potential appreciation and the paying down of the mortgage over time.

Many clients have asked, "Why would I let someone take this over and have it remain on my credit?" The answer to that is that if you can't sell your home based on price, then you can sell it by offering favorable terms. There are a lot of good buyers out there who don't have perfect scenarios to be able to buy a home, but they have the down payment, and they also have good cash flow on a monthly basis. As a seller, the benefits to you are that you can create some profit out of the underwater property for relocation or whatever you need. You can also move on and get where you are going without the worry of being a typical landlord who's fixing toilets in the middle of the night. You can also create a buffer for yourself in the event that something goes wrong and keep that money in a separate account.

If you feel like you are in this situation where you are looking to turn the home into a rental or want to do seller financing, please find a realtor who has experience with these types of scenarios. You will never regret having them on your team to make sure that you are not getting yourself into a scam or into unfavorable terms. You will also want to verify the value of your home with a realtor, to make sure that your terms are favorable and also advise you in the event that you have equity in the home to sell.

NOT A ONE-SIZE-FITS-ALL SOLUTION

The strategies I am presenting here are not a "one size fits all" solution. With all the variables there are, what may be a great solution for one family may not be a good fit for another. So don't read all of this and come to a specific conclusion without consulting with the professionals first.

All the options that I have spoken about in this chapter deserve to have a book written on each one. I am only briefly describing what they are here so that at least you might know what direction to go in. If you would like more detailed information on these topics, then please go to my website at www.brianpitcher.com and purchase my book: *Should I Stay or Should I Go? A Homeowner's Guide to the Housing Mess.* I have received a lot of feedback from homeowners who have saved their home from the information in its pages. Or if you would like to email me questions directly about your specific situation, I will be happy to analyze it and get back to you or line you up with a good short sale agent in your corner of the country. I look forward to helping you.

Brian@SaveMyUtahHome.com

About Brian

Brian Pitcher is one of the foremost experts in short sales in the country. He has been interviewed by many well-known organizations about his expertise, such as "The Short Sale Specialists Network," Keller Williams International, Prudential Utah, and many other smaller organizations. Brian is one of the experts that other "Short Sale Specialists" call when they get stuck on their short sale transaction. Not only has Brian closed over 250 short sale transactions over the past five years in his own business, but Brian also owns a short sale negotiation company where they have closed thousands of short sales over the past five years. Almost any agent can complete a short sale, but Brian is the agent that you go to if you do not have a cookie-cutter situation.

Although Brian's team, "Pitcher Group Real Estate Experts," does a lot of short sales, they also sell retail homes regularly, typically in 30 days or less. When clients are short on equity in their home, they consult with Brian on their options so that they can move on and accomplish what they are looking to do. If they have the equity to sell then Brian makes it a very smooth transition.

If you need to consult with Brian, regardless of what part of the country you live in, feel free to email him at brian@SaveMyUtahHome.com to set up a phone appointment. You can also visit his site at www.SaveMyUtahHome.com. He is happy to help whenever or wherever he can.

CHAPTER 11

"I'M NOT GOING TO GIVE IT AWAY"

BY ANDREW GAYDOSH

There are very few statements that are said to me on a daily basis that I can truly count on hearing. Outside of the "I love you daddy" and "Have a great day" that I hear from my wife and children, I can honestly count on hearing at least once or twice a day the dreaded *"I'm not going to give it away."* Having sold thousands of homes in my career and sometimes attending two or three listing appointments a day you can imagine how frustrating it is to hear these words time and time again. Early in my career it would often rattle me to hear those words from my clients' mouths as I knew it was one of the most important discussions I could have with them. Billions of dollars are lost every year by home sellers due to the incorrect positioning of their homes in the market relative to what it is actually worth. Much has been written about the negative effects of pricing your home too high. My intent in this chapter is not to teach pricing strategy nor the negative ramifications of incorrect positioning in the market, but rather it is to identify the alternative options that sellers have if they are not willing to sell their home in today's market because they feel like they "don't want to give it away." I also want to illustrate the true benefit or loss that may occur by choosing the path to wait and sell later.

In my younger years I tried just about everything to help my sellers understand that you are not giving your house away if you sell it at true market value. I tried being firm and direct; I tried being empathic. One year I even had T-shirts made up that I would wear under my dress shirts. They had "I'm not going to give it away" printed on the front of them. When I heard the sellers say that dreaded phase during my listing presentation I would unbutton my dress shirt and show them my T-shirt. I tried hard to look like superman coming to save the day. The sellers would look at me like I was crazy. I would say, "I was waiting for you tell me you were not going to give it away." It was a great icebreaker. I would then go on to explain to them the importance of pricing their home at its true value and that it was important enough that I even made a T-shirt for the occasion.

OPTIONS IF YOU CAN'T SELL FOR WHAT YOU WANT

Due to the risk of looking like a Chip and Dale dancer and getting love letters from the grandmas, as I approached my 30s, I found more professional ways to approach the subject. I do, however, often threaten our team on occasion that I may bring back the retro T-shirt if our "list priced-to-sell price ratios" were to ever drop. In all seriousness it is my duty as their agent and Expert Advisor™ to help them understand the financial losses they will most likely incur by overpricing their home. If their home is not worth what they would like to sell it for in today's market, it is also important for me to advise them on their options as well as forecast their financial risks in delaying their sale. They really have three options:

1. Sell if for what it is worth today.

2. Improve the home to reach the value of the price they want.

3. Wait until the market gets better and sell it then.

Let's break down these options:

1. *Sell it for what it is worth today.* We already know sellers don't like this option. It often requires selling the home at a price that is below what the seller financially has into the home. They may have bought the home when the market was better and therefore paid a higher price, or they may have spent more money on the home after they purchased it. It is common that homeowners improve their home just after they buy it. They would naturally recoup the money they put into the home. Right? The answer is most likely no.

If the home is sold within five years of the work being completed, more often than not the homeowner will financially realize only a fraction of the money they spent on these improvements. (See the recoup percentages tables for home improvements on www.AndrewGaydosh.com/HomeImprovementRecoupPercentages.) Over time it is more common to recoup the money spent on the improvements; however, in the short term it is not likely. In both of these situations the seller may have to take a loss on the home by losing a portion of the money they paid for the home, the money they put into it, or the equity they once had in it. In many cases it is common that sellers have to bring money to closing just to sell the home and move on.

2. *Increase the value of the home through improvements.* This is not the best option for many homeowners. The cost of these improvements often surpasses the increased value of the improvements to the prospective buyer. Paint and carpet are often the best returns on value to increase the price of the home. A quick facelift by a do-it-yourself homeowner may just do the trick. Sweat equity is usually the price these homeowners will pay to successfully get the home price up to a satisfactory level; however, sellers may not have the skills or the time to complete these tasks themselves and may need to hire a professional at a higher price, therefore, defeating the purpose. It is true that if you have a home that is in overall good condition, yet it is functionally obsolescent, you may be able to increase the value of the home with improvements. For example, take a nice home that has been well maintained over the years that is having a hard time selling because it does not have a bathroom on the main floor. It is possible that a half bath could be added to the first floor, adding more value than the cost of the bathroom. The goal is to add enough value to cover the cost of the improvement and to make up the value that the home was lacking with respect to the desired sales price in the first place. In summary, option number two is possible yet risky. It is not the best option for most homeowners.

3. *Wait until the market gets better and then sell.* This option sounds the most logical if the homeowner has the luxury of time. Right? The reality of the situation is that it will most likely cost the seller more money than he or she will gain by selling in the future with

property appreciation, even if they find themselves in a down market today, with future home values expecting to increase in the near future. Before you can answer that question you have to figure out what the homeowner's intentions are for their future move. One of the skills that separate the average frustrated real estate agents in the marketplace today from the successful agents that are Expert Advisors™ is their ability to properly advise the client based on their wants and needs in conjunction with identifying the market trends for the future. If we know where the seller wants to go and we track where the market is heading, we can typically determine if selling now vs. later is a good option.

HOMEOWNERSHIP VS. COST APPRECIATION EXAMPLES

Let's look at three examples of homeownership costs vs. appreciation gains in comparison to three different seller scenarios. As you know variables in homeownership, such as price, taxes, insurance costs, etc., vary widely throughout the country. Let's pick Dayton, Ohio, an average market in the average Midwest. Using $100,000 increments as examples we can illustrate the impact of selling today vs. waiting until a future date. Let's also assume that the economy is on track and homes are appreciating at a 2 percent increase per year on average over a two-year time frame. We will look at just a few consistent expenses associated with homeownership, as additional expenses, such as HOA fees, maintenance items, etc., are not applicable to all homes. These examples will not take into account the debt service if these homes are financed or the opportunity cost of the money if a seller does not have a loan. Using all these variables would be far too lengthy for our simple illustration and would only make the results even more obvious. Furthermore, it would not change the outcome of the trend in the results.

In this first example the seller is downsizing from a larger home to a smaller, more affordable home. They are selling a home valued today at $200,000 and buying a $100,000 home. The question is if they should wait two years until the market increases enough to get them $8,000 more in a sales price (they need $208,000 to break even), or should they take their losses now and move on? We first have to determine the net appreciation after both scenarios.

Current market value of a home is $200,000

$200K x 4% appreciation (over a two-year period of time at an average 2% per year) = $8,000 gain in sales price at the end of two years. Two years from now the home will have a value of $208,000.

VS.

Current market value of a home is $100,000

$100K x 4% appreciation (over a two-year period of time at an average 2% per year) = $4,000 gain in sales price at the end of two years. Two years from now the home will have a value of $104,000.

The difference in the future gain in the appreciation of the $200K home vs. the future gain in appreciation of the $100K home is $8,000 - $4,000 = $4,000. You will make $8,000 in appreciation by waiting two years; however, you will have to spend $4,000 more on the house you will be buying. Your net would be $4,000.

Now let's look at the expenses associated with owning the homes for two years:

HOME EXPENSE COMPARISON

Costs of owning the $200K home vs. the $100K home after two years:

$200,000 home	vs.	$100,000 home	
$6,000		$3,000	Taxes (approx. 1.5 % of the home value per year on avg.)
$2,000		$1,000	Insurance ($200K home at $1,000/$100K home at $500/yr.)
$7,200		$4,800	Utilities ($200K home at $300/mo. $100K at $200/mo.)
$15,200		$8,800	Total Expenses (for taxes, insurance and utilities)

There is a $6,400 difference. (The $200K home will cost $6,400 more in general expenses over a two-year period of time in comparison to owning the $100K home for two years.)

Now that we know the net appreciation and the differences in expenses, let's finish the comparison of the two scenarios.

Selling the $200K home today vs. two years from now and buying a $100K home (using the future net gain and general holding expenses for both homes):

Financial gain in waiting two years, with appreciation on current $200K home:	+$ 8,000
Added costs for owning existing larger and more expensive home for two years:	-$ 6,400
Home (expense comparison from above)	
The added price you have to pay for a $100K home in two years:	-$ 4,000
Ownership cost of larger more expensive home and future price for $100K home:	-$10,400
The net loss in waiting two years to sell $200K home and buying $100K home:	-$ 2,400

This scenario proves that waiting two years would not be a good financial decision for the seller. It could be worse yet: With a flat market and no appreciation, they could end up losing $10,400 because they would not have the $8,000 gain in appreciation to offset a portion of the loss. This analysis does not even take into consideration the cost of borrowing the money. In times when interest rates are very low, it makes even more sense to take advantage of low interest rates on the new home purchase. If the interest rates go up in the future like they often do after a period of low rates, these losses can even be more magnified by the fact that future mortgage payments on the new home will be much higher in comparison to today's payment. It could also affect the ability for future buyers to purchase your home as the affordability will be less for more people. The higher the mortgage payments, generally the fewer buyers in the purchasing pool.

If you look at a second example of buying a similar priced home in the future it becomes a wash, assuming interest rates do not go up. Basically you may get the $8,000 more for the home you are selling, yet you will have to spend $8,000 more in the future. You will risk paying a higher payment if you finance the home due to the potential of higher interest rates in the future.

Selling a $200K home and buying at $200K home:

Appreciated gain in home value after two years	+ $8,000
Increased costs for owning a $200K home (taxes, insurance and utilities)	- $0
Added cost for buying a $200K home in the future	- $8,000
Net gain after two years	**0**

In the last example, if a homeowner is moving up from the $200K price range and buying a home in the $300K range, it may make sense to wait if certain conditions apply. The financial swing would be the same as the first example, yet netting $2,400 instead of losing $2,400. The seller would net this after two years if the interest rates stayed the same or lower. The risk is if the rates move up, a person financing a home could realize a negative financial result if the rates increased as little as a half a percentage point. In this case you would probably want to go ahead and sell and buy now to play it safe. If the rates are high now and you expect them to drop in the future, it may be the only time you would want to hold off in selling your home. The problem with that scenario is that for such a small net of $2,400 there are a lot of associated risks that could ultimately cost you thousands of dollars over the lifetime of your homeownership. The safe bet would be to sell now and buy now when you know what the market conditions are as opposed to speculating.

Selling your $200K home today vs. selling it two years from now and buying a $300K larger more expensive home:

Financial gain in waiting two years with the appreciation on the current $200K home	+ $8,000
Costs savings for owning a smaller and more affordable home while you wait	+ $6,400
Total of the appreciated gain on the $200K home and the cost savings of keeping smaller home	$14,400
Cost of future appreciated purchase price for $300K home in two years	- $12,000
Net gain in waiting two years to sell	**+ $2,400**

There are well over 100 variables involved in the home-selling process. I can tell you from my experience of selling thousands of homes in my career that very few of these variables are unpredictable. In this chapter we looked at just few of them relative to appreciation, expenses and time. Like the hundreds of other variables, these have a predictable and logical relationship to one another and to the outcome of the sale. Our comparisons prove that in most cases it is best to sell now rather than wait for a better market. More often than not the better market will just cost you more money. The reluctance to "not giving it away" may cause you to "give even more away" in the future.

ABOUT ANDREW

Andrew Gaydosh, also known as the "Midwest Real Estate Guy," is a best-selling author and real estate expert. He is often sought by the media and real estate organizations throughout the country for his insights and expertise on the real estate industry and the Midwest real estate market. Andrew has been seen on NBC, CBS, ABC, and FOX affiliates as an expert guest on the "New Masters of Real Estate" television show. He is most recognized for his featured role in the five-part real estate series "Home First Home" that was broadcasted nationally on Better TV. He has been ranked as a top 100 real estate professional in the county by the *Wall Street Journal's* "Real Trend" report and has been a top-producing agent from the moment he started selling homes after graduating from the University of Dayton. While attending UD, he was a four-year letter winner and co-captain of their Division One men's basketball team. Shortly after graduating, Andrew became one of the youngest broker-owners in the RE/MAX Organization. He is a RE/MAX Hall of Fame award winner and has also won the top national awards honors with GMAC Real Estate and Better Homes & Gardens Real estate. One of Andrew's most notable awards is that he was honored with the prestigious "30 under 30" recognition by the *National Association of Realtors* magazine. This award is given to the 30 most successful and influential agents in the country under the age of 30.

Andrew is the managing partner/team leader for Andrew Gaydosh & Associates Real Estate in Dayton, Ohio. He currently works with BH&G Real Estate and is active in the day-to-day operations of managing his team and acting as an Expert Advisor™ to his clients. His team consistently ranks as one of the top producing teams in the Midwest region with sales over $20 million a year. Although he is very active in his business, he is regularly hired to be a speaker at industry events and media productions.

Andrew, his wife, Dawn, and their three children live in the Dayton, Ohio, area. They are very involved in the community in which they live, work and worship. When you don't find Andrew selling homes, you will find him at the kids' sporting events or spending time with his family and friends at Lake Lakengren. Andrew feels blessed to have worked with his mother and father over the years, both of who are top producing agents. "I feel very fortunate to have the opportunity to work daily in an industry that I love, with great clients, family and friends. Our tremendous successes have been the result of all these great people. It is a pleasure being able to now give back to an industry that has given me and my family such a wonderful opportunity."

To learn more about Andrew Gaydosh and his real estate organization, media appearances, books, and educational materials, please visit www.AndrewGaydosh.com.

CHAPTER 12

THE 30 DAY TEST DRIVE

BY AL STASEK

It was 1989, the year of my 16th birthday, and my dad, Big Al, tracked down a 1981 Ford Pony in the Cleveland area newspaper, and told me to grab my coat…we were going to give it a test drive! As I grinded through each gear, riding the clutch, and wrestling the wheel to get it to turn a corner, I knew it was perfect and I had to have it. I'll never forget that day. Beyond the facts that it was my first car and once the keys were in my hand, it meant immediate freedom, I believe the bigger reason it felt so good was that I had complete control over the situation. If I loved it, I could buy it. If I liked it, I could think about it and get back to the nice man the next day. If I wasn't comfortable with the way it handled around the curves, or I felt it didn't pick up the way I hoped it would, or even if I just wasn't feeling cool behind the wheel, I had an option of walking away. I was in total control of the outcome. I did not feel trapped into buying the car, even after driving it around for an hour. Even better was that though it was a used car, it came with an aftermarket limited warranty so if anything went wrong in the first three months, I could bring it back to the dealer and it would be fixed… perfect! Of course I ended up buying that 4-speed chick magnet and burned the clutch out in four months! It was a great car, and although it had its share of repairs, I was very proud of my decision. Looking back, I wouldn't change a thing.

WHY SELL YOUR HOUSE WITH A GUARANTEE?

Hiring a real estate professional to sell your home in today's economy without performance guarantees is like buying a car without test driving it and without a performance warranty—yet home sellers do this every day! Signing a listing agreement shouldn't feel like a close-ended decision. Frequently when a home seller calls a real estate agent to come to their home to talk with them about listing it for sale, it's the first time they are meeting. First impressions are very powerful, and if the agent is a polished salesperson, the seller may feel comfortable enough to sign a listing agreement for six, nine, or even twelve months that very night!

It's kind of scary when you think about it. A one-sided business relationship with almost zero accountability has just been formed. There is nothing in most standard broker listing agreements that holds the listing agent accountable to the seller for performance, communication, or the client's overall satisfaction that everything that was promised to be done will actually be done. Most of the time the agent has all the control. Every month, our office gets calls from home sellers who are stuck in a listing agreement with our competition, and they want out! Maybe it was that nice lady from their church who advertises in the weekly bulletin. Or it was their neighbor who claimed to be the expert in selling homes in their neighborhood because he's lived there for 20 years and knows the construction and wiring of these homes inside and out. They all have one thing in common—they hired an average frustrated agent (AFA) to help sell their home, but what they needed was an Expert Advisor.

TRAPPED IN A CONTRACT

Joe and Sally Green raised four boys in their humble Bay Village Ohio Cape Cod home. They loved to entertain, filling their house with family, friends and neighbors every weekend. Holidays, birthdays and graduations were regular events at the Green home, and there was always plenty of food and spirit to go around. Joe took pride in having the greenest lawn with the straightest lines in the neighborhood, and Sally loved planting her perennials and meticulously maintaining her garden. It was the only home the family knew, but after over 40 happy years of building memories and living the good life on the edge of Lake Erie's coast, they found that raking the leaves, cutting the lawn and planting new flowers every year wasn't the fun it used to be. Now empty nesters, Joe and Sally agreed it was time to downsize to a smaller, more manageable home to live out their golden years together.

They called one of the local realtors who they noticed had a few signs in yards around town, invited her over to discuss what were the steps they needed to take, and get some guidance through a process that they haven't experienced in over four decades. They sat nervously waiting for her to arrive. After all, this was much more than a real estate transaction to the Greens; it was a life transition, and they had no idea what to expect. Much to their surprise, the agent didn't suggest they touch up any of the walls with fresh paint or consider doing any repairs or minor upgrades that would enhance the marketability of the home. What's more, the agent suggested a price that was much higher than any of the homes that were currently for sale or had sold in their neighborhood. But who were they to question the advice of someone whom they considered to be the "neighborhood expert." After a couple of hours, Joe and Sally signed a 12-month listing agreement to market and sell their lifelong home, and all they could do was trust and pray they were being led in the right direction.

Four long months went by, and they sensed something was just not right. Fewer and fewer calls for showings was soon followed by no buyers coming to see their home at all! To make matters worse, they hadn't heard from their listing agent since signing the listing agreement and began wondering why they hadn't received any communication. After calling their listing agent they were offered no explanation except that the market was tough and they should just sit tight and be more patient. Sally suggested they reduce the price to perhaps attract more buyers, but this idea was quickly shot down, and they were again told the right buyer will come along—just hang in there. Frustrated and exhausted with the process, Joe took matters into his own hands and called my office to ask for a second opinion.

When I arrived at their home, Sally greeted me with a warm Irish smile. Joe was waiting to show me his basement (man cave); it was his pride and joy. He handed me a cup of coffee before beginning the tour. As I walked through their home, memories of the last 40 years were hung on every wall and placed neatly on every bookshelf. Immediately I had the feeling of a warm home and a family filled with love.

As we sat at the table together drinking our coffee, I gently explained step by step what we would need to do to get their home ready to sell fast and for top dollar. Although the news wasn't the easiest for them to hear, they listened with open minds and promised to get to work immediately with the help of their kids and some of the preferred trades I referred. There was only one last problem: the current listing agreement. Joe explained to me that he tried calling their agent's manager asking to be released from their agreement, but had no luck. That broker only offered them a different agent within their company but refused to release them. This left them no choice but to take the home off the market and wait more than six months for the listing to expire.

Once the Greens finished the needed prep work I recommended, they were ready to get the home relisted. But the last thing they wanted was a repeat of the previous experience. There was no way they were going to be roped into a long agreement with no accountability tied back to it. They were not going to stand for little or no communication this time around. If their next agent wasn't going to live up to the standards they promised, they wanted to have the right to fire them immediately and find a better option. Luckily that is exactly what my agreement promised.... accountability in writing!

They immediately signed a new listing agreement with our exclusive "30 Day Test Drive" and "Communication Guarantee." We scheduled a photo shoot with our staff professional photographers, and within 24 hours, we lit up the internet with dozens of great photos and professionally written ads describing their home and everything it had to offer. The result was an all-cash sale in less than 30 days for over 98 percent of asking price.

SATISFACTION GUARANTEED

Joe and Sally trusted our powerful Expert Advisor home selling system, and the results paid off. Not just in selling fast and for top dollar, but in a seamless transition to their next home. The fact of the matter is the average frustrated agent only sells about eight homes per year. Even with good intentions, most don't have the experience or resources to fulfill the expectations that home owners should demand when hiring a professional to assist them. Accountability is a word everyone likes to talk about—until it's time to get some!

Hiring an agent that offers performance guarantees like our 30 Day Test

Drive is a vital component of an outstanding home-selling experience. When hiring a real estate expert for the job of selling your home, be sure there is some built-in accountability in the agreement you sign. Never trust your home to an agent whose marketing plan consists of pounding a sign in your yard, entering it into the MLS, and praying another agent sells it. Only trust your home to a Certified Home Selling Advisor (CHSA), because only CHSAs have a proven, repeatable home-selling system, backed by market research, to sell homes for up to 18 percent more than traditional, average agents. Best of luck with your next home sale and may your experience *move* you!

About Al

Born in a post-World War II housing project in Brooklyn, Ohio, called Brooklyn Acres, Al admittedly had humble beginnings. He attributes his strong work ethic to his parents, Al Sr. and Kathy. They worked double shifts and multiple jobs, and eventually settled in Parma, Ohio, where they raised Al and his brother and sister. In order to make ends meet for the family, Al Sr., who was a full-time union dockworker, also sold real estate part time. Every day, after working on the docks for long, arduous hours, he would come home, shower, and head out to hustle real estate deals.

"I remember sitting on the floor next to my dad's desk one fall evening when I was about 9 years old," All recalls, "listening to him perform the same cold calling routine he went through every night. Without fail, he would get yelled at, hung up on, and sometimes even threatened. I had heard it all before, but on this night, seeing the pain in his eyes as he struggled to make a better life for us, I promised myself that I would never put myself through what he was dealing with; I would never be a real estate agent."

Thirty years later Al and his team, Stasek Group, have grown to be the number-one RE/MAX team in his market and have helped over 170 families buy or sell a home in 2012. His marketing arsenal is famous for selling his clients' homes for more than 4 percent higher than the average, and in a fraction of the time. Stasek Group's "Buyer Advantage Program" offers unique value and benefits to home buyers who hire Al's team to represent them in their home purchase.

"I dedicate this chapter to my wife, Patty, and two boys, Aiden and Matthew, for giving me my 'why' every day. We're delivering the highest level of service. In January 2012, we opened our first Stasek Group office. We have an outstanding 10-member team, and every single one of them I would enthusiastically hire again."

To contact the Stasek Group about their popular 30 Day Test Drive and how you can sell your home for up to 18 percent more, go to www.18percentmore.com, or call their headquarters at (877) 925-1018.

CHAPTER 13

AN ANALYSIS OF SUCCESSFUL HOME SALES

BY TOM DAVES

A few years ago, my clients, Jim and Mary Adams, were looking for a new home. As sometimes happens when working with a couple, her wishlist for their new home differed slightly from her husband's wishlist. After showing them several luxury homes, we arrived at the ideal property for Mary. She fell in love with the home; the gourmet kitchen was perfect. She could see herself whipping up brunch for friends and family and hosting holiday gatherings. Mary also loved the steam shower and the cork flooring. Jim, however, was not sold on the home 100%. He desired a mancave/media room that the home did not yet have, and he wasn't budging. Then, Jim saw her. In the garage, the owner had a pristine, red, 1957 Chevy. Jim fell in love.

I could tell that Mary wanted this house; it was her dream home. Jim needed some encouragement. I asked Jim if there was anything that would persuade him to make an offer on the house. Jim said he would buy the house if the car came with it. Instinct and experience both told me that it never hurts to ask. I drafted the contract offering for Mr. and Mrs. Adams to purchase the home at a reasonable price with the '57 Chevy included. The sellers happily accepted. Aside from the obviously comic value of an old car conveying with a new home, I share this story to illustrate that sometimes the most important thing you can do when buying or selling a home is to think outside the box.

Thinking outside the box of conventional tools has kept me the #1 National Keller Williams Agent overall (out of over 80,000!) five out of the last six years. What that means to my clients is a guarantee of top-notch service from a proven industry leader. I am grateful for the lives that I have changed by helping people to buy and sell homes, but I want more. I want to teach people what it takes to list and sell 500 homes per year.

Hiring an expert Realtor—I am a member of the National Association of Expert Advisors® (NAEA)—can net a seller 18% more on average than they would if they hired a Realtor with limited experience. Experience makes a difference. I have 35 years in the real estate business; it is a passion of mine. I want to share my passion with you.

Multi-Channel marketing is the way to go when you want to sell a home. You seek the right combination of referrals and repeat buyers, new clients and branding. Branding includes signage, radio, media relationships. The larger your sphere of influence; the greater is your opportunity to combine the right buyer and seller for sales success.

Many buyers and sellers make the mistake of thinking that any Realtor is competent enough to handle their real estate transaction. Many are qualified, it's true. Nevertheless, there is a distinct difference between good and great. Good gets the job done; great satisfies needs that a client might not know they have or did not know was available.

Hockey great, Wayne Gretsky said, "I skate to where the puck is going to be, not where it has been." His words became my motto long ago. Many people, misunderstanding Gretsky's quote, skate to where the puck already is. It isn't enough to skate to where the puck is –- the "greats" of the world anticipate where it will be and get there first. That's how my team manages every real estate transation in which we are involved.

Who plays on a winning team? Our team is comprised of full-time, dedicated real estate professionals. Real estate *is* their day job. Realtors who work only part time, or dabble, in real estate are not marketing your property full time or searching for the right home for you except for a few hours a day. That's important to buyers and sellers because missed marketing opportunities equal missed sales.

An excellent agent is the most important tool you have in buying or selling a home. They should have experience and be able to guide you through the process. Their professional networking will sometimes open doors for you that may not have been available without them. Their professionalism and negotiation skills will protect you and your investment throughout the process.

A strong team implements cutting-edge strategies and tools to obtain maximum exposure in the market for every home. The key is to develop a custom marketing plan for each property that meets and exceeds the seller's needs. When selling your home, look for an agent who will provide the following:

Professional Staging Services- Home staging prepares a property for showing. Beyond a thorough cleaning and polishing that every home requires for listing, home staging accents a home's best attributes while creating a buzz in what might be under-noticed areas. For example, a home stager might create a cozy reading nook in an area of the family room that previously was unused space.

Create Exposure across Platforms- Most homebuyers currently begin their search on the Internet, so a home's debut should be a virtual tour of the home linked to the Realtor's own website and listing on the local MLS. Next, resourceful Realtors will also advertise the home on a property specific website and leverage top real estate consumer websites. Very savvy real estate agents will also utilize social networking such as Facebook or Twitter to market homes to their followers.

Personal Opportunities to View the Home- Agent tours and open house luncheons create intimate opportunities for smaller groups of people to see the listing. Agent-to-agent advertising also creates a buzz about a particular property in a way that simply uploading to the MLS will not.

Target Audience- While a widespread reach is excellent to help a home sell, marketing within specific communities can be exceptionally effective. Luxury homes, for example, might be a dream for any buyer, but when selling a luxury property it is most important to reach qualified, luxury buyers. Advertising in luxury home magazines helps attract the right attention for a luxury home. You want your agent to target the appropriate audience for your home. One great question that I always ask clients before I list their home is, "What inspired you to buy this home?" It's logical that future buyers will notice and appreciate similar features.

A reputable agent will research the area to determine the target market for a home before listing or advertising it. A neighborhood in which the last ten transactions have been to single professionals is not likely to be the best neighborhood to market to families with small children.

Mass marketing- Radio and television advertising, and newspaper advertising are broader and far-reaching but they cost money. Part time Realtors will rarely have the resources to pay for such advertising.

Qualifications are important. However, finding a solid, professional agent means looking beyond their resume and into what makes an agent effective. You can use the following questions as your starting point in hiring your licensed, professional real estate agent.

Why did you become a real estate agent?
You'll be able to see what passion they have for their chosen profession and how that passion can help you. If the agent isn't excited about selling homes or helping you to find your dream home, what will compel him or her to work hard for you?

Why should I work with you?
When you ask that question, you are really asking for their sales pitch. The answer will give you an idea of how well they will be able to sell your offer to the other agent and seller when the time comes.

What do you do better than other real estate agents do?
This gives the agent a chance to tell you what they are great at.

How long have you been in Real Estate; how many homes have you sold?
This will help give you an idea of how effective the agent could be in finding your home. It also tells you how hard they will work for you and how much experience they really have in negotiating winning real estate transactions.

What are the most common things that go wrong in a transaction and how would you handle them?

This questions not only prepares you for potential issues that may arise, but also should give you some confidence that your agent knows what he or she is doing and knows how to overcome obstacles.

What are some mistakes that you think people make when buying their first home?
This information will give you an idea of how knowledgeable your agent is as well as provides opportunity for you to avoid pitfalls.

Who are the other professionals with whom you suggest we work, and what are their credentials?
Your agent should have a list of people they have worked with in the past who have proven themselves. This includes loan officers, contractors, inspectors, and even house cleaners and landscapers in some cases. It's in their best interest for you to have the best on your team to ensure you are able to find and close on the home of your choice.

Do you have an assistant(s) who helps you?
An agent who can focus on your needs and desires, instead of the paperwork, can be helpful. Often agents will have assistants or Transaction Coordinators working with them to ensure everything goes smoothly so they can give you their undivided attention when needed.

Can you provide me with references or testimonials from past clients?
You wouldn't hire anyone to work on your home or to work in your business that you had not vetted thoroughly. Do your homework and talk to references from each potential Realtor.

Remember that when you choose an agent to help you buy or sell a home, you become part of the team. As part of the team, there are certainly things you should expect from your agent, but remember to be reasonable. Here are some tips to help you build a better relationship with your real estate team:

- Don't expect an agent to call you instantly when you leave a message, but do expect a call back within 24 hours or a reasonable amount of time depending upon the situation.

- Buyers do not pay commission. The seller pays a set commission that is decided before they list their home on the market. Your agent does not receive payment until you have the keys in your hand.
- Refrain from calling your real estate agent late at night or early in the morning; send them an email instead. They have a life and family too.
- This is probably one of the most important transactions in your life. A seasoned real estate agent does this everyday and understands the many problems that arise during the process. Try to keep the big picture in mind and follow your agent's advice.
- Your house/or the house you are buying is a commodity. Supply and demand within a neighborhood play an important role in pricing and timing of a sale. Try not to become overly emotionally involved in the purchase of a specific property until escrow has closed.

A home does become a commodity the moment a "For Sale" sign hits the yard, but I understand that for clients, this is personal. Whether buying or selling a property, a client still develops his own personal relationship with the property. It just has to feel right. That's why the greatest thing I offer my clients, in addition to my experience and expertise, is the chance to build a strong relationship with them. When I understand what is important to my clients and close to their hearts, I can get us to "yes" much sooner.

Relationships are the final, critical piece in the real estate puzzle. Strong relationships with clients build rapport and understanding. Strong relationships between a Realtor and bankers can mean more financing options for a client, or a better understanding of the client's budget and how to stay within it. Strong relationships between a Realtor and repair specialists, inspectors and home stagers mean quicker responses and less lag time.

About Tom

Tom Daves epitomizes integrity, energy, hard work, and creative service in every detail of your real estate transaction. Tom grew up in the Sacramento area and started his sales habit at the age of ten, selling a San Francisco newspaper to Sacramento neighborhoods. He has continued rising early and has since built a successful career in real estate for over 37 years in the Sacramento area, and is the #1 National Keller Williams Agent overall (out of over 80,000!).

He has worked every aspect of the industry representing sellers, buyers, investors, and banks, in both the residential and commercial market. Tom is a family man with a devotion to God, his beautiful wife, and three children. An athlete by nature, in the winter he is an extreme snow skier taking his challenges from Heli skiing treks in Canada to the Palisades at Sugar Bowl. Cycling is a year round passion. In the winter after a fresh rain you will probably find him on his mountain bike on the Clementine Loop in Auburn. Summer belongs to road rides like Iowa Hill, French Meadows, Folsom Lake loop, or riding around Lake Tahoe. He continually challenges himself on one of the west's premier cycling events "The Death Ride" from Markleeville he rides a grueling 129 miles, ascending over 16,000 feet!

Tom has been trained and inspired in sales by some of the best from Dale Carnegie, Tom Hopkins, Jim Rohn and others. He uses his experience and foresight to proactively address details before they become a problem. Tom and his team work with clients to provide "Raving Fan" customer service in every detail of the transaction, from the first phone call all the way to close. He leads, trains, and motivates his team to communicate with you better consistently. Five words you can count on from Tom Daves: love, integrity, commitment, passion, and fun.

CHAPTER 14

LESSONS LEARNED: A STEP-BY-STEP GUIDE THROUGH THE REAL ESTATE PROCESS

BY LUCAS HOWARD

The year is 2002, I'm young, ambitious, and sick of paying rent, so I decide it's time to buy my first home. A family member had been renting a home, and they told me they were moving out, and that the owner was interested in selling. It was a cute home, and I thought it would be a good first home, but what did I know. I was a 22-year-old young man who knew nothing about real estate, and didn't know that I should be contacting a realtor. I made an offer for what the seller was asking and didn't even try negotiating because it seemed like a fair price. Plus, because I was dealing right with the seller, I was afraid of offending them. Inspections, what are those? I didn't even know that was an option, or that there were professionals who did this for a living…I was clueless.

Fast forward to after the closing. I am now a happy homeowner, right? I was, that is until all the problems began. The first thing I discovered was that there had been some foundation issues, then I noticed the roof was leaking, then the water heater went out, and did I mention that I had paid way to much for the home? I quickly learned that all of this could have been avoided, if I had contacted a local realtor to help educate me, and guide me through the process.

I began my career in real estate in 2004, and I absolutely love being a realtor. I get to meet so many amazing people, and it's so rewarding to me being able to consult, educate, and help guide clients through the real estate process. Because of the experience I had when I purchased, I am extremely passionate about making the home buying and selling process as smooth as possible for my buyers and sellers, and to give them the peace of mind that I never had.

Here are the basic guidelines, steps, and part of the process explained so that you'll have an idea of what you'll be looking at throughout the process. I could write an entire book on the topic, but this is to serve as a guideline, and to help further educated before you begin your journey into homeownership, or simply a refresher for those who have been through the process before, because let's face it, you don't purchase a home every day.

1. GET PREQUALIFIED

Before you start shopping for a house, you should talk to a loan officer. They will be able to provide you with valuable advice about the mortgage processes and can help you get prequalified for a loan. You are not the professional nor do you have to know everything about the loan process; this is what a loan officer is for. So the first step in the home buying process is to get prequalified to buy a home. You would contact a loan officer either from where you bank or a referral from friends and family.

Once you have chosen a loan officer, they will help you find the right loan to fit your needs, explain mortgage rates, and talk you through all of your financing options. Getting prequalified for a mortgage is not the same as applying for a mortgage. When you start the prequalification process, the loan officer will run a credit check, and gather basic financial information that will decide how much money you can comfortably afford to borrow. You will then be provided with a prequalification letter stating the amount in which you are able to purchase.

Your prequalification letter can help you start your home search process. It is necessary to have this letter so that you are able to put an offer in on a home. The seller wants the security of knowing the potential buyer has done their due diligence by making sure they're are able to buy before they accept the offer and take their home off the market.

2. USE A REALTOR/BUYER'S AGENT

As if my story above isn't reason enough, some major misconceptions people have is that they can save money by purchasing a home right through the listing agent. The important thing to remember is that the agent is hired by the sellers to negotiate on their behalf, and when you hire and sign a contract with a buyer's agent, they are legally bound to look out for your best interests. If you were to not hire a buyer's agent and went through the seller's realtor, you would have to keep in mind that they were hired by the sellers and are legally obligated to look out for the sellers' best interest. For example, if you were to inform the seller's agent that you can go as high as $150,000, then the realtor is legally obligated to pass that information onto the seller, which could hurt you in negotiations.

A buyer's agent will guide you through the entire process, from start to finish. They will help you locate all available homes that match the search criteria that you are looking for, assist you in negotiating the best price, guide you through the home inspection process, and be right by your side, holding your hand all the way to the closing table and beyond.

3. FIND THE RIGHT AGENT

When looking for a realtor, start by asking your friends and family for referrals. Once you've located some agents, interview them by asking them questions, such as how many homes have you sold in the past year (which may be an indication of how active they are in the market), what's your process for helping me buy a home (they should know the process frontward and backward), do you provide references (any good agent should be able to provide you with references). After meeting with a realtor and asking them these questions, you should have a good feeling about which agent would be the best fit for you.

4. LOCATE YOUR FUTURE HOME

Once you've sat down with your lender and figured out, not only what you qualify for but what payment range you're comfortable in, sit down with your realtor and let them know what you're looking for in your ideal home and location. They will then assist you in locating the available homes that match your criteria and help you narrow down the list until you've found "the one."

5. MAKE AN OFFER

Once you've found that perfect home, you can now work with your realtor on making an offer. There is a lot to consider when making an offer, such as what have similar homes in the neighborhood sold for recently? This will give you a good estimate of the current market value of the home. What is the mood of the market? If it is a seller's market, the houses are moving fast and close to the asking price, and if you really want the house, consider offering close to the market value of the house, or even full price. This will ensure that you are a serious contender, even if the seller gets multiple offers. If it's a buyer's market, you might want to leave more room for negotiations after your initial offer.

6. OFFER ACCEPTED—NOW WHAT?

Get a Home Inspection!

As you read with my personal experience as a first time buyer, skipping out on this step to save yourself a little money can cost you major money down the road. Also, having your Uncle Joe or cousin Tom look at the home does not constitute a good and thorough home inspection. Ask for referrals on a good home inspector. If major defects are found during the home inspection, you will have several options. If it's a serious defect, you could choose to walk away from the deal altogether, or you could reduce the purchase price for the amount of repairs, or what's more common, you could have the seller make the necessary repairs.

Mortgage Application/Appraisal/Order Title Work

At this point, the inspection process is completed, your realtor has sent your completed purchase agreement into your lender, and you will now meet with your loan officer to complete your mortgage application. The mortgage application is a detailed document that is provided by your loan officer that applicants must submit to lending institutions in order to obtain approval for a loan to purchase a piece of property. Borrowers must show their ability to repay the loan and must submit information on their debts, income, cash reserves, amount of down payment, and have a good credit rating.

When applying for a loan, the following documentation will be necessary for loan completion. Some may not pertain to every situation, but this will give you a feel for what to start collecting:

- Your social security card
- Pay stubs for the last two months
- W-2 forms for the past two years
- Bank statements for the past two or three months
- One to two years federal tax returns (typically only need if self-employed)
- A signed contract of sale (if you've already chosen a your new home)
- Information on current debt, including car loans, student loans and credit cards (loan officer will be able to verify from credit report as well)

Employment Income Verification

You may need the following items to verify your income:

- Names and addresses of all employers for the last two years
- If you work for a large company, you may want to call human resources and ask what address should be provided for employment verification
- W-2's for the last two years (and perhaps even federal income tax returns forms the past two years)
- Pay stubs for the last two months

Self-Employment Income Verification

If you're self-employed, you may need to provide:

- Year-to-date profit and loss statement and balance sheet
- Signed tax returns for the last two reporting years (business and personal)
- Other income verification

For Income From Other Sources, You May Need to Furnish:

- Social Security and disability payments

- Pension income
- Dividends
- Child Support
- Alimony
- Bonuses
- Overtime
- Rental property income

Asset Verification

Your assets may need to be verified through:

- A gift letter (if you are receiving a monetary gift from a relative)
- Statements and records for the last three months that include account names, addresses, account numbers and balances for the following accounts:
    - Checking
    - Savings
    - Credit unions
    - Mutual funds
    - IRA, 401(k) and other retirement plans
    - Securities (stocks, bonds, life insurance)

Debt Verification

The following information about your debt may also be required:

- The most recent statements or payment booklets for present creditors
- Car loans
- Outstanding student loans
- Credit card accounts
- Name and address of present landlord, along with the last 12 months cancelled rent checks
- A complete copy of any divorce decree or separation agreement to document alimony or child support

- A copy of documents related to a bankruptcy, if applicable
- Explanation letter for any judgments, with a copy of release/satisfaction
- Explanation letters for other delinquent credits of record (late payments)

Additional Documentation

You may also be asked for these additional items:

- A list of your addresses of residences for the last two years
- If you were a full-time student at any time in the past two years, a copy of your diploma or transcripts
- Relocation agreement (if you were transferred into the area)
- A check for application fee (if required by institution)
- If you are a resident alien, evidence of permanent residency issued by INS

You will also be required to obtain homeowner's insurance. This required insurance protects you against loss or damage due to theft, fire, or certain weather related hazards. In some areas, it may also be necessary to obtain flood insurance.

At this point the documentation collected is submitted into the lender's underwriting department, and an appraisal will be order by your lender. The appraiser will visit the property and ascertain that the price you're paying is in line with other values in the area. They will also order a title policy to ensure the property is free and clear of any liens.

Congratulations, your loan is now out of underwriting, and it's time to close! Many times we close at a title agency. Where ever you meet, have your signing arm in good shape, because there is a small mountain of paperwork for you to sign. Once you have signed yourself into a happy stupor, the closing agent will make sure your transaction gets recorded at the register of deeds. At this point, you get the keys from the seller, and walk around the room giving everyone a high five because you are officially now a proud homeowner!

About Lucas

Lucas Howard is the "Rain Maker" for the Lucas Howard Group and has been serving Grand Rapids and West Michigan in spectacular fashion since 2004. He and his team of real estate expert advisors specialize in the West Michigan market and reside in Grand Rapids, Michigan. Lucas developed his successful business by simply being committed to helping home buyers and sellers, by educating and empowering them to make confident real estate decisions that are in their best interest, even if that means not buying or selling a home with him. Lucas is known for his positive attitude, joyful personality, and relentless pursuit to better himself so he can bring a higher standard of service to his clients.

If you're interested in working with Lucas Howard and the Lucas Howard Group, you can connect with us at: www.lucashowardgroup.com

CHAPTER 15

HONESTY, THE BEST POLICY

BY BEVERLY HERDMAN

Knowing your prospects wants and needs and asking the right questions is like having the master-lock key to real estate success! If you are selling your mother's home or helping her purchase a home, you would know her about as well as you know yourself. Of course it would be easy to be up front with Mom. You would search properties that fit her needs, or tell her that she is not realistic with the asking sales price of her home.

Why is there that uncomfortable tendency to hold back our knowledge from a potential seller or buyer? We listen and let them dictate their wants and needs, simply nodding our heads in agreement. We wouldn't do that with our own family; at least I would hope not. Are we afraid of losing the deal? Afraid of disappointing, because we want to please? Let's face it, we all want everyone to like us and use our services. So it appears on the surface that if we tell them what they want to hear we are developing that relationship and they like us. We get the deal. Score!? On the contrary.

Isn't this oxymoronic? Think about this situation for a minute. The "right now" of doing it their way may appear to be well and good, but what about when the home doesn't sell because it is overpriced? What about when you aren't able find a home in the buyer's price range because it is unrealistic, or you find the perfect home and they can't qualify for a mortgage?

Through the years of listing appointments and buyer consultations I certainly have my share of stories. The most prominent are divorce and retirement situations. Sellers are depending upon the realtor's expertise to sell their home so they are able to move forward into the next chapter of their lives. Although, the homeowner feels it is in their best interest to walk away with as much money as possible, for obvious reasons, is it really in their best interest to tell them what they want to hear? If they are overpriced and think they can sell at a number they want, their retirement can be held up and parting ways with a divorce can become much more stressful for the entire family. Asking the right questions and getting to the heart of what is most important to the seller is truly the best solution.

> *Agent:* Mr. Seller, what is most important for you? Selling your home so you can retire and be near your family or the amount of money you walk away with?
>
> *Mr. Seller:* Both! With a smile. No really, it is the amount of money I walk away with, I really need xyz for it to make sense and make the move.

Now, start to ask the right questions.

> *Agent:* What does that number look like to you?

Here is where the realization starts to take place. The seller wants a particular number. Based on the market research for the home to be sold, the agent knows the number is unrealistic. If the home is listed at the seller's price, when will this seller be able to move forward and retire? The seller's home is going to exceed days on market, and the seller will become frustrated after wasting months. Chasing the market results in a prolonged retirement as well as having to lower the list price because the home is now stigmatized with days on the market. Due to the seller's frustration with loss of time and money, he gives up on the possibilities of moving.

Now, let's rewind and set a realistic expectation by setting the proper tone. Determining motivation (understanding that motivation changes the longer the house stays on the market, which can be costly) is of utmost importance.

Agent: Mr. Seller, after reviewing the market statistics and the amount of money you want to walk away with, would you like me to tell you what you want to hear, or the reality of the market and the realistic number to expect?

Mr. Seller: Well, I do want to move and would like to hear what I want, of course, but I guess I need to know the reality.

Every time, this is the response I hear. There is now permission to be completely honest. The right question has been asked and a tone has been set.

Sellers need to see and understand how costly chasing the market can be. The agent needs to be fully equipped with market knowledge to show the seller how detrimental it is to overprice. This is when negotiation skills, market knowledge, and showing on paper the probabilities of selling at certain prices are important. Seeing is believing; negotiations start between agent and client before the home even goes on the market. The agent's job is to sell the home, but keeping the seller's best interest is the number-one priority. If it will not sell at a number they need, the agent's position is to be honest with the seller. The seller will either be comfortable with the number and move forward, agree it is not a good time and wait, or list with another agent who will price it at the higher amount. I have seen this first-hand, time and time again. The most likely outcome? The seller will come back because you were the one who was honest; they were just not ready to hear it. This is big-picture thinking, not right-now thinking. Right-now thinking does not build a long-term business.

I had a seller who was a FSBO (for sale by owner). He was desperate for a certain amount of money. We looked at the market comparables, average days on market, and broke down the numbers at three different list prices. The closing expenses put him with a list price at the peak of the market. I disclosed to him, I could not make any promises with this list price. At the top of the market for this home size, it would need to show like a model and we were far from that. The home was listed on the market with the understanding that after two weeks we would re-evaluate. Two weeks went by and I had to pull the honest card. With the amount of showings we had, I believed we could get very close to the peak price. The bad news? The home would have to be vacant and professionally cleaned or the price would have to drop significantly.

He chose the first option. Tuesday we removed the home from market temporarily while he moved his family out. We put it back on the market the following Monday. Tuesday, the first folks through the home brought us an offer and my seller got the number he wanted. The most chilling part of this story is, the week he was moving out he lost his job. Had I not been honest with him he would have still been in the home missing opportunities of a contract. Upon losing his job and the panic of having to sell, we would have had to decrease the price to "get rid" of the home.

Can you see how honesty is the best policy? This is a core value of our company and something we stand by. Integrity is such an important aspect of any business. Buyers and sellers deserve to know what is reality and the ability to create a plan to obtain the goals they are looking for. This was a concept that has been a natural part of the way we do business; I assumed this was how every agent worked. Interviewing with sellers and purchasers who are on the unsuccessful round two or three with an agent and hearing stories of inadequacies is nothing short of frustrating to me. This is where I have learned that our business practices are different from the average agent. The buyer side of business is really no different when we hear story after story of frustrated buyers who are not being educated on the market and not understanding why they need to be preapproved prior to looking at homes or how to write a reasonable purchase offer.

The average buyer can't wait to start looking at homes. We are heavily leveraged on the internet for maximum lead capture, allowing access for buyers to view the homes on the market. We receive emails and phone calls with immediate demands of "I want to see this home today; can you show me now?" When we speak with these buyers, they have been viewing our website and conducting drive-bys all over the county looking at homes. (Just saying, gas is expensive.) When asked, "Have you spoken to a lender?" The common response is no. Where is the importance in this you ask? Lending dynamics 101. This is like going to the pharmacist and telling them you need a prescription for something you have not been diagnosed with. You first need a consultation with the doctor to determine the ailment. After the doctor has evaluated the situation, he can prescribe the proper medicine. Looking at homes and writing a contract is no different; the situation has to be assessed and both financial and credit conditions need to be evaluated. Once everything has been assessed, the lender can provide the pre-approval with their signature. Today's strict loan conditions make it imperative for buyers to know expectations of qualifying for a loan. Looking at homes first is putting the cart before the horse and creating a roller-coaster of emotions for the buyer.

The agent needs to know their buyer. What is their current living situation? Renting? If yes, is it month to month or a length of term? This can determine time frame of closing. How much is being paid currently for rent. This sets an average limit of a comfortable payment and also helps us to understand a price point. Do they own a home? Do they have to sell in order to purchase? The need to keep the buyer realistic is imperative. This means having an in-depth knowledge of the market so you can convey the process of expectation. Knowing what you can get at a certain price point is important. If they are saying they want "their cake and eat it too," but you know they are going to have to go to Timbuktu to make that happen, they need to know and not be lead to believe differently. What is most important: distance from work; a large yard; single family, fixer upper; and garage? There has to be an understanding of compensation and motivation. It is our job to relate to their needs and ask the important questions. Why would it make sense to drive buyers all over creation for a home they will never find or may not qualify for? Knowing and understanding expectations up front makes for a much healthier relationship as well as saves hours of wasted time.

It all comes down to client consultation and education. We have seen agents jump at the request to show a home to the potential buyer without any questions being asked. Most buyers come to us with the expectation of writing a "low ball" offer. The main question to be asked by the agent is "Do you want a deal, or do you want a home?" Follow up with "If this home were listed at the price you want to offer, would you offer the list price or would you offer less?" Most of the time they just want to feel like they are getting a deal. It is our job as their agent to educate on market value. Again, the negotiation starts with the client before an offer is even presented. It is imperative to know your comparables to substantiate value without letting your client overpay. If they are being unrealistic with their demands for an offer we need to tell them what is realistic and work in their best interests. Knowing how badly they want this home is imperative. Do they want it because it can be a good deal, or is there an emotional connection to it? Now the question becomes "If I called to tell you the seller took another offer that was better than yours, how would that make you feel?" This is how you determine how to write the contract. If unrealistic demands are made, the purchaser may end up losing a home they are in love with. Is this working in the best interest of the buyer if they lose a home they love, because they were not educated properly? We have helped buyers who have written unsuccessful offers with other agents, losing home after home because the agent would not explain to them to dynamics of writing a proper offer. How frustrating can that game be?

The burning question to any agent should become what is in the best interest of my client? The only way for an agent to be sure of this is if there are enough of the right questions being asked of the client. This should be a primary focus of any agent.

This was the exactly the reason why I became an agent. We had worked with one agent and had written two offers over the course of a couple months and lost both. It resulted in us giving up. Instead, to satisfy our desire for a different community, we built on an addition and decided not to move. Well, I will tell you, it didn't work. We had now outpriced our home in our neighborhood, and it did not change our desire to want to be in a different location. We attempted another agent and started round two. We wrote three more offers and lost all three! We lost five homes in the course of two years, Really? The agents were not asking us the right questions; they assumed we wanted the best price. Were they working in our best interest? We wanted a home, not a deal, and we didn't know any better; they were the experts, or so we thought. This is why I have such a desire to understand our clients' needs and wants, and I am adamant about asking the right questions.

The importance of the buyer or seller understanding how a particular agent conducts business is imperative to the success of the entire transaction. There is a lot of overpromises and underdelivering? How can a typical consumer understand the difference? The answer is simple. Is the agent asking enough questions to understand the client's situation? If the consumer is telling the agent what they want, and there are not enough or any targeted questions being asked by the agent, that's a red flag. If the client's demands are accurate and reasonable, questions still need to be asked to know how to properly negotiate in the client's best interest. A successful transaction starts with a client-to-agent relationship. Every relationship requires proper communication. To have proper communication, the right questions need to be asked and the proper expectations set.

About Beverly

Beverly Herdman, owner of Wine Trail Homes, LLC, affiliated with Keller Williams, is commonly referred to as the energetic optimist. Beverly is known for her in-depth understanding of their company's market area and keeping the clients best interest as a number-one priority. Her entrepreneurial attitude keeps her seeking for the highest levels of training to be the best and most knowledgeable team for her clients. She started her real estate career in 2005 for more of a challenge in life and business. Since then, she has attended several workshops, trainings, classes and conventions. Beverly is a firm believer in using the expertise of a coach, both personal and professionally. Her purpose in life and what gets her out of bed in the morning is to assist others in getting out of their comfort zone and living a life to its fullest potential with purpose.

CHAPTER 16

THE VILLAGE EXPERT ADVISOR

BY GLENN STEIN AND MICHAEL VERI

Most of our initial introductions to clients begin innocently enough. It may be by way of a referral, ad call, or email off an ad. My introduction to Mary came when her daughter called me off a sign in front of one of my listings. Mary's daughter came to visit for the week and was helping her mother shop for home. Mary needed reassurance that the move she was considering was the correct one. Many times a senior may need guidance from a son or daughter. This usually ends up in one of several categories: 1) The parent asks and is met with "I just don't have the time," 2) the parent is afraid to ask or does not want to bother anyone, 3) the parent gets a lack of patience ("Mom/Dad, just do it already"), or 4) worse yet, the parent has no one to rely on. I have often had to play the role of son for many who did not have anyone to rely on. Mary's case happened to be the third scenario. Her daughter just did not have the patience. This is where the need for an expert advisor comes into play. An expert advisor must have patience with clients.

The Client Conundrum

Now for a little bit of background information. Mary is a 78-year-old analytical person who needs a lot of information before she makes a decision. She is very active (kayaker, golfer, card player, board member) and enjoyed her life other than the fact that she was using her nest egg to stay in The Villages. Also, Mary had lost her husband years ago (the last time she bought a home was before his death), and he always made the financial decisions. Naturally, she was nervous, indecisive, and hesitant. My job as an expert advisor is to provide comfort and confidence in the real estate transaction.

THE RIGHT QUESTIONS

Now I needed to ask questions to fill in the missing pieces. It is important for the expert advisor to ask questions so that she or he can help to the best of their ability. Where, why, what, when are some of the questions. The answers to the questions are that Mary would like to travel, go to the movies, eat out, and treat others if she wants—immediately. The dilemma is her community, The Villages. Florida provides so many wonderful things (it's Disney World for retirees) to do, but there are fees and dues to pay for this lifestyle. However if you want action, The Villages are the place. Mary cannot afford to live in her home, which has a mortgage ($900 per month), and pay all the fees ($600 per month), but she would be miserable living outside The Villages. You have heard the stories: elderly people who retire and all they do is sit at home watching the idiot box.

PROVIDING SOLUTIONS

Expert advisors also provide good information and are problem solvers. This is where I come in and talk to Mom and ask questions and review the options. It is important for me as an expert advisor to ask questions, listen, be patient, and act honestly in favor of my client. I asked and I heard a woman who needed to stay in The Villages because her friends and activities were there—in short, her life was there. She was receiving pressure from her daughter that she was living like a "rich person" and could no longer afford to be in the community and she should move closer to her a few hours away. The advice from her daughter was sell her home, use the money to buy another place outside the area, and get away from the fees. My advice was sell her place, use the equity left in her home buy a smaller home in The Villages, with fees of only $300 per month, rather than $600. By doing that, she would save $300 per month, reduce her mortgage payment from $900 per month to $300 (a savings of $600), and most important, still be near her friends, enjoy all the activities, and do all the things she could not do before. In total, Mary would save over $1,000 per month by reducing her monthly fees, mortgage payment, property tax bill, utility bills, and overall maintenance of a smaller home. A big win. In my mind, selling her current home and moving to a small home was the right thing to do.

HONEST TO GOODNESS

In the middle of this, there was a constant back in forth between mother and daughter. Sell, don't sell, move here, move there, stay in The Villages, move out of The Villages. Once it was settled that she was selling, then we could get down to business to price the home correctly. Within a week we had a contract on her home.

Part two was find another home. We found the right home for her. It was within her budget, and it would save her a minimum $600 a month. It would allow her the financial freedom to stay in The Villages and enjoy life, because she sure wasn't by digging into her nest egg every month just to cover expenses. In fact, it was so perfect, it was the only property on the market that she could get into. We had to move quickly because, naturally, we had competition; other buyers were circling. So it was crucial that we not low-ball the offer. On the surface it would seem that offering less to get the "best deal" would be in the best interest of the buyer. In this case, if Mary loses this home, she loses much more than just a few thousand in potentially overpaying for the home. She loses the ability to afford The Villages and the joy of her life, the activities she enjoys. I needed to tell Mary the truth about the correct price of her home and to act quickly to buy the only option for her. Mary realized I was telling her the truth, sold her home, bought another, saved money and is enjoying her life. Expert advisors are honest.

The most enjoyable part of my work as a broker has been helping people get what they want. I have sold many, many homes, and in doing so, I have learned how to have patience, be a calming influence, ask the right questions, give good information, and be completely honest. So number one when looking for your expert advisor is to look for five key characteristics: patience, calm demeanor, good communicator, provider of information, honesty.

WHAT YOU NEED TO KNOW BEFORE YOU BUY OR SELL A HOME

As you can see from the home buying and selling process with Mary, there is a lot more to buying and selling a home than there is to buying almost anything else. This is because for most people this is the largest financial asset that they own, and not only is it a large financial transaction, it is highly emotional. Your home is the place where you make memories that last a lifetime and can influence generations. Who doesn't have a memory about a summer or holidays spent at grandpa and grandma's house? Think about your own life and how prominently your home is present in those memories—your house, your yard, your neighborhood, and your neighbors. All these things that influence who we are as people start with our surroundings.

Throw in the fact that most people only buy or sell a home a few times in their lifetime, and you can see why most people feel like they are on an emotional roller coaster when buying or selling their home. This is also why it is important to make sure that when you are making decisions about buying or selling a home that you have an expert advisor who is not emotionally attached to your home to give you unbiased advice so you can make the best decision for you and your family. You should look for a professional who is not just looking out for themselves and selling a home; you should look for someone with the heart of a teacher who will treat you like family and only give you advice that they would give their own family.

You also want to make sure that the professional giving you advice knows what they are doing and has done it on a regular basis. Don't be fooled by how many years they have been an agent. The sad fact in the real estate industry is that the average real estate agent sells four homes in a year. So someone could have been in business for 20 years and been involved in only 80 real estate sales. A good agent should sell a minimum of 24 homes a year to be proficient and knowledgeable about the home buying and selling process.

Would you allow a doctor who only performed four surgeries a year to operate on you, or do you feel that his skills might be a little rusty? The same is true in real estate. The skill sets required to successfully navigate the ever-changing real estate market require constant exercise of those skills and education and training on an ongoing basis. This is true now more than ever with the way financial regulations, insurance, and the mortgage market have and still continue to change in response to the real estate and financial downturn. An expert advisor constantly works on improving their skills and will invest in education to make sure that they have the latest and best information available to help advice their customers.

An expert advisor will be focused on you. They will ask you a lot of questions so that they can make sure they have an understanding of your situation and what goals you are looking to achieve. Every person has different goals and your home sale or purchase does not deserve a one-size-fits-all approach. Sometimes a home may require a small investment in time or money that can bring a seller tens of thousands more in their sale, or a buyer can save thousands of dollars on their purchase by asking the seller the right questions. Wouldn't you like to have that kind of advantage in your next real estate transaction? That is the type of results that hiring a true professional who is focused on what is best for you can achieve.

When selling a home, most people make two critical mistakes. First, they let their emotions dictate. This is natural and can end up costing you a lot in your home sale. This causes a seller to add what I like to call "emotional value" to their home and want to price the home for more than the market will bear.

The second mistake is made by many real estate agents also. This is when they take a narrow look at the real estate market and just look at what most agents refer to as a CMA (Comparative Market Analysis). This is where you take three homes that recently sold and are similar to your home and look at how much they sold for and determine the home's value based on what those homes sold for. This may look like a logical way to determine a home's value, but unfortunately, it is just one piece of a much larger puzzle. While what the home down the street sold for does have an impact on what your home is worth, there are many other factors. Did that home have 12 cats inside that used it as a toilet? Were the owners under financial pressure to sell because of a divorce, death, or job loss? Was it the only home for sale in your neighborhood when it sold two months ago, and last month five of your neighbors had to relocate, so now your home will be the sixth one on the market, giving buyers a lot more to choose from?

In real estate, the basic law of supply and demand is a dominant factor, but so are other factors like condition, differentiation, cooperation, location, exposure, marketing, and negotiation ability that will ultimately determine how much your home sells for. If you are selling by owner, then you need to have a plan to make sure all items are handled, and it is imperative that you obtain total market knowledge before you place your home on the market to make sure you position it correctly for maximum value. If you are hiring an agent to sell your home, make sure they have a plan for managing all the different aspects of the marketing and sales process.

Whether you are going to hire a professional or try to navigate the real estate marker yourself, please make sure that you have all the relevant information to make the best decision possible.

About Glenn and Michael

Glenn Stein is a husband and father of two. He graduated from Arkansas State University and has been licensed in real estate since 1998. He started selling in high volume in 2000, and in his first year he sold 32 homes. He has sold as many as 132 homes in 2004 and over 1,000 properties in his career. He started his own company in 2004, Realty Excutives Ocala, and in The Villages Florida. As broker-owner, he created property management, commercial, and bilingual divisions of real estate. In the real estate downturn he has taught and trained many agents how to serve clients and build their businesses in the process. Glenn has studied the psychology of buyers and sellers and believes that understanding how people think is helpful to having a successful real estate transaction.

Michael Veri has been a top-producing, full-time real estate professional since 1998. With consistent multimillion-dollar sales performances for over a decade, he has been one of the most sought-after agents in both the Midwestern and Southeastern United States, focusing on sunny Central Florida. Michael both contributes and hones his skills nationwide at some of the real estate industry's highest profile "think tank" venues. His passion in business is making the often complex transaction of buying and selling a home as simple, smooth, and efficient as possible for his customers, offering a range of assets from the perfect family home to investment and commercial real estate. Michael maintains his consistent success by using a team approach, implementing cutting-edge IT, and focusing on the most pleasurable experience possible, whether it is a purchase or sale for his customers. Michael has been a part of the paradigm shift of IT and internet marketing for the real estate industry, starting as early as the late 1990s. In fact, a significant portion of his business relationships are directly from the internet as well as conventional marketing. Michael can be found on the web at www.MichaelVeri.com and www.TheVillagesHomeSeller.com.

CHAPTER 17

CORE CULTURE: BUILD YOUR TEAM FROM THE INSIDE OUT TO PROVIDE THE BEST EXPERIENCE FOR CLIENTS

BY JASON IRWIN

Congratulations! You closed your first transaction, asked for a referral, and you think you are well on your way to a successful real estate career. You think to yourself, "I am hungry, I will generate my own leads, I will host open houses, I will show houses to buyers, I will take care of my own listings, I will take care of my own bookkeeping, I will be my own runner," the list goes on. Those are all great qualities and to have ambition is a great trait to have to be successful in any business. Things are going well, business is growing, although you find yourself working more hours each week, taking time away from your family and other responsibilities. You don't think about that because all you see is your business growing and you bringing home more commission checks. Then one day you wake up, go through your morning routines, although a bit more lethargic than normal, you arrive at your office, and—bam!—it's like you hit a brick wall. You walk into your office, and you have buyers calling you, sellers calling you, escrow and title companies calling you, lenders calling you, the list goes on—not to mention the hundreds of emails you have waiting for you.

I bet more than a few of us can relate to the above story. We all start out hungry and want to conquer the real estate work, thinking we can do everything. The fact of the matter is we can't. We can't do it all and expect to continue to grow. I ran into a couple of those challenges, but I quickly overcame them. I will mention shortly the most important things one must implement to run a successful real estate brokerage. First, although we all want to make money and be the best we can, we can only do that by providing the best service possible to our clients. Without clients, we have nothing, including commission checks.

I learned through school and previous work experiences that the most effective way to service our clients' needs and to make sure they have the best home buying/selling experience possible is that I couldn't do everything by myself. I knew to best service my clients' needs I needed to have a team around me, each member having their own responsibilities. I will admit, I am somewhat of a control freak when it comes to work, but I had to learn to delegate. Also, I knew I not only had to hire and form a team, but I had to make sure I formed a team that believed in me and bought into the culture I wanted. Finally, I knew I could not just go out and hire just anyone to fill certain positions. I had to hire methodically, in a certain order. All of these factors were imperative for me to put together my team so that I could not only continue to grow my business but also service my clients' needs at the level they expected and I guaranteed. In essence, I had to build my team from the inside out, from the core. No amount of money invested in marketing, etc. would serve the same purpose and produce the same results. It all starts with the team; it all started with me.

THE TEAM

When I got to the point where I could no longer do everything myself, I knew it was time to start building my team. My eight years of working for my family's company helped make this process easy for me. I was always told, over and over, the first person I needed to hire was an admin person, or who I like to call my assistant. Within three months, my revenue grew by 50 percent. Just this past month, I promoted my assistant to the CEO of my office, giving her full control of office operations. I am still the owner, and the one board member, which still gives me the final decision, but giving her the new title has already paid dividends. And, I am not worried at all about my losing my assistant, my CEO, anytime in the new future.

I had no idea how important that hire was, and to this day, my admin hire is still the most important hire in my business. After six months, I almost doubled my revenue. Having an assistant allowed me to focus on the three things that mattered most to me: going on listing appointments, negotiating and closing deals, and prospecting. (The three areas where I make money.) I still follow that today. It's when I notice I start to veer of course and not focus on one of my main three goals that I realize I need to hire more staff.

It was at this point I brought on a buyers' agent. I personally prefer to work with sellers and listings, and many new agents like to work with buyers, so it made perfect sense. My buyer agent helped with prospecting and taking care of buyer leads. Once again, my business grew even more, and I wasn't working any more hours. Actually, I was home much more often, and business was going better than ever.

A couple months later I hired another buyers' agent and two field reps to take care of my properties and listings. Recently I did some research and spoke to other agents and brokers in the industry and found out about inside sales agents. What a novel idea. I could bring an ISA (inside sales agent) who focused on my sellers and setting up my listing appointments. I recently brought an ambitious person onto my team and I have more listing appointments than there are hours in a day—it's fabulous. And yes, once again revenue shot up and grew rapidly.

Having a team gives me such an advantage with working with my clients because they know they not only have me working for them; they have an entire team. I have yet to be able to put a price on what's that worth to my clients.

Now, it's not as easy as just hiring people to fill positions; there is a lot more that goes into it. Let me explain.

HIRING THE RIGHT TEAM

I wish it were as easy as just hiring people and plugging them into positions. I mentioned earlier that I made sure I brought on staff that fit the culture I wanted clients to see and feel. To this day, I tell every one of my clients that whether they are talking to me, anyone on my staff, or even my vendor partners—escrow, title, lender, etc.—when they get off the phone with any of them, they should feel like they are talking to me, and if they don't, I tell my clients to let me know.

The only way to provide superior service is if everyone on the team buys into the company culture. Obviously I can't control escrow, title, my lenders, or any of my other numerous vendor partners, but within my office, I can control that. I am diligent when interviewing and hiring staff for my team.

Not only do I interview them thoroughly, but I check their references, and what I would like to call my secret weapon. I give them all a DISC profile test. The best way I have found to make sure I bring the right people onto my team is by using the DISC profile. The DISC profile is a behavioral assessment. These behaviors are grouped into four categories: (D) Dominance, (I) Influence, (S) Steadiness, and (C) Conscientiousness. Not to go into detail on each, but for example, I would not bring onboard someone who scored extremely high in D if I was looking for an admin or an ISA. For an ISA, I would look for someone who scored high on S, or steadiness. The ISA is on the phone all day setting up listings appointments, so I would also want them to be an I. And since they would be talking on the phone all day, I wouldn't want them to be a high C, because then they would not pick up the phone, fearing rejection.

I will be honest, I am not perfect at every aspect of running a real estate company. I know my strengths and my weaknesses, and by using the DISC profile, it has helped me add members to my team who are better in certain areas that I would have normally considered a weakness. But building my team from the inside out has all but erased my weaknesses, or at least my clients don't know what they are.

I use the DISC profile to help me hire my team, but using the DISC profile is also supremely helpful when working with clients. The more you know about them, the better positioned you are on how to approach and work with those clients. Try it; you will be amazed.

After the interview, checking the references, having them take the DISC profile, and bringing them onboard, it doesn't stop there. For every client that calls or walks through the door, I have to make sure they are all treated with the upmost respect and professionalism. To help guarantee this, I am always coaching my team—from my admin to my agents to my field reps—praising them for jobs well done, but I *never, ever* criticize anyone on my team in public, I do that in private. I don't find criticizing team members in public is good for team moral. Finally, I am constantly raising my own standards, and by doing this, the team sees that I do what I say I am going to do. I find that is one of the best ways to continually build trust and respect.

CONTINUED EDUCATION

My grandfather told me a long time ago, well, a while ago, that education is important. That stuck with me, and that's why I attended college and furthered my education by getting my MBA. I felt like I had achieved everything. Then my grandfather told me, "Jake (as my grandfather has always called me), all you have accomplished is getting your degrees, and all that proves is you have the ability to learn. It's up to you how you use what you learned, and on top of that, you will never stop learning, and the day you do, you might as well call it quits."

For years I couldn't wrap my arms around what he meant. Sixteen years later, I know more than ever what he was telling me. It's one thing to get an education, but what does that get you, where does that get you. Once I got into real estate, I realized something profound: It didn't take much at all to get my real estate license, heck, anyone can get it. With just a few hours of study time, you can pass the test, and you can technically sell real estate. I had an "aha" moment. It's not just about getting an education or getting your real estate license. To be the best, to be the market expert, to be able to give my clients 110 percent service, to be better than others in my market, I had to take continued education courses. I started taking them, even partnering up with, in my opinion, the top real estate coaches in the industry, and I instantly saw how I could serve my clients even better and help them have the best home buying/selling experience possible—more than I ever thought possible years ago when I got into real estate.

I now not only offer continued education courses to my staff, but my goal is to get them involved with my real estate coaches as well—all paid for by me. Yes, I offer them, but my team knows that they better jump onboard because my culture is reaching higher levels, and by doing this, my clients' experiences are unbelievable. I have clients who tell me that they have never been treated so great and never had the entire transaction, from beginning to end, go so smoothly. I still believe there is no better way to know how well we did than to receive referral clients, but even better is hearing clients tell me they used to hate—yes, I have heard the word hate—working with real estate professionals, but now I completely changed their perception. More than any commission check could bring, hearing that brings a smile to my face.

BOTTOM LINE

Everyone has their own idea of what they think works best. I can speak on what has worked for me, and my business is growing, and I am about to open a second office. To give your clients the best possible experience, here is something to look at: If you look at your employees, salespeople, and home buying and selling customers as clients, you will hold yourself to a higher standard of service and care for these people. Ideally, your core belief should be that you know all of your goals will be met if you do everything you can to help these people be successful. When you operate from this belief system, your results are better, your relationships are stronger, and you will forever have an endless flow of business and good quality people coming to you.

Treat everyone like they are a valued client and your success is limitless. I always make myself accessible to all my staff, and it is an unwritten rule that work time is work time and play time is play time. I take care of my staff, maybe to a fault, but I can tell you clients can see when they walk into the office that not only are we professional and we know what we are doing, but we also work together as a team, for each and every clients' needs. At the end of the day I can lay my head down on my pillow knowing I did my part helping to change a clients' life with their biggest investment they will ever make, and I wake up every morning looking forward to who my team and I will be helping that day. Life is good. Being a real estate professional is good.

About Jason

Jason Irwin is a realtor with Irwin Group Real Estate in Newport Beach, California. Jason received his bachelor's degree from the University of Central Florida, with a major in finance and a minor in marketing. He also received an MBA from the University of Central Florida. Growing up in a family where both grandfathers were in construction—one in home development and the other a project manager for the development and construction of Walt Disney World in Orlando, working directly with Walt Disney, and his father in construction as well as his uncle—construction was in Jason's blood, although he took a different route and went to work for Merrill Lynch right out of school.

After two highly successful years at Merrill Lynch, he moved out to California to work for his family in the construction business which is where Jason got his first taste of real estate and real estate investing. After working for the family business for eight years, Jason decided to dive head-first into real estate in one of the worst economic times our country has ever faced. His philosophy was "if I can succeed now, when things do turn around, I will have quite the head-start on most everyone else." Jason's passion is helping clients with all of their real estate needs and forming long-term relationships with each and every one.

Only three years into his real estate passion, Jason is on the verge of opening his second office in Irvine—his first office is in Newport Beach—and each day he wakes up enjoying what lies ahead for him and looks forward to how he can help people change their lives by helping them with their biggest investment most will ever make. By doing that, Jason looks forward to having and living a higher quality of life and being able to provide for his family and give back to his church.

For and questions or for more information, we would be happy to help. Contact Jason at Jason @IrwinGroupEstatere.com as well as our company's website at www.IrwinGroupRealEstate.com. We can also be reached at (949) 933-3768. Irwin Group Real Estate is located in Newport Beach at 2549 Eastbluff Dr., Ste. 140, Newport Beach, CA 92660.

CHAPTER 18

IN CONTROL: HOW TO PRICE YOUR HOME TO GET TOP DOLLAR

BY JASON JAKUS

In late September Linda and David Brown were looking to sell their four-bedroom home on a golf course. They saw that their neighbor Adam Franks just sold his home after being listed for only two short months. The Browns were talking to the new owners, Marge and Jack Holiday, who mentioned that when they were searching for a home they had limited choices because there are not many homes currently on the market.

During the process of interviewing realtors, the Browns discovered a lot about the home-selling process, including what they needed to do internally and externally to get their home sold for the most money. The punch list from the realtors interviewed included improving the curb appeal, painting two of the four bedrooms, and replacing the carpet upstairs, which they worked through during the following three weeks.

After the Browns selected which realtor would be best to represent them, they had the realtor, Mr. Bryant, into their home one last time. When Mr. Bryant arrived to the Browns home he had prepared several documents, which explained pricing principles and pricing strategies.

Over the next 60 minutes, Mr. Bryant reviewed the sales process and listing agreement.

3 QUESTIONS TO PRICING YOUR HOME

The conversation included Mr. Bryant telling Linda and David that there are three major questions that need to be asked when selling a home. These questions set the strategy and principles for pricing the home.

First, what is the timetable for the sale? This is a critical question because pricing a home too high may cause it to stay on the market longer than the desired timetable, and sometimes will force the home to sell at a lower price because the seller ends up chasing the market, continually reducing the price, and this causes some consumers to think there is something wrong with the property.

The second question is what is currently on the market that is comparable to the property they need to sell? If you price above these similar homes, chances are the lower-priced properties will attract a buyer quicker.

Lastly, is there anything you can do to increase the value of the home? After you have reviewed your home's attributes and features, ask yourself if there is anything you can do to improve the value. Replacing outdated appliances or refacing cabinets are inexpensive and can add tremendous value.

Mr. Bryant walked the Browns through the two pricing principles—absorption rate pricing—and average price per square foot. After this, he went through six comprehensive pricing strategies.

During the review of the listing documents, Mr. Bryant suggested a listing price of $399,799 for their home based on both pricing principles and strategies.

THE MOST IMPORTANT QUESTION

After thoroughly explaining the pricing strategy, Mr. Bryant asked the toughest question of a seller: "Where do you want to position your home in the market?" The Browns asked if they could have a few minutes to discuss it, and Mr. Bryant left the room and went outside to return some phone calls. After about 20 minutes deliberating, the Browns informed Mr. Bryant that they had determined that they would like to get top dollar for their home, so they were going to list the property at $439,000.

Even though Mr. Bryant knew this price would place the property at the top of the market, and was higher than he recommended pricing it, he accepted the listing agreement since it was a referral from his Uncle Tim.

Every Tuesday for 30 days Mr. Bryant contacted the Browns to review the activity on their property, which was not favorable. During this time, Mr. Bryant only had two showings. The Browns stated that they were concerned because at the 30-day mark Adam Franks had over 15 showings. Mr. Bryant stated that this is the power of the pricing principles and strategy. Mr. Bryant referred back to the original list price for Adam Franks' home when he first put it on the market ($398,430), and it sold for $391,800 in only 60 days. Mr. Bryant spoke at length with the frustrated sellers, and they finally agreed to a price reduction of $9,000 to $430,000.

After another long 30 days and only one showing, Mr. Bryant set up a meeting with the Browns at their home. He again revealed some staggering numbers of what homes sold in the past 60 days, and what they were listed and sold for. Being completely frustrated, the Browns agreed that they were being greedy and lowered the price to $399,799, the price Mr. Bryant originally suggested two months earlier.

THE ONLY THING YOU CAN CONTROL

There are many things that are in your direct control when selling your home, but the most important is pricing the home competitively.

Every time I meet with an anxious seller, they always have two questions at the top of their mind: What are you going to do to market my property and procure a buyer, and what is my home worth? When it comes to pricing, there is a delicate balance between the psychology and the strategy of pricing a home to position it in the marketplace. The psychology of pricing is leveraging value in the actual number, while the strategy is the process of gaining visibility based on price. It does not matter how well a home shows, or where it is located, if the price is fouled.

The price of products and services is always a result of supply and demand. I recently went to a real estate conference where I paid $16 per day to park my vehicle during the conference. I stayed two additional days for a little rest and relaxation once the conference was over. The same hotel was now charging only $9 per day for the same parking garage. I asked the parking attendant about the change in price. His response was perfect, "We always charge a premium price for parking during conferences. The number of spaces never change, but during an event we get three times the usual number of cars needing parking." In marketing this is referred to as supply and demand, which simply put is price is based on what the market demands and what supply is available.

DETERMINING VALUE

There are three principle ways to determine a home's value. The first one is absorption rate, which is examines comparable homes sold within a specified time frame, and the level of current inventory. The next way is a blended price per square foot approach, which involves looking at comparable sold properties and determining average sold price per square foot and applying that price to the square footage of the subject property. The final principle to pricing a property is using a third-party vendor and obtaining an un-biased opinion from a licensed appraiser.

Absorption Rate Pricing

I have a unique way of looking at a home's price. If I was selling yellow rubber ducks out of a storefront and I had sold 1,830 rubber ducks in a year (closed transactions), which equates to 153 rubber ducks per month, and I currently had 500 ducks (active inventory), that would be 3.27 months of inventory.

When using absorption rate pricing, you will need to use comparable homes in your analysis. You will need to be vigilant about location, square footage, amenities and condition.

An example would be looking at Heritage Farms, a subdivision in Paradise City, a beachfront community in Florida with single-family three-bedroom homes. There were a total of 10 properties sold in 12 months, with nine homes currently on the market. The absorption rate is 0.83 and there is seven and a half months of inventory. The highest price home that sold is $200,000, and it was on the market for 12 months. The lowest-priced comparable home sold for $165,000 and sold in two months. This could be plotted on a graph showing months on market on the left, and price on the right. You would be able to visually see that the median home price was $183,000 and sold in five months.

Using this example, a realtor could walk into a listing appointment in Heritage Farms and show a seller on a simple graph that if they price their home above $184,000, it will take more than five months to sell. Using this visual, I ask how soon do they need to sell their home. When the seller responds within 90 days, I pull out the graph and show them the price they need to be at based on absorption rate.

When I first started in real estate, I was at a listing appointment and prepared a high-quality Comparable Market Analysis (CMA). The customers challenged my comparable properties, throwing out statements like "our kitchen is nicer than that one" and "that property did not have the landscaping that ours does." As I researched their objections, I found that I did not agree with them. I thought the house that sold for more money actually had a nicer kitchen and that the landscaping on the other property was superior. The lesson that I learned was that these are buyer preferences and have absolutely nothing to do with price, or perceived value.

Today, Fannie Mae's Form 1004MC and Freddie Mac's Form 71 both require that appraisers calculate days on market, inventory levels, and absorption rates for the comparables and the immediate area around the subject home. When banks are pricing foreclosure, REOs or even approving short sale prices, they are looking at absorption rate as well. This pricing principle is timeless and is based on hard numbers, not opinions about nicer cabinets, tile or other features.

In real estate, anything less than a six-month supply of inventory is considered a seller's market and anything more than six months is a buyer's market.

Blended Price Per Square Foot Pricing
The next pricing principle is blended price per square foot, using a minimum of four comparable sold properties. These comparable properties should be as similar as possible to the subject property in regard to bedrooms, baths, location, features and age.

Using the comparable sold homes, add up the total amount of square footage and divide that number by the number of comparables used to determine the average square footage. The next step is to find the average price of the sold comparables by adding up the sold price and dividing that by the number of sold comparables used. Next take the average price and divide that by the average square footage to get the average price per square foot. You will then multiply the average price per square foot by the square foot of the subject property.

Here's an example:

Sq. Foot: 3213 + 2983 + 3235 + 3099 = 12,530 / 4 = 3133 avg. sq. feet

Sold Prices: $394,000 + $399,343 + $401,300 + $389,900 = $1,584,543

$1,584,543 / 4 = $391,956 avg. sold price / 3133 = $125.10 per sq. foot

Subject Property: 3100 sq. feet X $125.10 = $387,810 list price

SELECTING A PRICING STRATEGY

After a decision is made on which pricing principle to use, the next area to review is the pricing strategy. Pricing strategy is how the actual price obtains the most exposure through pricing. These strategies are used to get the home noticed and found.

Electronic Price Tiers Pricing

The first pricing strategy is electronic price tiers. This strategy of pricing includes being found on internet search websites, which use an Internet Data Exchange (IDX) search engine. These IDX search engines allow consumers to search for homes by home type, bedrooms, baths and price, and are found typically on realtors' websites. Price ranges, usually in tiered increments of $25,000 or $50,000, segment the pricing criteria. If a customer is searching for a four-bedroom single family home for $250,000 to $300,000, and your home is priced at $249,900, it will not show up in the search criteria. However; if a consumer is searching for homes from $200,000 to $250,000 it will show up in this search, but it will look like the most expensive priced home in the marketplace.

This strategy is also valid on major search platforms, such as Realtor.com and Trulia.com. If the home is not within the searched threshold, it will not be found. It is important to know how each of these property search engines is broken down.

Psychological Pricing

The next strategy is psychological pricing. This is a marketing practice based on the philosophy that specific prices have a psychological influence. The strategy is simple and through dynamic testing is proven to work. In an IDX or MLS, the prices are standard, usual numbers, which means it is common to see prices like $190,000 or $320,000. The Non-Standard Numbers strategy pricing will look like $191,481 or $321,213. A few experiments that I have conducted with pricing revealed that the psychological pricing numbers get more attention.

The Negotiation Factor

The final strategy is the negotiation factor. When purchasing a high-ticket item like a vehicle or home, most people are accustomed to negotiating and not paying full price. In the MLS, your realtor will be able to determine the ratio of sold price to list price. This can be calculated by using the same four comparable properties used to determine average price per square foot. Add up the list price and divide that by the number of comparables used. This will give you an average listing price. To figure the ratio, you will divide the sold price into the listing price.

$391,956 avg. sold price / $402,231 avg. list price = 0.974 sold to list price

BACK TO THE BROWNS

The next 45 days flew by for both Mr. Bryant and the Browns. As the three of them walked into Winged Foot Title Company, the Browns thanked Mr. Bryant. The home had over 30 showings and had multiple offers, driving up the final sales price to $402,000 with a quick close. As they entered the conference room, Mr. Bryant asked Linda and David Brown "So how do you feel about the process?" The Browns smiled and responded, "It is all about pricing your property right for the market." After the closing, Mr. Bryant handed the Browns a closing gift, and the Browns handed Mr. Bryant two referrals for neighbors that were looking to sell.

The bottom line is that you must conduct your research, understand your objectives, hire the right realtor, and use smart pricing principles and strategy to get your home sold for top dollar.

About Jason

Jason Michael Jakus, known as "the bold negotiator," leads the real estate practice of Leisure American Realty, LLC, and the The Jakus Realty Team in Southwest Florida. Jason specializes in marketing and selling luxury, golf and waterfront homes. Jason also practices commercial real estate, and his firm offers full-service property management. With over 12 years of experience in real estate consulting, valuation, investing, and marketing, he is recognized as a leading expert in real estate sales.

Jason is also the managing partner and CEO of Platinum Edge Solutions, a comprehensive consulting and training company. Jason is a national speaker with 13 years experience working as a consultant, Certified Business Coach and Peak Performance Strategist, assisting Fortune 1000 companies in execution and strategy.

Jason trains real estate agents in the art of negotiating, marketing, branding, technology and valuation practices. Jason has earned his Short Sale and Foreclosure (SFR), Broker Price Opinion Resource (BPOR), and E-Pro designations through the National Association of Realtors®. Jason is a sought-after "Voice of Real Estate" and has made appearances on NBC, and is a featured contributor on real estate for two newspapers in his local market.

To book Jason to speak at your next event, go to www.PlatinumEdgeSolutions.com or contact him at (239) 931-9779. If you are in the market to sell your home, you can obtain his free report *7 Steps to Selling Your Home in 30 Days* by going to www.JakusRealtyTeam.com, or contacting him at (239) 931-9779.

CHAPTER 19

SELLING YOUR HOME THE RIGHT WAY: 3 "P's" FOR GETTING TOP DOLLAR

BY JEREMY BACK

"For every disciplined effort, there is a multiple reward."
~Jim Rohn

Often my team and I hear people talk or joke about the three "P's" of selling a house: post a sign in the yard, put it on a Multiple Listing Service (MLS) or a website, and pray it sells. These are small parts in the process that are involved with the sale, but unfortunately these are the only steps taken by most For Sale By Owners, and disappointingly most real estate agents. That is why in 2011, 58.4 percent of the homes placed on the market nationwide didn't sell, and if they did the homeowners often took an 11 percent reduction from the asking price. Add closing costs to the table, and the homeowners walked away with almost 18 percent and even 20 percent less than they desired. In this chapter I will discuss the successful steps required to sell your home in any market for the most amount of money.

"The majority of men meet with failure because of their lack of persistence in creating new plans to take the place of those which fail." ~ Napoleon Hill

Just like anything that is sold in the world today, selling your home simply comes down to a few factors: market exposure, competition, supply and demand, the right price to attract the market, and great negotiating skills with experience to bulletproof the transaction. Using these factors and having them work for you can lead to a very successful sale of your home. I have successfully incorporated these factors into my own three "P's": being proactive, utilizing professionals, and establishing the price to attract the right market.

BEING PROACTIVE

Proactivity is simply taking the steps you need to drive the market, or in selling a home, the ability to drive the maximum number of qualified buyers you get to your home in order to get the highest price possible. Visualize with me that you are going to an auction house to buy a few items. You walk in and look at the items and take your seat in excitement to purchase hopefully with the right bid for the price you want to pay. In your seat you begin to look around and you realize you are the only one there with the auctioneer and his staff. No one is there to bid you up! You now can control what you want to pay. Now imagine you enter the auction house, look at the items you want, and you have hard time finding a seat. There is excitement in the air, and now you are worried about getting the items you want. You start to wonder if you should bid a little higher because you really want it, and you become willing to pay a little more for the item you want. As a seller it is an easy choice: You want a packed house for your home to get you the most money possible.

Let me give you an example of how proactivity sells homes. In 2011, I had clients who were ready to buy a bigger home and take advantage of rates and pricing. They had purchased their home through me in 2007 for $260,000 and they were ready to sell in 2011. The clients were experts in staging and design one of them worked for a large furniture and lifestyle company. Their beautiful home showed like a model, but they were facing a huge problem: the market around them had turned upside down. Similar homes in their neighborhood were selling in the $230,000s and below. Their beautiful home would stage better than any of the others in that neighborhood and compared more like the next neighborhood down the road.

My team and I immediately began to prospect for buyers. We called everyone in the neighborhood and asked them to invite any potential friends or family to come by and see the home. If they knew anyone who wanted to move into the neighborhood this was their chance to get the word out and pick their neighbors. We followed up with an open house invite and door knocking then prospected the realtors in the area that were successful and also had homes for sale that could be potential move-up buyers.

By taking a proactive approach we were driving the market to the house: We had over 11 showings from potential buyers in the first couple of weeks, which was good at the time and for the area. We focused on the phone prospecting and followed up with emails, while informing the real estate agents in the area that this home was ready for one of their buyers and that this home would be a smooth transition working with my team.

UTILIZING PROFESSIONALS

Utilizing a professional is my next big "P" in selling your home. In the example that I'm using we leveraged multiple professionals. Because the wife was amazing at decorating homes and furniture, we already had a professional staging appeal, which is huge to attracting potential buyers. When potential buyers walked into the home, they didn't see my client's pictures or awards, or my clients living in the home. They saw a professional-staged home that looked ready for them to move into. If she was not a professional, we would have talked to the homeowners about getting a professional stager. The average cost of staging is around $550, including items purchased, and half the stagers get it done in three hours or less.

A professional photographer is another important piece. We hire one to give us over 25 amazing pictures that could be advertised on the web, in print, and the home's own personal website or tour that is built to sell the home. Most home buyers start online, and the number-one thing they look at is pictures, so if you want those phone calls, then you need the best pictures. A lot of buyers in this marketplace need to see great pictures because they do not have the best imagination. So the pictures need to be professionally done so that the buyers can see exactly what you are offering and become attracted to the home.

A professional inspector was also called in to take any surprises away, such as plumbing, roof, or other problems with the house that my clients might not know about. It allowed us to be ready and either fix the problems or to inform the buyer before their inspection that we are aware of the problems and that the house is being sold "as is." In my experience, this can save sellers up to 3 percent on their home alone, and keep the sellers in the power seat while negotiating. We worked with a professional home warranty company that gave my sellers free coverage while it was listed, and also a great advertising piece to drive in buyers.

A professional showing service paid by my team allows agents to set appointments to show your home, and you know that the appointment is being set. Our service is available from 8 am to 8 pm. That is a lot more availability and it is easier for the agents to get in touch with the showing service than myself, if I'm in appointments most days with my phone off. Plus, I know most the homeowners can't drop what they are doing and take these calls all day. The showing service also provides a huge service in helping me get feedback from buyers and agents who look at your home. This allows us to adjust marketing, staging, and pricing by understanding what the market thinks about your home.

We also worked hard with professional real estate agents to alert them that your home is for sale so that the agents will bring us a buyer through phone calls, the MLS, and emails. The majority of homes in any market are sold between multiple brokers, so it's important to get the information out to them, and have a good reputation that other real estate agents want to work with my team on the deal and sell your home.

SETTING THE RIGHT PRICE

Price is the most important "P" of my three "P's" in selling your home. Without the price being in a range that attracts or allows the market to become interested in your home, most of the other efforts are wasted. With the price range set correctly, it allows me to get the market to the front door of your home with the efforts described above.

Price is also very interesting because if you price it too low, you lose a lot of money; anyone can sell a house under market value. It takes a proactive agent with a plan to get you the highest price from the market you are selling in.

Back to my earlier example: We listed that house for $259,900. Remember I told you that most of the homes in that neighborhood were in the $220,000 to $230,000 range. Not only did this home show better than all of those homes, but it also had an extra bedroom and bathroom than the average homes in the area. I thought these factors meant we could still drive the market to the house. I was correct but not without some naysayers. I had a neighbor actually take the time to call me back after our initial phone calls; she told me that we will never get the price and that we are way overpriced. I thanked her for the information and asked if she knew anyone who wanted our home at any price or if I got the price when was she planning on moving?

We ended up with several interested buyers for this home, and at the price we set. We put the home under contract for $260,000 in 38 days and closed the home with no problems 21 days later. If you are wondering, yes it did appraise for the purchase amount. By following a plan of proactivity, using professionals, and pricing in a range that can deliver the market of qualified buyers to the home, we were able to deliver a full-price offer. What would have happened if we followed the first three "P's" approach? My clients might have been like all the other homeowners and just accepted "average" and took an average price for the neighborhood? How much money would they have lost? How would this have affected their next home purchase and the lifestyle they wanted? For most people your home is your largest asset and investment and an important piece in your lifestyle, wealth, and life enjoyment.

Through an intentional plan of being *Proactive, using Professionals, and setting the right Price,* you create an attraction with buyers. It isn't about chasing buyers around in the market; it's about positioning yourself so that the buyers and market are attracted to you. When you are always chasing buyers or creating no exposure for the home, you put yourself in the situation of the empty auction house with one buyer—if you're lucky—and your price is going to go down. When you follow the plan and get multiple qualified buyers to see your home and want it, you create the excitement and energy to sell. That is when multiple offers come in. It's when you get market value for your home and even higher. That is success when buyers are on edge because they know other buyers are there looking at your home also. When these interested buyers start making offers to you, they will tend to spend a little above because they want your house. They don't want to lose, and trust me, their agent doesn't want to keep showing houses, so he doesn't want them to lose either. That is a win in real estate when you can attract and close with a well-qualified buyer for a price you want to sell at.

About Jeremy

Jeremy Back in an Associate Broker in Utah and has worked in real estate for nine years. He has sold large developments, new construction, condos, investment properties, estate, single family and land. His real estate career started in high school when he worked for a local title company and did property searches. He used this experience to buy and work on some property investments while serving as an air traffic controller for the Utah Air National Guard. In 2004 he received his real estate license and never looked back. He focuses on consulting his clients to make educated decisions through market report, trends and certain indicators. Education has been an important part, which he pursues daily. He has studied with some of the best coaches in the industry, such as the Mike Ferry Organization and Kinder Reese. His license is currently with Red Rock Real Estate in St. George, Utah. He practices real estate in Washington county.

Jeremy enjoys spending time with his family: his wife, Lindsey, and their three children, Kylie (8), Easton (5), and Mason (10 months). As a family, they enjoy spending time in the outdoors at the family cabin and attending sporting events, especially the Utah Jazz.

CHAPTER 20

8 SECRETS TO GETTING TOP DOLLAR IN ANY MARKET

BY JOHN SELLERS

Selling your home can be a perilous task. As a realtor with 20 years of experience, I can tell you that there are many different scenarios homeowners can find themselves in during a real estate transaction. You have probably heard horror stories from friends and family if you have not personally experienced it. Some stories have to do with a realtor not doing the right job. Many have to do with the market conditions. Others have to do with the buyers not qualifying, the house not appraising, or any multitude of things that can be found by a home inspector.

There are eight secrets that I have learned over my career to not only get you top dollar compared to other homes like yours, but to also sell quicker and easier. As I explain these secrets you may say, "These are so obvious." The majority of them are simple, but rarely do I see people implement them fully to their complete advantage.

Each of the secrets when done individually will have a real positive impact on the sales price. However, when they are combined in the right order, the compounding effect will make you look like a magician.

Implementation of the eight secrets will take planning, time and careful execution. The results can potentially help you sell your home for 10 to

15 percent more! You will also see the marketing time cut significantly and help you have the experience be really positive!

The following story illustrates what the typical home seller experiences versus the one that uses the eight secrets.

Two men are each given an axe and the task to cut down identical-size trees. Their deadline to complete this assignment is 30 minutes. The large, burly man is impatient and just starts chopping wildly with all of his force. The second man, who was quite slight physically, disappears with his axe for 15 minutes. Upon returning with exacting precision and efficiency he has the tree cut down in 10 minutes. In the meantime the large man is whacking away with his muscles aching, beads of sweat rolling down his face, and he takes the full 30 minutes to complete the assignment.

When both are done, they sit down together and the large man is angry. How could it have taken him a full 30 minutes of chopping and the other man who was half his size, only 10 minutes? The smaller man humbly shared that he had spent the first 15 minutes sharpening the axe and getting expert advice on calculating the correct angles to chop for maximum efficiency with a super sharp axe. So when he approached the task he looked superhuman, but really all he did was get some great advice, do some planning and a little bit of prep work.

Do you want your home selling experience to be like the first man or the second man? If you chose the latter, then pay close attention to each of the secrets and implement as many of them as you possibly can for exceptional results.

SECRET #1: PRELISTING HOME INSPECTION

The common practice is for the home inspection to be done after the home is under contract. This is one of those times when it is wise to see what the masses are doing—and do the opposite!

The home inspector's job for the buyer is to list any defects, safety issues, work not up to code, pests or termites, upgrade suggestions and maintenance. When defects with the house are found, the buyer is back in the driver's seat. Now you are going to have to fork over cash that was not planned for repairs or play chicken with the buyer as to whether they will cancel the contract if you do not do as they request.

Selling a home with a prelisting inspection is so much easier and puts you as the seller in the driver's seat. The biggest concern sellers seem to have is what if significant damage or defects are found. This rarely happens, but if it does it is better to find out beforehand so that it can be dealt with calmly and rationally. In contrast to after you have made your moving plans and have lost leverage in negotiating. At this point you can decide to make full disclosure of the issue and sell the house "as-is" or make the investment to repair.

For all the little items, the seller makes the repairs and then calls the inspector to do a re-inspect. The home inspector returns a clean report. Now when the buyer has the home inspected you will have nothing to worrying about and will not be blind-sided. If you provide the report to the buyer up front, they will feel more confident about offering you a higher price and may choose to not even have their own inspection.

Below is a short list of real advantages for the seller:

- The seller can hire a top-notch ASHI Certified Inspector rather than being at the buyer's mercy.
- The seller can assist the inspector and clarify anything of question beforehand. This does not usually happen when it is the buyer's inspector.
- Helps the seller realistically price home if defects exist.
- Can help seller ask a higher price if repairs are complete or do not exist.
- Seller has time to get competitive bids and make repairs.
- Removes the buyer's overinflated estimates from the negotiation table right up front.
- Giving the buyer the report provides full disclosure for legal reasons.
- Making the report available to the buyer before they make the offer along with explanations and receipts of repairs is an excellent marketing tool.

SECRET #2: EXTERIOR HOME PREPARATION

Curb appeal is always talked about, but so few home sellers actually take the time and spend the little amount of money to make it work in their favor. The first impression that a potential buyer has will set the stage for their whole visit to the property.

First thing to do is have the front yard mowed and edged. The edging really provides a crisp, clean look that buyers notice. Make sure that the flower beds are weeded, and if possible add some fresh mulch or bark. Trim the bushes and trees so they are not touching the house and do not overwhelm the property.

Next look at the windows in the front of the home. Repair or replace window screens that are sagging or damaged. If the window trim needs a fresh coat of paint, make it happen, and you will be surprised how much more the house will "pop."

How does your front door look? Is it damaged and need to be replaced. Replace the door handle if it is old and unattractive. If the door is not in good shape, make sure to put on a fresh coat of paint and include the trim. In most situations you want to pick a color that adds contrast to the rest of the house. Many homeowners choose to paint the door black or red. However, if you are not sure, the easiest thing to do is to drive around the neighborhood and look at the colors for your area that stand out.

Some fresh potted plants that are flowering are a great added touch as well. There are many more things you can do to the exterior, but these are the easiest and will get the highest return on investment.

SECRET #3: INTERIOR PREPARATION

First thing you want to do is give your house an extreme cleaning. For most people if you have the money it is worth hiring professionals to do this because they see the dirt that homeowners have just gotten used to. If buyers see your home unclean, then they will assume in many cases that the house is not well cared for, and they offer less money.

Next thing you want to do is patch any nails holes, and touch-up and repaint as necessary. If you have too many nail holes it is best to paint from corner to corner. Once that is done, look down at your baseboards. In most houses they are due some attention, and if not taken care of, greatly distract from the home's appearance. Try Mr. Clean Magic Eraser to really get the baseboards spiffed up. If they need paint or touch-up, take the time as it will be well worth it.

Rent a small storage unit. What furniture can you remove that will make the home feel bigger? Take three quarters of what is in your closet to storage. Ideally your closets should be only half full.

SECRET #4: PROFESSIONAL STAGING

Hiring a professional to help you stage your home for sale will make you money. According to National Association of Realtors, professionally staging a home can increase the sale price by up to 10 percent!

Home staging is about creating illusions. It is about creating the illusion that the house is everything the buyer wants and they could make it their own. It goes beyond cleaning, painting and simple decorating. It is an art to create the right mood. Staging can make your house look cleaner, warmer, brighter more loving and best of all will take the buyer's eye away from the imperfections that every home has.

Professional stagers are like artists. They take either a blank canvas if your house is vacant or work with what you have to create a gorgeous portrait. They have many secrets on how to take the simple and transform it so it is most appealing.

Stagers can supply large pieces of furniture if needed. However, in most cases, they are working with the seller's furniture and adding many of their own accessories to help create the illusion.

Staging a home can cost anywhere from $500 to $5,000, depending on your location, size of home and amount of furniture that is required. According to a survey done by Home Gain in 2009, home staging typically provides a 586 percent return.

SECRET #5: HOME WARRANTY OFFERED

According to Gallop Polls 8 out of 10 buyers want to have a home warranty. *BusinessWeek* noted that they want it so bad that they will pay up to 3 percent more for the home.

The good news is that many home warranty companies will warranty the home when it is listed and not require payment until closing. This way if a system crashes while the house is listed, all the seller will have to do is pay the small deductible. Should the buyer not want the warranty, the seller is not liable to pay for all the benefit they received during the listing contract.

This is another tool that enhances the buyer's peace of mind and makes them feel more comfortable about moving forward with your home over others.

SECRET #6: ONLINE MARKETING

You can do everything to prepare your home for sale, but if you don't have an excellent marketing strategy, you are not going to get top dollar and the house will languish on the market.

In today's tech savvy world over 90 percent of all buyers start their search on the internet. The top 5 sites that you want to be on for maximum exposure are:

1. Realtor.com
2. Yahoo Real Estate
3. Homes.com
4. Zillow.com
5. Trulia.com

When buyers are searching the internet, they are first trying to find homes of interest to them. Once they have found homes of interest, then their goal is to eliminate as many of them as possible so they only have a short list to visit. This is why you need to carefully select the best photos of your home and choose to showcase the parts of the home that attract buyers to your house rather than distract. By staging your home, your pictures will stand out against the crowd. Professional photos are recommended.

Craigslist in most markets is a must. This is the first place buyers seem to start their home search and it is free for you. Craigslist will allow you to post the same property every 48 hours.

SECRET #7: CORRECT PRICING STRATEGY

You can have the most incredible home in the world, in the best location, and have used all the strategies already mentioned, but if your home is overpriced, it will not sell. As a matter of fact, depending on the overall market conditions, you will not even get buyers to visit your home.

The old way to value your homes worth was to have a CMA (Competitive Market Analysis) completed. The CMA is not a bad place to start, but there is much more to accurate pricing!

First you will need to understand what the national market is doing, then your city and then your neighborhood. Once you have those factors, you will want to understand how many months of inventory there are in your area and in the price range of your home. Has the inventory been going up or is it going down?

Based upon the data gathered, you can make a truly educated decision on how to maximize the price of your home sale and still accomplish it in the time frame you desire. Interpreting the data can be tricky, but the basics are that the lower the months of inventory within a local market that is trending up, the higher you can price. Conversely, the higher the months of inventory within a local market that is slowing down, the lower you are going to have to price the home based upon previous sales if you want it to sell.

SECRET #8: HIRING A REAL ESTATE EXPERT

Hiring a great real estate professional for most homeowners is the key to implementing the secrets we have been talking about. The realtor should have the contacts and resources. I am always amazed by the poor choice of realtors that so many buyers and sellers decide to hire.

There are three factors when you hire a realtor that must be present. The first is you must like them, then you must trust them, and then the most important is that they be a top producer that is incredibly competent.

Some Questions to Ask Agents When Interviewing

1. *How long have you been in the business?* Generally you're going to want at least three to five years experience.
2. *How many transactions have you done in the last year?* Be very concerned if the agent has done less than 25 transactions.

More is not always better, but be concerned if someone is inexperienced, and they are not doing at least two transactions a month.

3. *What is your personal online strategy?* **How** many unique visits does your personal website get per month and how many registrations? Since over 90 percent of buyers start their search online, you better get this one right.

4. *Do you have references?* Written testimonials should be part of their presentation.

5. *Ask them what the current absorption rate is and how many months of inventory of homes like yours are on the market.* Based on these factors are homes like yours in your area trending up or down? If all they do is pull out comparables or a CMA, be concerned.

6. *What is their marketing plan for your home?* It better be more than putting up a sign and a lockbox and putting it in the MLS.

7. *What does your team look like?* To get the service you deserve, the agent must have staff so they can spend time working for you and not doing all the details.

8. *Ask them what top seven things you should do to increase the sales price of your home and to help it sell quickly.* For your sake I hope they talk about at least five secrets mentioned in this chapter.

Only implementing one or two of these secrets will have a positive impact. However, it is when you layer them on top of each other that the results make you look like a magician!

About John

John is the CEO of The John Sellers Group, which is one of the highest producing real estate teams in Southern Oregon. John has been in the real estate industry for over 20 years. In addition to real estate sales, he has been an industry trainer on how to treat your clients so well they will be compelled to refer their family and friends. He has also originated over 500 mortgage loans, owned a large portfolio of rental properties, and rehabbed for resale over 25 homes. John's wealth of experience and knowledge is leveraged every day so that his clients can experience exceptional results, whether buying, selling or investing in real estate.

The John Sellers Group invests their resources in cutting-edge marketing, technology and training while never forgetting the business is about people. He has built his group so that each part of the client experience is served by the team member that is gifted in that area.

Family is a huge priority to John. He has been married to his wife, Jill, for 21 years. They have three children: Zach (15), Sophia (13) and Jacquelyn (8), which seem to keep them busy with school events, music, dance and sports. When they get a break, they love to spend time at the beach, in the mountains skiing, and traveling.

John graduated from Medford Senior High and then went on to get his undergraduate degree in business administration from Azusa Pacific University.

If you would like to contact John, he can be reached at (541) 773-SELL, or John@JohnSellersGroup.com.

CHAPTER 21

CRACKING THE CODE ONLINE: GET THE UPPER HAND AND SAVE THOUSANDS WITH THE POWER OF THE WEB

BY CARLOS GERMAN

In the past eight years of working with thousands of homebuyers and sellers, I've seen the trend toward online home search increase dramatically. Its impact on the real estate industry, however, is not quite what you might expect. There's no shortage of online resources, all claiming to be the end-all and be-all in real estate and promising to help you achieve your real estate goals with ease. Indeed, one of the biggest problems faced today by homebuyers and sellers is information overload. From thousands of online articles, Multiple Listing Service (MLS) websites, and national portals, it's not surprising that so many people get the wrong advice and lose thousands of dollars in the process.

In this chapter, I will uncover six secrets to getting the upper hand and saving thousands with the power of the Web. If you are a home seller, you'll learn a little trick to make sure buyers don't undervalue your home by using automatic online valuations, learning how to specifically target the kind of buyer that is truly bound to love your home, and understanding the importance of a "deep, not wide" online marketing approach. Once you learn all these tricks and employ them, you'll be a top dog in the selling game and will never leave an extra cent on the negotiating table.

If you are a home buyer, you're about to learn the one key strategy you must know to uncover the seller's real bottom line price, how local real estate statistics can give you a huge advantage in negotiations, and how to narrow your search like a seasoned pro to highlight only the best deals.

As for the real estate professionals reading this chapter—sit tight, you are about to learn some of my biggest secrets on how to get top dollar for your sellers and great deals for your buyers by giving them the tools necessary to crack the real estate code. They'll be eternally grateful to you for it.

Let's get started.

SELLER Web Secret #1: Have a deep—not wide—online strategy to showcase your home on the Web.
As mentioned earlier, thousands of online resources are available where you could showcase your property for sale, and many real estate professionals show you how they will present your home on ALL of them. The reality is that over 95% of those websites receive very little traffic, so wouldn't it be better if you or your representative spent that time making sure your property shines on the 5% of websites that get all the traffic?

Instead of sending your property to hundreds of websites and never looking back, the best strategy is to narrow the field, targeting the 5% most visited websites and going deep on those websites by adding extra photos, links to videos, personal notes, and content that is often not allowed in the MLS but can be presented on other portals. The average home seller typically relies on their agent syndicating their property on hundreds of websites with only the details allowed by the MLS for syndication. For this reason, carefully using these portals and manually augmenting your listing gives you an upper hand that could make you thousands as a home seller because the perceived value of your home will be much higher than that of the other listings.

BUYER Web Secret #1: The advantage of local market statistics, how to find these statistics online, and how to use them to gain an edge in any negotiation.

Eighty-nine percent of homebuyers start their search online and yet most will rely on national portals that are often out of touch with their local market. Well, their loss is your gain—this trick will give you a true edge. Stop using national portals because they represent the first hits on search engines. You need to find yourself a local expert who markets specific communities and can recount what's happening in the area and the current market trends. On the surface, this information may seem like a distraction— you want to see homes and you want to see photos. But wouldn't you also want to know what the absorption rate is for a given community? How many months of inventory there are? And even the average days on market and how much on average sellers are discounting their prices before they sell?

Arm yourself with these statistics and gain a massive upper hand on the average seller who may not even be aware they exist. The absorption rate tells you how quickly homes are selling in a given community, the supply of inventory indicates how overcrowded the market may be, and the average list-to-sale price ratio shows how much of a discount is prevalent in the area. The next time you make an offer, write a cover letter describing area market trends and how you landed at your given offer price. You'll be surprised by the degree to which some sellers are uninformed, and your shedding some light into the matter may make them more likely to consider your offer.

How do you find these local websites? Instead of searching for "city real estate," try searching for community information, state of the market, or a specific zip code. On my website, www.CarlosAndTeam.com, you can see an example of what I'm talking about. Browse through one of our community pages and you'll find an array of statistics and local community information that gives our clients an edge. Find something similar for your local market, and you'll be on your way to saving thousands on your next real estate purchase.

SELLER Secret #2: Target your prospective buyers directly online through Facebook ads and search engine pay-per-click advertising.

If you only knew the profile of your home's perfect buyers—what they liked, where they lived, and how to contact them to inform them that your home is finally available to purchase? Well, you actually do! Who were you when you first bought the property? Where did you come from? What did you like? You get the picture—it's very likely that the next buyer for your home has a very similar profile to yours when you first purchased the property.

How is this helpful? By knowing all these variables, you can target these buyers online and unleash the power of the Web to your advantage. Let me introduce you to Peggy and Frank. They bought a home near Disney World because they love the parks and wanted to be close by to visit frequently. Not only that, but they understood their children and grandchildren were more likely to visit them if they lived near such a nice attraction, which meant a lot. When Peggy and Frank decided to sell their home, I interviewed them and asked them why they purchased the property. Once I learned their original motivations, I captured an idea of the target buyer for this home and added the following elements to our marketing strategy.

I created a Facebook campaign for people who liked pages related to Disney World on Facebook. I also targeted the age group most likely to buy this home, the areas from where those buyers came, and married users likely to buy a home of such size.

I created a pay-per-click campaign on the top search engines to target people searching for homes near Disney World, jobs near Disney Word, schools near Disney World, you name it.

Can you see how this simple strategy could bring you face to face with exactly the type of buyer who would be interested in your home? This trick of the trade will give you an advantage every time because the buyer who is likely to pay the most for your home is the buyer who understands all of its benefits and features, not just "Joe Buyer" down the street who wants a house of a given size and doesn't care how close to Disney World it might be.

BUYER Web Secret #2: The one thing you must know to get the seller's true bottom line—it's easy to find online but few people know about it.
The bottom line number—the precious secret sellers withhold even from their real estate agents. That's right! Oftentimes not even the seller's representative knows the true bottom line price a seller is willing to

accept. With that said, some quick online searching is all that's needed to uncover a seller's biggest secret.

It all boils down to reverse engineering. What if you knew how much the seller owes on their mortgage, what liens they may have, whether they have a second loan, and even whether they own other properties? Armed with this information, and then doing some math to determine all possible closing costs, you'll probably arrive at the seller's true minimum price. Whether the seller will accept that price is another matter, but at least you have a good estimate of his or her bottom line. From this vantage point, you can push hard to ensure you stick as close to this bottom line as possible during negotiations. Ideally your real estate expert advisor will be in the ring fighting for you, and you can remain on the sidelines, advising him or her to take another jab.

Finding this information is so easy that it amazes me most buyers don't know it. A simple Web search for "county public records search" will yield a website where you can dig up this precious information. Beware of paid-for websites; this information is available for free online by searching for the seller's name and then digging up all public records associated with that name. Let's say you discover a seller has a mortgage for $173k, back taxes of $3,400, and closing costs of $22,000. You know the seller needs about $198k to break even. Depending on how long the home has been on the market, its true market value, and the statistics we discussed in the previous buyer secret, you could even target a price lower than $198k, forcing the seller to bring money to the closing table. This is very powerful information, and either you or your real estate professional should be unearthing these details before any offer is made.

SELLER Web Secret #3: Take control of online home valuations and online buyer listing comments by forbidding them on most websites.
You've probably never heard of AVMs and VOWs—heck, you may be thinking they're a new brand of luxury car or something. Well, I hate to break it down to you, but AVMs and VOWs are actually your enemy, often having an adverse effect on your ability to receive top dollar for your property. Automated value model (AVM) is a technology that places an automatic valuation of your home next to your listing online. At virtual office websites (VOW), buyers can leave comments on your property for others to see.

Let's step back for a moment. Home prices are still recovering after the market collapse, so most online auto home valuations will "appraise" your property at less than your desired price. Why would you want to have a guestimate of your home's price, or comments from other buyers for that matter, next to your home's listing online? This could cost you thousands because buyers will receive inaccurate home valuations and think your property is worth less than it truly is.

How do you get rid of such a menace? It's very easy, actually. Be sure your real estate professional disallows both of these elements in the MLS. I personally have all my sellers approve these changes in my listing agreements with them. By opting out of these two settings, your home won't get automatic home valuations on most websites, and comments under your listing won't be allowed, thus protecting your property from misinformation and, in turn, ensuring a prospective buyer won't get the wrong impression and try to knock your price off a few more thousand dollars.

BUYER Web Secret #3: Find properties like a pro and be the first to know when a new listing matching your criteria enters the market. You have learned about getting the best deal on a home and how to possibly save thousands with our previous two buyer tips, but how do you find a great home in the first place? Let me teach you some advanced techniques.

One key to beginning your home search is to find a website that features an arsenal of tools aimed at narrowing your search and helping you to scout the best deals with ease. On our website, www.CarlosAndTeam.com, buyers in our local market can find homes by setting up a landmark, for example: Disney World, an employer, a family member's home, or even a favorite restaurant. Then buyers can search for properties within a pre-determined number of miles from the set landmark. In addition, each property suggested has the distance to this landmark prominently displayed—and all this is done automatically by our technology. That tool alone is very helpful and powerful—it can make your life easier as you search for a home.

In addition, find a website that allows you to search for homes by price per square feet. This tool allows you to search for properties below market value once you know the average price per square foot in a given community. If amenities are important to you, make sure you are using a website that allows you to search for homes in golf communities, gated communities, or even developments that allow vacation rentals. Some of these market-specific options won't be available on national sites, so try to find a great local brokerage website with the tools and options you need.

Lastly, stop putting up your guard to websites or real estate professionals willing to send you instant notifications the moment a home matching your criteria enters the market. This is an invaluable service—in my company, we only provide it to select clients as part of our Buyer's Edge Program. Sure, you may get some personal emails from an agent to see how things are going, but you don't have to reply. Just use the service, be in the know, and find out when properties enter the market before anyone else.

The other option is for you to spend hours upon hours searching for homes online, stumbling onto inventory that's not even presently on the market. National non-brokerage website are known to have over 30% of their inventory out of date and/or off the market, so being notified immediately is very important because while other buyers waste time on those out-of-date websites looking at expired listings, you'll be getting fresh information delivered right to your inbox.

About Carlos

Carlos German is the founder and CEO of Carlos German & Team Real Estate Advisors. He also serves as seller specialist for the central Florida office. Carlos is originally from the Dominican Republic and came from very humble beginnings. In his native country, even electricity and water are scarce resources, so when he migrated to the United States at the age of fifteen looking for better opportunities, he cherished every little resource and opportunity available and gave his best to make sure he could become a success.

Carlos grew up with a curiosity for technology, learning to write computer programs at a very young age, and eventually learning to develop websites and set up computer networks. He started his professional career as a tech lead for an IT firm. When he began his journey in real estate, it was a natural step for him to employ all his knowledge of technology to grow his business.

Today, Carlos German & Team Real Estate Advisors dominates the search engines in its markets, and Carlos is regarded as a leader and innovator in the community. He was recently chosen as one of six young, accomplished professionals to appear in the cover of *REALTOR® Magazine* for their "30 Under 30" feature, he was recognized as a REALTOR® "30 Under 30" along with 29 other top-producing young agents from the U.S. and Canada. In addition, his roles have included directorships for his local and state REALTOR® associations, speaker at engagements where he teaches technology strategies to peers, and chairman selected for the local chapter of the Young Professional Network of Realtors.

By following his passion for technology and real estate, Carlos developed a powerhouse website that features tools not seen anywhere else in the market. He prides himself on his "Distance To" search tool, which allows homebuyers to find properties near their favorite locations, and his "Community Search" search tool, which allows homebuyers to find local communities based on the amenities important to them.

In his spare time, Carlos enjoys watersports, spending time with his wife Rosemary and son Hector, and reading about amazing companies and entrepreneurs who have changed the way we live today.

For more information, visit his website: www.CarlosAndTeam.com

CHAPTER 22

NET WORKS: HOW REALTORS MUST USE TODAY'S NEW MEDIA AND TECHNOLOGY TO GET AHEAD

BY LEO ALBANES

I love it when a client wants to buy a home but is confused on how to find great deals with all the information on the internet today. The Fitzpatricks were a great example of a family who learned how wonderful and easy the internet could be.

I'll never forget the day: Jim and Sharon walked into my office after making an appointment off one of my websites they just stumbled upon while searching the web for property in Florida. Jim mentioned that previous realtors had showed him tons of homes but nothing they liked. The other realtors simply didn't listen, let alone understand what his needs were. All the other realtors just wanted to drive around, looking at the property *the agent* wanted to show, not the property the client wanted to see.

My first question to the Fitzpatricks was if I could make sure the homes they saw would *only* be homes they liked, would they work with me? The answer was unanimously yes, of course.

If I could make it that easy for them, they would definitely allow me to represent them with their home purchase. So I had to educate them a little. I explained how I would be able to search the local MLS database, enter specific criteria they wanted, then send results to their email. They would be able to click on a link to a personal webpage that I set up for them. From there, they would be able to see all the listed information on each home, multiple pictures, take virtual tours, and sometimes videos of the home's interior and exterior. They would also be able to view the property from aerial satellites photos, be able to zoom in for close-ups, and rotate the image 360 degrees, all as if they were there at the home.

They immediately asked where they could sign up! Once I entered my clients' criteria, I let the software do the work. It would alert my clients automatically by email any time a new listing matched their criteria or any existing listing had a status changed, like reduced price. The website I provided enabled them to mark each listing as a favorite, possibility, or rejection, and type in any notes on a specific listing. This enabled them to organize the chaos and allows me to interact with their notes.

I told them that a great realtor makes their website interesting, easy to find and use, making it easy for the consumer to find the perfect home. With me, they had nothing to worry about. True to my word, Jim and Sharon took just a few days and decided on one of the six homes we saw, where they now happily live.

SIFTING THROUGH THE CLUTTER

The Fitzpatricks are like many people I work with: They wanted a home but didn't know where to look with all the internet clutter. After all, in the old days, when someone wanted to buy a home, all they had to do was find a local paper or magazine. The ads were always there. Now, online marketing has picked up where printed ads left off. There are hundreds of pictures, phone numbers and listings stretched across too many websites to count. The huge amount of new information out there doesn't help. It's disorganized, and it just confuses people who want to buy or sell a home and aren't sure where to start.

The number one complaint I hear from new clients is that they couldn't find any decent information before they came to me. I'm here to tell you what I've done right.

EASE OF USE

If you want customers, your website must be easy to find and full of the options home buyers want to use. I've seen countless real estate sites that don't make any sense. We're living in a new technological era, where everything is at your fingertips.

Realize that more than 80 percent of real estate transactions start online! The search engines are the gateways to the web's information. You must get educated on how the internet works and understand that to stand out, your information must be the most accurate to what the searcher is looking for, the simplest web page, the easiest to understand, and no distractions—only subject matter.

You also need lots of pictures with links to more information on the picture or subject matter and don't forget videos. YouTube is owned by Google, so videos rank better than text and will get you to the top of the search engines faster.

Here are the basic components of a website that delivers results:

- A *uniquely branded website* that is user friendly and easily navigable
- Strong *calls to action* to entice visitors to use or inquire about your services
- Relevant, *original content* to establish authority and resourcefulness
- Strong *link popularity* to build credibility with the search engines
- *Videos*. If a picture is worth 1,000 words, how many books can a video write?

Having a website on the search engines is one thing but knowing how to market a real estate business online is another. There are too many competitors in the arena right now, so unless you are doing something to set the standard, the chances of your real estate business getting the exposure it needs online is going to be pretty slim.

CALL TO ACTION AND CONTACT INFORMATION

When designing a site, remind yourself that you're just dealing with people, and people want useful tools, not a mess. Ask yourself: Would I use this service? Most of the time, websites only need good pictures, some important information, and a way to contact an agent.

One thing realtors forget more than anything is a "call to action" or "squeeze page" to get their contact information out to the masses. A "call to action" is anything that helps the client to get the ball rolling after they've found information they're interested in. It's the next step, and I can't believe that some realtors forget to include it. Your "call to action" and contact information has to be there, and it has to be easy to find.

OPTIMIZATION

Let me introduce a term that shouldn't be new to any of you: search engine optimization, or SEO. If your site doesn't come up in major search engines like Google, Yahoo or Bing, it might as well not exist.

Also, if it's not near the top of the Google search page for your area, the customer will go someplace else. Educate yourself on the subject or hire a reputable company to optimize your website landing pages. Pay per click (PPC) is another option, but you still need a good web page.

Your money is better spent optimizing. Once your site is fine-tuned, people will visit it organically, reducing (PPC) costs.

Here's a SEO tip: Whenever I post a picture or new listing, I will optimize that listing by attaching keyword tags to the caption and description, and also geo-tag its location. Search engines love this stuff and will match whatever the perspective client is looking for. For example, when a listing picture is being viewed, the consumer will run the mouse over the image. A text box appears with the description of the picture containing the niche keywords that the prospect is searching for online, linking it back to you.

Each of my listings include the maximum amount of pictures allowed, instead of just four or five. (The search engines will rank your listing higher with more pictures. On your listing don't forget to include pictures and videos of the area/community). *Remember content is king!*

SEEING THE BUSINESS IN NEW WAYS

One thing I've noticed about doing business online is that you have to go to the customer. For example, I pay to advertise my listings and my image on large, one-stop realty sites. They're huge and have top ranking in the major search engines. Many people like to start their housing search there, staying anonymous until they are ready to speak with someone.

Needless to say, they generate more traffic than any one company's site. Some of these real estate sites include Zillow.com, Trulia.com, Realtor.com, Real Estate.com, etc. These sites are like supermarkets that sell fruit from many different farms. If you make sure your fruit is front and center, it's a fact that you'll get more eyes on your product.

And then there's social media—listen up! Here's the thing: I am not an adamant social media fanatic. But in today's competitive market for business, you have to be. No smart realtor will ignore social media outlets like Facebook, YouTube, LinkedIn, ActiveRain or Twitter. I use them all the time because my future clients spend much of their lives there, writing status updates and talking to their colleagues and friends. When they decide it's time to find a home, they'll start talking about it and searching things about it on social media. And I'll be there to help answer any question they may have.

All of this social media exposure can be outsourced and be done automatically for you. There are many companies that will manage your social media outlets, all for a couple of dollars a day. They will write current real estate topic and niche market articles for you, automatically updating and maintaining your social media accounts weekly so you can spend time doing what you do best—negotiating real estate deals.

PEOPLE TRUST EACH OTHER

Another very important thing to remember is that people trust each other more than they trust you as the realtor. Until you wow them, a customer will trust their friends first, past customers second, and you a distant third.

Never underestimate the value of customer testimonials. They are your online resume. Great reviews will get you noticed and contacted guaranteed.

Better yet, use video recordings. Once you've finished a deal with a happy client, and while they're still excited about their new home, get them in front of the camera and record a video testimony.

Ask anyone and they'll tell you that information is much easier to digest in a video than it is in big chunks of text. Plus, videos are very easy to optimize and get better search rankings.

Here's a tip: Shoot the video in front of your sign and the home that was just purchased. Bring a big "*Sold!*" banner.

WORK IS SOMETIMES BETTER OUTSOURCED

More and more, successful entrepreneurs outsource work that used to be done by full-time employees. With a new employee, you have to train and trust that they can do what they've said they can. For those reasons, I've adopted a different approach. When I can, I'll hire professional freelancers to do certain projects on a contractual basis.

For example, in the past, when we needed to write articles for real estate magazines, we looked across our office for whoever the best writer was. That person had to stop what they were doing and write.

Now, I ensure that job goes to an online outsourcing company so my people don't fall behind. I also outsource when I need to market myself, listings, and services on the internet, which requires SEO and a steady stream of new content to stay relevant.

That's where successful businesses are going—streamlining when they can, opting to hire on demand, using project-by-project contracts. I advise you to look at your company's to-do list and ask yourself what tasks can be hired out.

BITE THE BULLET: HIRE AN ASSISTANT

I've saved my best piece of advice for last. Whatever you do, hire an assistant! Once you do it, not only will your efficiency double, but your profits just might double too.

Think about it: As an agent, your work is out in the field, showing houses and meeting people. Once you execute a contract, the paperwork and follow-up for closing should be done by someone else, with updates sent to you at each stage of the process.

What few people understand about this business is that once you sign the contract, a whole series of tasks come into play. For example, inspections, building permits, title search, pest inspection, mortgage lenders, appraisal, etc. If a real estate agent has to do the bureaucratic work of finalizing the paperwork, they will lose valuable time that could be spent generating new business. If you hire an assistant, even part time, to take care of the paperwork, you'll be able to spend more time out in the field making money.

FINAL THOUGHTS

In my time as a realtor, I've learned to balance my knowledge of the internet with timeless people skills that helps me sell homes. Stay sharp, continue to learn, get help with your online strategy, seek a mentor, expand your network, and get to know the people you're working with. They could be sending you your next referral.

It doesn't have to be rocket science. Just be fair, be honest, be humble.

About Leo

After growing up in the tropical city life of Miami, Leo moved to Chicago to take on corporate America, where he says he honed the competitive edge he brings to real estate today. After trading futures commodities in the pit, he says, "You really learn how competitive this world is and to have even a small edge makes all the difference." Leo was a former commodities broker at "The Chicago Mercantile Exchange," where he quickly moved up the ranks by being aggressive, responsible, hard-working, and most important, a man of his word.

Leo decided to move into real estate when he moved back to Southwest Florida, where he became a real estate broker in the Punta Gorda area. With knowledge of technology and with the internet just beginning to explode, Leo saw an edge to incorporate the new tech into real estate.

The internet is the future in real estate, and as always, Leo wants to be the leader of the pack, spending time learning and teaching others various aspects of technology and new media available for realtors, like LeoAlbanes.com (www.LeoAlbanes.com) and Search Homes in Punta Gorda (www.searchhomesinpuntagorda.com/); popular blogs like Punta Gorda Fl Realtor (http://puntagordaflrealtor.com/); and networking sites like Facebook, LinkedIn, Twitter and ActiveRain.com. Leo also launched his own TV Channel, Punta GordaHomesTV (http://puntagordahomestv.com/), where he streams video feeds of homes he tours.

He's excited about the ability in today's world to use this technology to allow clients to literally sit in their own living rooms and make buying their dream home happen. With today's technology, you no longer have to "drive by" to view a home. With Google or Bing maps, you do a "fly by," seeing homes not only in aerials but close-up bird's-eye view (angled shots), with 360 degree views of the properties.

Leo Albanes has quickly become known as "The Negotiator," a savvy realtor, who believes in good, old-fashioned customer service, where the client is No. 1. In the end, it's all about quality service. "Whatever the customer wants, I'm there to provide," he says.

CHAPTER 23

PRICE ISN'T EVERYTHING: BOOST YOUR ODDS OF GETTING YOUR DREAM HOME WITH THESE LITTLE-KNOWN STRATEGIES

BY MARC CORMIER AND TANIA IVEY

At the Tania Ivey Real Estate Group our job is to make our clients the best-educated buyers or sellers in the market. We often come across buyers who have been looking for months, sometimes years, and have not purchased a home; and in most cases, it is because the buyer and his/her agent have not implemented an action plan. This is the largest purchase in the buyer's life, and they are willing to make it without a plan? That's like Rocky Balboa getting into the ring with Apollo Creed without training or a manager! Succeeding without preparation is called luck.

Does anyone really think by showing a prospective buyer 20, 30 or even 100 properties that he/she is doing the buyer a service? A weak agent—yes I said it, a *weak* agent—is the agent that fails to take the time to understand his/her client's needs and wants. Why would a buyer want to work with an agent who doesn't take the time up front to understand a buyer's needs? The agent should spend at least an hour to uncover the buyer's needs and desires. The goal should be to spend an hour or more up front to uncover the buyer's needs and desires. Then find the perfect house within the first five properties that the agent shows. If that fails, then another meeting of the minds needs to occur because something is getting lost in translation. An agent's job is not to show every property in the MLS but rather to *find* the property that matches his/her client's needs.

Around the country, the real estate markets are constantly changing. The notion of one big real estate market is a fairytale; they are individual markets. Real estate is all about the local market. Tania and I have serviced the Washington, DC, metropolitan areas for almost 20 years. You may be familiar with some of the local cities we've serviced: Bethesda and Potomac, Maryland; McLean and Langley, Virginia; Washington, DC; and Loudoun County, Virginia. Real estate is impacted by the national mortgage industry; however, a house selling in Potomac, Maryland, is not influenced by a house selling in Maumelle, Arkansas.

The following 15 points that Tania and I are about to discuss are relevant in 99 percent of the markets throughout this country. These points will help position a buyer's offer so that it's more likely to be accepted, which should also not cost the buyer any additional money. Imagine making a stronger offer without even raising your offer price. When a buyer is being properly represented, these are all points his/her agent should address with them. Remember, agents are not all the same, just as doctors and lawyers are all not the same. In every field of work, there are winners and losers. Make sure the person you are counting on is a winner; otherwise you may end up being the one taking the loss.

First and foremost, your agent should speak to the listing agent and find out the status of the property in addition to the seller's most favorable terms. Flat out ask "Besides price, what else is the seller looking for regarding the terms of the contract?" One thing that may sound silly or nonsense is to make sure that the offer is completely and correctly filled out. It will amaze you to see the lack of common sense in certain aspects of real estate.

> 1. Know the absorption rate. Realtor.com states that in order to know this, you must recognize and understand the following factors: the time frame, the number of homes sold during this time, and the number of active homes (Realtor.com, 2011). Knowing this and reminding the seller that currently there are

X months of inventory on the market help remind them that you, the buyer, have choices.

2. Match the seller's ideal closing date.

3. If you are in a position to remove the appraisal contingency in a contract, that is huge in today's market for a seller. To make sure this extremely aggressive strategy is right for you, consider it carefully and heavily consult with not only your agent and lender but the broker too. I've seen offers that the seller accepted a lower offer, which had the appraisal contingency removed. This may be the riskiest strategy as well as one of the boldest.

4. Do your home inspection prior to submitting an offer or at least within the first three days after contract ratification.

5. Do your termite inspection within the first two days after contract ratification.

6. In your offer, cap your home inspection repair items to a specific, limited dollar amount.

7. Have your mortgage lender write a "strong" approval letter versus just a "plain-ol' run of the mill" preapproval or prequalification letter.

8. Use a well-known, reputable and *local* lender, I repeat *local lender*.

9. Offer to let the seller stay in the property for a few days after closing at little to no cost (I strongly suggest consulting with your agent regarding security deposit).

10. Have your title company begin title work immediately upon receiving the contract. They need to make an introduction to all parties within the first 24 hours of receiving the contract.

11. Avoid a bidding war. One of the easiest ways to stay out of a bidding war is to act fast and decisively. If you see it, like it and want it, make a strong offer right out of the gate. Don't be like Agent A in the story below. Make an offer so strong and desirable that the seller is afraid to lose your offer.

12. Handwrite a note to the sellers. In some cases, a hand written note to the seller, introducing your family to them and telling them how much you want the house, can be extremely powerful. Let them know you are planning to raise your family in the home, just as they did. Make the connection and bring the seller into the "emotional zone."

13. Time the delivery and presentation of your offer. It's a shame that technology has replaced some of the good old fashion methods of communicating. We consistently try to merge the old with the new and want to keep the things that benefit our clients' ability to win without costing them more in terms of money. This technique is so important and yet has died off like the dinosaurs. Ask a listing agent and most will tell you that 99.9 percent of the offers they receive are emailed to them. The buyer's agent has not attempted to build any type of rapport. I'm always impressed and reiterate this to my seller when a buyer's agent actually personally delivers their offer and introduces themselves to me and my staff. Real estate is all about human interaction, and we all know we would rather do business with people we know. Your agent should be trying to get to know the listing agent. You want the listing agent to impress upon the seller that they (buyer and listing agents) have "met." This should make you stand out among the other offers as someone who really wants the property. That's a connection the other offers are not making. When a buyer's agent simply asks if they can bring over their offer instead of just emailing it, that is a major wow effect! That "wow" can be the difference between getting the house of your dreams or losing out to a competitor. You shouldn't have to ask your agent to deliver your offer, but if you don't, I can almost guarantee it won't happen (unless you are working with the Tania Ivey Real Estate Group Inc.). This simple method will make your offer stand out from the crowd.

14. Keep your offer clean and concise. If a home is listed for sale at $400,000, and you offer $400,000 but ask for 3 percent seller subsidy, *you are not offering full list price*! I cannot tell you how many times both buyer's agents and buyers say, "We

are offering full list price." No, you are not; you are offering 97 percent of list price, not 100 percent. Remember, you are buying the house to live in, raise your family in, and create memories in. With the historically low interest rates we have as of the writing of this book, the additional $12,000 will actually increase your monthly mortgage rate around $50 per month. You need to determine is that worth you losing your dream home?

15. Finally, in some cases, you may simply have to decide if the best strategy for you to achieve your dream house is simply to bid above the list price. Remember that if you maintained the appraisal contingency and the property fails to appraise for the contract price, you and the seller re-enter negotiations and in many cases, the price is adjusted down to the appraised value.

WILL YOU BE THE WINNER OR THE LOSER?

The following true story illustrates and highlights the difference between a winning offer and a losing offer. Tania and I represented the seller, which allows us to be able to share the schedule of events and monumental mistakes that cost a buyer a home that he loved:

In Fall 2012, we listed a property that had been listed by another agent for a few months. The property hadn't sold, and the seller wanted a top-producing real estate agent that was capable of moving product. We immediately repositioned the property and had the seller make some simple, but impactful modifications costing less than $100. We relisted the property and within a week we received multiple offers. Agent A contacted me within the first three days of showing the property and said his client had interest. He had asked if there were any offers on the property, and I had replied that there were not. I told him that we were expecting an offer within the next few days and the conversation abruptly ended. Agent A made the mistake of not consulting with me, as the listing agent, to see what the seller was looking for in regards to contract terms. Three more days passed before he submitted his client's offer.

When devising the offer, I suspect that the conversation between Agent A and the buyer went something like this:

Agent A: They don't have any offers.

Client A: What do you think we should do?

Agent A: Let's offer a low price and see if they counter.

Client A: OK, but you do understand I want the house.

Agent A: I understand, let's talk tomorrow. I'm going to get you a steal of a deal.

Within hours of Agent A's offer arriving into our office, Agent B calls in, and she begins to ask questions like "Do we have any offers? What is the seller's plans after the sale? Will she need someplace to stay? How soon does she want to close?" As I was walking out of my office to present Agent A's offer to my client that night, Agent B's offer came in. I briefly reviewed it, put it in the folder and headed off to my client's home, with not one but two offers within a week of repositioning her property.

At our client's dining room table, I presented both offers. Agent A's offer was low, and it contained almost every contingency known to man. Then I explained Agent B's offer to my client, offering list price, putting close to 50 percent down, closing within the time period my client had hoped for, and best of all removal of the appraisal contingency. The appraisal was of concern to both Tania and I, and we conveyed that to our client when the price was being established. The property was in fantastic condition and had been upgraded well beyond anything else in the development. Since the real estate meltdown and overregulation of the appraisers, it was almost certain that an appraiser would disagree with the price established by a willing buyer and seller. With the successful closing, a new price point has been established in this community. My client, a widower in retirement, did not want to go back and forth negotiating one offer against the other. She wanted to move on with life, so she countered a few very minor items and ratified Agent B's contract the following day.

That afternoon Agent A found out his offer was not accepted. He called me highly upset to say, "Why didn't we have an opportunity to counter? My client really wanted that property! My client is very upset!" After he finished his rant, I asked him, if your client wanted the property, why did you write such a weak offer, to which he replied *"because we expected to get a counter."*

I will conclude this chapter by asking the question, If you (the client) want the property, why let your agent submit a weak offer? This is not a marathon; getting a contract ratified is a sprint. Ask your agent if this the strongest offer you can submit. Ask "What can I do to improve my offer, other than simply raising the price?" Tell your agent to get your offer submitted immediately after signing to curtail any chance of losing the property to another offer that came in earlier. By delaying the submission of the offer, this allowed Agent B to submit her offer. Remember to strike fast and hard. Otherwise, you might find yourself in a bidding war that could have been avoided. Get the property under contract as fast as you can. When a market shifts from a buyer's market to a seller's market, you may not see it coming, but if you are not observant, it will hit you like a freight train.

One last golden nugget of information to not overlook: Have your lender call the listing agent and talk up the ability to close and the possibility of even closing earlier than the established settlement date.

About Marc and Tania

Marc Cormier was born and raised in the hustle and bustle of New York City. He graduated from Brown University with a Bachelor of Arts in both urban studies and organizational behavior. Marc is uniquely interested in the science of human behavior, which has allowed him to innately understand his clients' needs/desires. He has even continued his passion through several post-graduate, executive-level business courses at Dartmouth University, Wharton School of Business, and MIT. Purchasing his first investment property at the age of 21, Marc has spent the last couple decades of his life immersed in real estate in several different markets in the U.S. Using his experiences from the Army (former Army Officer), as a negotiator, and as an entrepeneur, Marc has developed an unparalleled ability to read between the lines in a consultation to deduce a clients' needs and desires. Settling down in the Metro-DC area over 10 years ago, Marc has matured his sharp sense of understanding combined with dedication to always provide his clients with the most up-to-date information and strategies so that his clients have the best opportunity to secure the property of their dreams.

An accomplished realtor, Marc holds the distinctions of a Certified Distress Property Expert (CDPE), a Certified Short Sales Expert (CSSE), a Seniors Real Estate Agent (SREA), and a Certified Divorce Real Estate Expert (CDREE), and many other certifications. Marc has been recognized as one of the Top 1 Percent of Realtors. He was also a runner up in the Ernest and Young Entrepreneur of the Year Award.

Tania Ivey was born and raised in the beautiful and lush Montgomery County, Maryland. She has flourished for over a decade in the Metro-DC residential real estate market. She is devoted to finding her clients their homes of their dreams and thrives off of these successes. Her long-standing career in real estate is attributed to her keen sense of understanding clients' desires/needs and analyzing the available inventory to find the home that best encompasses both sets of characteristics. Intuition and instinct have allowed Tania to discover the location of the best homes, deals, and/or steals in the DC area. In real estate, experience and knowledge is what separates a good agent from the pack. Tania knows the best neighborhoods, the best school systems, and the homes that best suit her clients' desires.

CHAPTER 24

YOUR START DOES NOT DETERMINE YOUR FINISH: HOW TO RETIRE EARLY WITH REAL ESTATE

BY TRACIE TOM

Where you start in life, in school or in your career does not determine where you will finish or end up. Where you start only determines how far you will have to go and how hard you will have to work to get to your destination.

I grew up impoverished and in the foster care system. On the day I turned 18, I was no longer part of "the system" or reliant on my family for financial support. However, I was also now on my own. My one goal was to make it, to be self-supporting and successful. I couldn't afford to go to college, and I needed to support myself, so I found a job. My first job was with Fruit of the Loom sewing at the local plant. Determined to make it and despite my lower-wage position, I was able to save $19,000 by the time I was 23 years old. I promptly took that money and purchased a piece of property. Friends and family told me I was nuts and that the land was Louisiana swampland. The land needed to be cut and worked. Two years later, when I sold that property for nearly $60,000, I proved them all wrong.

When I was very young, my aunt and uncle owned a very successful chain of funeral parlors. When we used to visit them, we had to drive past all the fancy houses in our beat-up old car that I affectionately called the "land barge." I was embarrassed. They had this gorgeous house and I was in awe. I wanted what they had, and I recognized that the owners of the funeral home made the money and the employees didn't.

I understood two things from an early age:

1. Money sitting in a savings account is about as useful as paying an employee to sit at her desk surfing the web.
2. Entrepreneurs are the wealthy people because they keep money moving and working.

Money should be working for you. I choose to keep mine employed all the time. After I sold my first property for almost 3 times what I had paid, I reinvested that money in a mobile home park. I put the $60,000 down on that $100,000 mobile home park that is worth $1 million today. Then, in turn, I invested the rental income produced from the sites in the mobile home park into the purchase of houses that I began flipping for a profit.

I retired at 35 years old on the income from my investment properties. When do you plan to retire?

This isn't rocket science, friends. I don't have a college degree from a major university. In fact, I couldn't afford to invest in an education and still support myself when I graduated high school. I invested in myself and in my business and learned through the school of hard work how to make a substantial living in real estate. By the way, I don't hold a real estate license either! If you will absorb what I teach you here, and replicate what I have done, you can retire too—sooner than you think.

SACRIFICE

You have to SACRIFICE along the way to keep things going.

Real estate appreciates. You have to be willing to do without in the short term to be able to invest and make money in the long term. Even if an investment loses value short term, it is still excellent for long-term income. At the time I bought my first piece of land, I needed a new car, but I kept driving my old car to save money. I could have paid cash for a car, but cars depreciate while real estate appreciates. Success requires sacrifice.

PRICE PROPERTIES COMPETITIVELY

Whether pricing property for rent or for sale, you want a quick turnover. Waiting for a house to sell or to find a renter willing to pay more in rent causes your money to sit idle. In 15 years, I have never had a property on the market for more than 3 months. I have never lost even one month of income on an empty rental. When flipping a property, stage the home for sale. You do not have to stage every room, but staging the dining area, main living space and master bedroom helps buyers to see potential. Enlist the assistance of a great, trusted Realtor who will help you price the property to sell quickly. It doesn't matter what you think the property is worth. Do your homework before you buy in a specific area so you know in advance how much you will be able to net from the property.

When renting a property, I always take multiple applications, interview on the telephone and then interview the best candidates in person. You do not want just any warm body renting your investment. The right tenant will stay with you for years. I have some tenants who have rented from me for over 5 years. Do not feel the need to charge the highest rent. I know people who charge high rent for their properties thinking that it will bring better renters. Actually, they have higher renter turnover. High turnover leads to greater wear and tear on the property. It also makes more work for the owners and leaves the properties empty for months at a time. Empty properties do not generate income.

LEARN TO LOOK BEYOND

I made $275,000 *profit* on one house that I flipped. I paid $60,000 for the 4,000 sq. ft. property because it had fire and smoke damage to the second story. Other investors looked at the smoke damage, and thought it was worse than it was, or they had to finance the purchase and the bank would require a long list of inspections and repairs before financing. I had cash reserves to pay for the property and complete the repairs, and, I had enough experience to know that tearing out drywall (an inexpensive repair) would eliminate most of the damage to the upper floor. I changed the damaged staircase to oak wood, eliminating the carpeted stairs and creating a focal point to ascend to the previously smoke-stained upstairs. I renovated the kitchen and updated it. The property quickly sold for a $275,000 profit.

WHENEVER POSSIBLE PAY CASH

Cash speeds up all processes. Once you have cash reserves, your negotiating and buying powers increase exponentially. Advantages of cash purchases include the ability to purchase at auction, greater leverage when purchasing, less headache than financing and money to get repairs and updates done quickly.

RESEARCH, RESEARCH, RESEARCH

Do your homework. Learn about the area. Most areas will be okay, some will simply appreciate faster than others will. The only caveats are known drug areas. Nothing kills the value of a property faster than drug-related crime. Lower income areas are still a good investment as long as the area is family-friendly. This is true for both resale and rentals. A few hours of research studying the market in your area or determining if a home is in a flood zone are a necessary aspect of your business.

If you plan to purchase the property to flip it, you need to find out what types of loans will be available for the property. If a potential buyer cannot get a VA or RD (real estate development) loan, you will be limiting your pool of potential buyers. You can generally find out online what bank loans are available for a specific address. Anything outside the city limits is usually eligible for RD loans. Available loans are also important if you plan to keep the property as a rental, as you will want to put down as little down payment as possible in order to keep your money working for you and not the bank.

KEEP YOUR MONEY WORKING

It is a good practice always to retain some properties as rentals to generate cash flow. Rentals provide income to sustain you in between, while you are renovating and selling other properties. As mentioned previously, cash keeps your money moving and working for you. A dollar sitting in the bank isn't doing anything for you; it might as well be sitting on Facebook.

BECOME AN EXPERT/MANAGE YOUR BUSINESS

You are self-employed. Remember that. If you are not working, your business is at a standstill. As owner and operator, you need to learn your business inside out. You wouldn't design a skyscraper without as much as a rudimentary knowledge of design and construction. The same is true of your job as an investor or a landlord. Make it your business to learn as much as you can about the industry; become the expert.

Learn which areas of town command the best rents or which neighborhoods are in the highest demand. You can search websites such as: www.realtor.com to see what properties are listing and selling for in an area. Locate reputable contractors, painters, Realtors, landscapers and plumbers. Be smart and find multiple laborers whom you trust to do those jobs. Some of your knowledge will come from references at first—later on, trial-and-error will have educated you.

You can make money even if you don't do the improvements yourself. In the beginning, I did most of the sprucing up of properties, such as painting and gardening. Now, I have favorite professionals to call upon. My favorite handyman works a day job and moonlights for me renovating my houses. My relationships with multiple, trusted laborers ensure two things: I know who to trust to make repairs and how expensive those repairs will be. You are the owner-operator of your business. Become the owner who can estimate repair costs on a property in less than 15 minutes, so you can get to the next steps of making an offer, rehabbing, and flipping the house.

I've shared with you the fundamentals of investing in real estate to rent or flip, but what will really make your business grow to the success I have had are the little extras I bring to my business. We always appreciate when people go that extra mile for us. We love the waiter who keeps the water glass filled or the doctor who stays in the room and really listens to our concerns for longer than ten minutes. Providing added touches in your real estate business keeps tenants happy and keeps buyers interested.

Over the years, I have developed a formula for renovating spaces for maximum impact. I will share my tricks with you if you promise to use them and create some of your own.

1. ***Paint:*** Choose several paint palettes you like and stick with them. I periodically research the color trends for interiors and exteriors of houses. It's easy to do, all you have to do is look through the latest swatches and look at books at your local paint store, Lowe's, or Home Depot. After you find several palettes that will appeal to a wide range of buyers and renters, you will be able to purchase paint in quantity and speed up the process of deciding how to update your properties. Never make the mistake of choosing colors that reflect your personality.

2. ***Staging:*** Stage your property with furniture and some accessories. I keep two to three sets of furniture on hand in storage to use to stage my properties for showing. The furniture coordinates with the paint palettes that I use most frequently so that the home has a unified and professional look when a renter or buyer comes to view it.

3. ***Quality Updates:*** Do not make the mistake of updating a property with cheap or low-end materials or appliances. Be mindful of your budget but use quality products. Appliances are a great example here because they catch buyer's and renter's eyes. You can purchase stainless steel appliance groups on sale several times per year. They update and modernize a kitchen dramatically and cost far less than new cabinets or flooring might. When selecting cabinets or flooring, choosing quality materials that are mid-range in cost will net you more in the end.

4. ***Unexpected:*** Throwing in benefits for the buyer, such as closing costs, get the buyer's attention. Change details buyers wouldn't expect; I change all the doors in every house that I flip. Doors show wear, and they date a property. Replacing them is an inexpensive update that adds value to the property.

If you are enthusiastic about owning, renting or flipping properties, you can start your business now. It starts with you, wherever you are today. Your start does not determine your finish. If you have savings in the bank already, start researching your area for the best investments. If you don't have even one dollar saved, don't worry. Start today. I am proof that you can start with nothing and still retire early if you are willing to sacrifice a bit in the short term and learn all aspects of your new business. Create a plan to save the money you need to begin; after all, every business has a business plan. Then, get out of your own way so your dream can take flight.

About Tracie

Tracie Tom's entrepreneurial spirit materialized when she was just eight years old and launched her first business – Spice Ropes, inspired by some that she saw hanging at a newly built Wal-Mart in Arkansas. She immediately bought supplies to make them herself and set out on a new venture. Within weeks she had profited close to $200, a tidy sum for an eight year old. She invested the profits into a button-making business and started a drop-ship company, all before high-school.

By the age of 25, she owned a portfolio of income-producing real estate. She took her love of real estate to an entirely different level when she decided to start flipping properties. By the age of 35, she was financially able to retire, but still continues to develop and flip properties. She is currently working on her personal memoir, *Soles*.

Her mission is to help business people succeed in the real estate market.

CHAPTER 25

MORE EXPOSURE AND BETTER RESOURCES = FASTER SALE AND MORE SELLER PROFITS

BY MICHAEL LaFIDO
AND LINDA FEINSTEIN

DIFFERENTIATE YOUR HOME

The first thing a real estate agent needs to do to get your home sold is to make your home "stand out" above the competition. Albert Einstein said: "The definition of insanity is doing the same thing over and over again, expecting different results." Nowhere does that hold more true than in real estate today. For decades upon decades, most "traditional" real estate agents rely on the same strategy to get homes sold: put a sign in the yard, enter the home into the MLS, host an open house, and maybe put an ad in the paper. Last year, 58.4 percent of homes that were listed for sale did not sell. While some Realtors® might attribute such a depressing statistic to the overall housing market or economy, we believe poor exposure and marketing are to blame. Why did the 42 percent of the houses sell while their competition did not? It comes down to differentiation. Effective marketing of a home relies on differentiating that home from every other home in its class.

There are over 115 variables involved in the home-selling process that must be identified and proactively managed to attract the highest possible offer. Differentiation when listing and selling your home in today's new economy is not optional when it comes to getting top dollar for your home. This chapter discusses some of the ways we have found works best to differentiate your home.

INVEST MONEY IN MARKETING

Exposing your home to the largest number of qualified buyers gets you the best possible price for your home. The problem is most Realtors® are too cheap and spend more on a Starbucks coffee each day than they do on marketing a seller's home. As mentioned previously, most agents rely on traditional marketing strategies in today's market, and unfortunately, fall woefully short of getting you the exposure you need to attract the largest number of qualified buyers through your home to get you the right offer for the highest price.

The problem in the real estate industry is that the average Realtor® only sells six to eight homes a year, which is difficult to make a living off that income, let alone have enough money to invest in marketing and continuing education to better their services. Most agents only invest 10 percent of their income on marketing and the systems to run their business. With the average real estate agent netting about $25,000 a year as of 2012, he/she only invests about $150 per month to run his/her business, including marketing for your home. This amount is certainly not sufficient enough to get your home the exposure it needs to attract potential buyers. It's not hard to see why most homes get such little exposure.

WARNING: An agent who isn't willing to spend any money to market his/her listing is just waiting to collect a commission check from someone else's hard work. The reality is that every product on the market has marketing costs associated with it; real estate should be no different. One has to spend money to make money. That is why The LaFido team's motto is "It's Not the Market…It's the Marketing!"

CERTIFY YOUR HOME WITH THE *VERIFIED* HOUSE DESIGNATION

We recognize from experience that many elements of the home-selling process can be distasteful or even scary. An appraisal that comes in too low or an inspection that turns up wood-destroying insects or mold will destroy a deal. Car dealers have for years relied on special reports that highlight the virtues of the cars they have for sale: car facts reports that even list what are know are defects to the vehicle.

Surely, such a report would give buyers greater confidence to make an offer on a home. We developed the "Verified House" program to create a transparency in the home-selling process, which increases buyer confidence. A "Verified House" will have the following completed before the house is for sale and goes on the market: an appraisal, a complete home inspection, a home warranty, and an updated title report. These reports are offered to buyers and their agents before they see the home. Copies of the reports are also left on the kitchen table for buyers to read during their viewing of the home.

HOME PRE-INSPECTION

The number-one reason contracts fall apart before the closing is home inspection issues. Knowing what pitfalls you'll encounter with an inspection and getting them resolved prior to listing your home can save you as much as 2 to 4 percent in repair cost vs. price. So instead of waiting until the home has an offer on the table before finding out what may be wrong with the home, we choose to answer the biggest questions before we list the home. In addition to cost savings on repairs, a pre-inspection will reveal any "deal killers" and positions your home to attract a higher offer.

APPRAISAL

Appraisals up front will detract buyers from making "low ball" offers. With websites like Zillow, many times buyers feel more educated than their agent. An appraisal will trump any of those website's suggested price. The latest research found that 26 percent of all homes that were under contract with a buyer, appraised below the contract price. So investing in an appraisal ahead of time will educate all parties.

TITLE REPORT

With so many short sales and foreclosures, there are a lot of horror stories out there. Buyers will have the peace of mind that a Verified House comes with a clean title (no contractor or bank liens). Ninety-nine percent of homes listed do not offer a title report ahead of time.

HOME WARRANTY

Offering a home warranty to prospective buyers helps your home sell faster and for up to 2.2 percent more. The peace of mind a home warranty offers you and prospective buyers is priceless.

1 PERCENT HIGHER SALE PRICE

Based on market research, a Verified House can get you up to 1 percent more for your home. Buyer's agents are more motivated to show a Verified House, as it has a greater likelihood of closing than does a nonverified property. Buyers, especially those who are relocating and have a very tight time frame for closing, like knowing what they are purchasing and that the home has already passed through inspections.

Visit <u>VerifiedHouse.com</u> for more information.

CLIENT COMMUNICATION

Did you know that 9 out of the past 10 years the number-one complaint of sellers is "lack of communication" with their Realtor®. Many sellers felt that their agent listed their home and then disappeared—never to be heard from again—until maybe closing. Part of distinguishing a home from its competition also involves distinguishing the Realtor® from his competition. We believe an agent should initiate communication with his client bi-weekly using whichever form of communication most appeals to the client. For example, one might ask the client if she prefers contact by telephone, email or via text messaging. Knowing a preferred method of contact up front means that both parties will get more from the communication and that one can reach the client more easily should anything arise with the property.

Make sure the Realtor® you are interviewing has a communication schedule so you are not left in the dark.

USE PROFESSIONAL INTERIOR DECORATORS AND STAGERS

Only the top 1 percent of Realtors® include a professional stager with their services. Eighty percent of real estate agents don't even recognize home decorators or stagers as being a vital portion of the home-selling process. A consultation with a professional staging expert will help you to determine what, if anything, needs improvement in your home to make it show the best while on the market. Market research shows professionally staged homes sell in as little as 30 days and for up to 6 to 10 percent more than homes not professionally staged. This is a critical step in the differentiation process.

- *Interior decorator:* A decorator helps the owner plan anything from a simple improvement in color, draperies, or fixtures to improve the way a home shows, to a major renovation designed with resale in mind. Simple changes like neutralizing paint colors or removing worn carpets can go more smoothly with a decorator's assistance. A decorator has no emotional attachment to the home and, therefore, sees the home with keen eyes trained to see potential. Oftentimes for the homeowner, redecorating a room themselves can feel like erasing memories. Decorators have no such notions.

- *Home stager:* Home stagers are similar to decorators in that they help the homeowner "stage" or rearrange rooms to look their very best. An experienced stager or decorator takes a room from ho-hum to holy cow! Adding an amazing light fixture in a foyer with 10-foot ceilings can be the one element that wows the buyer from the second they step through the door. Our favorite stagers and decorators have great connections to help purchase discounted price items for the homeowner. Ultimately, a staged home will sell in a shorter period of time and for more money than an unstaged home will. Regardless of whether one chooses an interior decorator or a stager, the goal is to stage the home for sale before the photographer shoots a single photo of the home for the fliers and MLS listing.

HOME DETAILING CREW

Preparing a home for listing involves more than moving some furniture around or painting walls. While those things are important, neither will mask a home that is filthy or requires maintenance. The top 1 percent of Realtors®, like us, who pride themselves in helping their clients manage the sale from beginning to end, will have a team of reputable people to assist homeowners in preparing their home for listing day. Window washers, handymen, painters, appliance technicians, and landscapers are all invaluable when getting a home listed. Even professional photos will not sell a home with filthy windows or loose baseboards.

HIRE A PROFESSIONAL PHOTOGRAPHER

Photos of a home listing will likely be the first image of the property seen by buyers and other real estate brokers and agents. Knowing that you never get a second chance to make a first impression, it behooves a listing agent to hire a pro to do the job. Before photos, the only things one has to recommend the home are price, location, and condition. Yes, a professional will cost more money up front, however, photos that show a home from the most advantageous angles will help the home get more showings in person than will a quick snapshot on the Realtor®'s pocket camera. Now, while retouched photos that "erase" the dead tree or the powerlines from the front yard are tempting, avoid them. Buyers despise showing up to see a home that was missrepresented in the photos. Such photos create a level of mistrust in the agent for potential buyers. Clear, quality photos with excellent lighting that display a property's nicest features are the goal.

Beyond improving a home to highlight its best attributes, the home cannot sell itself. Marketing a home remains the jurisdiction of the real estate professional.

PROACTIVE VS. REACTIVE COMMUNICATION

Before an agent even shows a property we have listed, that agent receives a telephone call to tell the agent a little bit about the home and to allow the agent to ask questions if necessary. After the home showing, we follow up again with that agent to elicit feedback about the property. If multiple agents give similar feedback or make the same complaint, one can bet that what they are saying is valid.

A personal touch is another way to achieve better relationships with other agents; for example, we choose to use personal staff to schedule showing appointments instead of a showing service. Agents come to rely on our attentive staff and know that they can get a showing scheduled quickly. Time is money, after all.

NEGOTIATION

Being a strong negotiator requires a thorough understanding of not only the real estate sales process, but also how to get from point A to point B without sabotaging a deal.

A top producing agent understands the principles of negotiating from a position of strength and knows what it takes to get you the results you want. Managing the buyer's expectations and their agents is vital. The top-producing agent probes the co-op agent to get information about the buyer to make sure you're in the best position to succeed.

GET THE RIGHT AGENT BY ASKING THE RIGHT QUESTIONS

Getting the most amount of money is not something that is left to chance. It is the result of proven, tested and measured strategies that produce overwhelming results for the seller.

What it really means is that the skills and abilities of your agent are what will get you more money when it is sold. And if your agent cannot prove to you beyond a shadow of a doubt that he/she is able to employ a proven repeatable system to get you those results…you will be leaving a lot of money on the table.

Differentiating a home from its competition is the responsibility of the Realtor® one hires. But what questions can one ask to determine which Realtor® to hire in the first place? As previously mentioned, ask the Realtor® what he spends per month on marketing. Other than that, ask the following questions of prospective Realtors® to help gauge their previous experience, success, and effectiveness:

- What is your average number of days on the market vs. the market average? If the market average is 158 days to sell, you want the Realtor® who sells homes much faster than 158 days.

- What is your average list-to-sell ratio? (In other words, the amount of money their listings actually sell for compared with the list price). If the home listed for $100,000 sells for $96,000, then your sell ratio is 96 percent. In addition, find out what the market average is for the sell ratio. If the average in one's area is 93 percent, then a Realtor® with an average of 96 percent is, generally, a better negotiator and marketer.

- Do you offer an easy exit guarantee in writing if I am not satisfied with your service? (In other words, can you fire the realtor?) The seller should be able to fire a Realtor® who does not market the property adequately. Remember, the Realtor® works for you.

Differentiation is our tested and proven system that takes the risk out of selling your home and guarantees that you'll get the best price for your home no matter what the market conditions are. As a rule, homes do not sell themselves. Sellers wishing to shorten the time their home is on the market, and/or who want to maximize their profits should hire a Realtor® with a successful marketing strategy who understands the importance of transforming the family home into a home that stands out in the market. When you hire an agent who is licensed to offer the "Verified House" system to seller clients, you are hiring someone that represents the top 1 percent of real estate agents in North America.

Remember, It's Not The Market…It's The Marketing!

About Michael and Linda

Michael LaFido and Linda Feinstein have both been recognized as two of the best real estate brokers and marketers in the country, focusing their business on helping sellers sell their home fast and for top dollar...even in this new economy.

For the past several years both Michael and Linda have been voted a "5 Star Agent" by their current and past clients. Less than 2 percent of all agents in Chicagoland were awarded this distinguished honor this past year.

With Michael's marketing system, sellers get his 201-point marketing plan and all the techniques discovered in his research that will allow sellers to sell their home in as little as 39 days for up to 18 percent more. All of his systems were developed *after* Michael interviewed and shadowed the country's highest volume Realtors® for the course of almost six years.

Last year Linda was top agent in DuPage County and the 68th biggest producer in the country, selling 94 million in volume. That is equivalent of selling 188 $500,000 homes.

Michael and Linda are very guarded of their selling system because other agents have secretly tried to discover their selling system. *Their systems are so advanced, they've had licensed Realtors® hire them to sell their own homes!*

Their office is the only real estate office in the state of Illinois that offers the Verified House selling system. For more information on that system, visit VerifiedHouse.com.

CHAPTER 26

SETTING THE SCENE WITH STAGING

BY PAULA DRAKE

After pricing a home correctly, the next most important step is staging your home. A correctly staged home with the right price will net you more money and result in your home selling much more quickly than a home that is not staged. The biggest objection many sellers have is that staging costs too much money. But for as little as $200, you can have a home staging service come into your home and do a touch up. They always first ask if there is anything you don't want them to touch or move, and secondly what would you like them to do with the items they won't be using. Staging isn't decorating; it's more like depersonalizing a home so that perspective buyers can imagine themselves living in it. This can mean removing family photos, piles of clutter, and even the cat's litter box as well as adding neutral color paints. Staging is a means of transforming your home into a style that is attractive to buyers and has been proved to sell homes faster and for more money.

Vacant homes sell for less than a home that is furnished. There are companies that that can bring in furniture to stage your home. Staging a home has always been part of the homeowner's responsibility, but it was often as simple as keeping the grass cut and picking up dirty clothes. The seller's agent would make recommendations if the owners were clueless about elements that turn off potential buyers. The late 2000's recession turned real estate into a buyer's market with increased inventory. Sellers had to look for any advantage to make their property stand out from the other homes on the market. U.S. research indicates that home staging can reduce time on the market by one-third to one-half and could get as much as 10 to 15 percent more than an empty home or one not properly staged. The whole purpose of staging a home is to have a potential buyer envision themselves living in your home. To accomplish this, your home environment has to be transformed into a style that buyers will find comfortable and with little or no work required to make it feel like their new home.

Staging works! A recent nationwide survey has shown that homes that have no market interest stay on the market for an average of 236 days. Homes staged by an accredited home staging professional are under agreement in an average of 7.6 days. Moreover, the equity increase is a minimum of 3 percent. Attractive homes do sell but after an average 32 to 42 days on the market. When a home is staged prior to going on the market, the average time-to-sale pending is 6.8 days, with the same equity increase of 3 percent. Having your home professionally staged by a certified stager is a great investment.

A PICTURE IS WORTH 1,000 WORDS

The next step after having your home staged would be to have your home professionally photographed. This will ensure proper angles and lighting. You have to remember people today are very visual and this will enhance their vision them living in your home.

The first time people will view your home will be on the internet. This is why pricing and staging and good photographs are important. Once they preview your home, they can picture themselves living there. This also can bring multiple offers, netting you more money. In homes that are not staged, people have a hard time visualizing themselves living there.

Most people look at several homes before making a decision. So going into a staged home knocks out the competition because the home that is staged is the one that people remember.

When a home first comes on the market, this is a crucial period. This is when you attract the most buyers because it's new to the market. When priced, staged and photographed correctly, it attracts the buyers looking in your price range and will create a price war.

So many times people want to overprice the home and not stage it and say buyers can always make an offer. This is a big mistake because when priced and staged right, buyers realize it and are afraid of losing the property, so they tend to make a full-price offer or close to it. When a home is overpriced, the buyer will wait for the price to come down and will come in with a much lower offer, which results in the seller losing money.

GIVE 'EM WHAT THEY WANT

Buyers today with the economy the way it is want to see the value in the price. They can't afford or nor to they want to do much to the home. The majority of the homes that stay on the market for a while or fail to sell are overpriced, and buyers cannot see the value in their appearance and condition. In a market like we are in, with a good amount of inventory where 58 percent of the homes expire or fail to sell, it's more important than ever to have your home stand out so that it will be one of the next homes to sell. The longer the property is on the market, the less you will net.

Staged homes that are overpriced will still take longer to sell but will get more activity. Without adjusting the price, you will end up netting less money. Today, more than ever, you need to price, stage and position your home in the market—not just on the market—to get the fastest sale and net the most money.

There are over 115 variables involved in the home-selling process that influence the price you can get for your home. If you proactively manage all of these variables, your home will sell at the top of the market, and if you ignore these variables, your home will attract much lower offers or worse no offers at all. The variables fall under the seven laws. Staging falls under the third law: the Law of Differentiation.

Here are some more staging facts for you. Professionally staged homes:

- Can sell for 6 to 10 percent more money
- Bring a return on investment from 251 to 569 percent
- Decrease market time by up to 50 percent
- Increase perceived value
- Attract higher offers

- Dramatically increase odds of selling

Builders are also a good example of getting their properties sold by staging. Ever go by a new development? A builder will always have a model home. When you walk in, it just seems homey. The furniture is just placed right in every room. They even have the table set perfectly. You can see your family living there, and it feels like home. Then you walk into the same home, but it's vacant. It's harder to visualize where to place your furniture or how it would look. It's just doesn't give you that same welcome-home appeal. Builders have been doing this for years. I guess we could learn a lot from them. People just get a better picture of what their home would look like and imagine themselves living there.

STAGING STORIES

Let me share some stories on how sellers needed to sell quickly and staging helped them net more and move on with their plans. I was referred to a couple by a past client to help his close friend sell their home so they could move to Florida. He had just been offered a job he has wanted for awhile and needed to be there in three months. I went over to preview the property. It was a three-bedroom, two-bath Cape built in the mid-'80s. They had recently put in a new kitchen with a center island that could fit four chairs. It had a new heating system and a finished basement with a laundry room, exercise room, and a large family room with recess lighting and an electric fireplace. The bedroom on the main level was a little small, but the two on the second floor were larger with another full bath. The home had a large deck that overlooked a private backyard.

At the time we were competing with 20 other homes on the market in their price range and only three a month were selling. We had to make sure this home was going to be one of the three a month. We had a staging company come in for touch up where it would show at its best and be ready for pictures. We had the pictures done and ready for the market in two days. Within the first couple of days on the market, we had five showings and an almost full-price offer.

The sellers were excited, and the buyers couldn't wait to get into their new home. Everything just fell into place, and we were able to close four weeks ahead of schedule. The buyers moved in, and the sellers were able to move on with their plans. They are very happy in Florida and have found a new home.

I'VE BEEN INSPECTING YOU

Another time I got a call from a realtor out of state who asked me to help sell her parents home for her and her siblings. The parents were deceased and none of them lived close by. I met with four of them and toured the home. It was a four bedroom, one and a half bath Cape with a fireplace living room and a two-car garage. It was built in the '40s and was dated. They couldn't tell me much about the home because none of them have lived there in over 15 years. This time not only pricing and staging was important, but they really needed to think about doing a home inspection. This way, we could address any of the problems that may come up and scare a buyer from the home or have to take less. The home inspection turned up faulty wiring, low water pressure, and water drainage problems around the home. They had these items taken care of up front. We staged the home, had the pictures taken, and the home went on the market. It sold in two and a half weeks. The home inspection went fine because everything that would have caused a problem was already taken care of. A young couple bought their first home and was very happy. The sellers were glad to see a young family moving into their parent's home and knew that their children would be just as happy as they were growing up in the home.

Once again it was important that they had listened and took my suggestion, or the home could have been back on the market after the home inspection was done. This happens more than people realize. You can price and stage correctly, and the sale can still fall through because of the home inspection.

Plan on the home inspection taking up to three hours. Once a home inspector comes in, he starts with the exterior. Then he goes around the outside to check for insects, electrical connections, water drainage problems, and the roof. Once inside they check for bugs, heating, electrical, foundation cracks, and signs of water in the basement. They check each level's outlets, plumbing, signs of water leakage, windows, and finally, the attic for signs of mold.

When they're done, they talk to the buyer and discuss each discrepancy. When a lot of discrepancies show up, it can get very overwhelming and starts sounding worse than it is. If the issues were addressed earlier, they could have been resolved or addressed ahead of time. This makes the buyer more at ease with the purchase and feels the home has been taken care of. If the homeowner has taken care of the little items, he knows the homeowner has taken care of the big items.

If a buyer walks from the home because of a home inspection, the home goes back on the market. If something major has shown up it would have to be addressed by either fixing the problem or disclosing it to the next buyer. A buyer has 10 days from the time the purchase and sales contract is signed to get a home Inspection. Some people want the home inspection done before they sign the agreement. The reason for the time frame is so if the buyer does walk, the home will not be off the market for any length of time. Sometimes a buyer will go forward with the sale but will want to negotiate the price.

A DECORATED HOME IS NOT A STAGED HOME

You can tell when a seller puts a lot of time, money and thought into the decoration process. For example, there are a lot of antique pieces that shows the home off well and probably took years to get it just the way the seller wanted it. The buyer falls in love with it, especially if it's to their taste. However, once they leave, they realize that it's all personal property and will be going with the seller. So they know the home will look totally different once they take everything down. A well-decorated property shows very well and you do get more showings than a home that isn't staged. However, it is hard for buyers to visualize their furniture in the home without all the decorations, so it doesn't net the amount that it would had it been staged. In this particular case, the sellers needed to move to the South Carolina. Seven couples came through the home, but we received no offers. We reduced the price $10,000 and received an offer the very next week. The sellers were able to move on with their plans. They both got the jobs they wanted and are happily living the life they dreamed of. I believe if the home was staged, it would have sold a lot faster. The home had a great layout but was overpowered by all the decorations.

Whether you want to sell your home at the top, middle or bottom of the market is all up to you. In this chapter, I talked a lot about the Law of Differentiation, expert staging, quality of life upgrade analysis, professional preinspection, and home warranty. There are six other laws that are involved in the 115 variables of the home-selling process and influence the price swing effect. Law 1: Law of Expertise; Law 2: Law of Differentiation; Law 3: Law of Exposure; Law 4: Law of Cooperation; Law 5: Law of Buyer Acquisition; Law 6 Law of Negotiation; Law 7: Law of Execution. For implementing each one of these laws, you can get an extra 3 to 5 percent more money.

For a free report, *The 7 Critical Mistakes Home Owners Make That Cost Thousands in Lost Equity or Worse Cause Your Home Never to Sell*, call me direct at (508) 675-1632 or email me at paula@pauladrake.com. Also, please feel free to call me or email me with any questions or concerns you may have involving the sale of your home. I would be happy to answer them.

About Paula

Paula Drake has been guiding buyers and sellers through the real estate maze for over 23 years. She is dedicated to helping people achieve their real estate dreams. The key to Paula's success is the personalized approach she takes to assisting clients with all their real estate needs and her extensive 23 years experience as an outstanding top realtor. Paula has experienced all types of real estate markets and all types of real estate transactions. She knows how to turn real estate dreams into a successful closing. Paula's mission is distinct: to provide unparalleled professional service and dedication to my clients during all phases of the purchase or sale of their valuable asset.

Due to the outstanding advice and service she provides, Paula has built a loyal following of satisfied clients. Her practice continues to flourish, thanks to clients recommending her friends, family members and business associates. A married professional, Paula resides in Somerset, Massachusetts. She has a daughter Jennifer, who resides in Dighton with her husband Dennis. She is the proud grandmother of a grandson, Joshua. Paula enjoys the satisfaction of helping people achieve the dream of owning their own home.

Generous with her time away from work, Paula serves her community as a member of the Greater Fall River Area Chamber of Commerce and also contributes to several local school activities and sports programs. In her leisure time, Paula enjoys travel, skiing, boating, and the thrill of watching her grandson compete in motocross and snowboarding. To learn more about how Paula helps people achieve their real estate dreams, visit her website at www.pauladrake.com, or contact her directly at (508) 675-1632 or on her cell at (508) 725-7294.

As we all know, buying or selling a home is one of life's most significant transactions, and there is a lot at stake both financially and emotionally. There has never been a greater need for a professional agent with experience, up-to-date knowledge, and a motivated support team to ensure a smooth stress-free closing, and help you locate a dream home in harmony with your personal lifestyle and family's values. I specialize in single-family listings, multi-family listings, condo sales and new construction. My clients include referrals, client resales, young families, first-time home buyers and investors. I look forward to exploring how I can help you.

Paula has received many distinguished designations throughout her career. Most recently she was recognized as a Certified National Home Selling Advisor .She has also been recognized as the Most Referred Realtor in Southeastern Massachusetts.

CHAPTER 27

WHY A TEAM?

BY RENEE BUTLER

The real estate profession is an ever-changing business. The idea of being a "solo act" real estate agent is nearly extinct. When observing the top-producing agents in the country today, they all share a common bond: a *team*! Having identified this trend through research and training, I have discovered that we must create a group of people who have congruent mind-sets to succeed and prosper in the real estate industry. To set yourself apart from the crowd, you must provide clients with the ultimate customer service experience, thereby allowing past clients to be your number-one marketing tool and creating a win squared.

The first step in building a successful real estate team is an analysis of your staff to determine the best fit for the roles outlined below. I am a strong advocate of the DiSC® personality test, which enables you to position people to be successful at what they do every day. In my business, this approach has created an environment whereby each staff member is excited to come to work and play a part in the growth and success of the business. Each position on the team has strong value due to the specifications and their expertise. This method provides each member with a great sense of accomplishment and a strong drive to push the entire team toward further success.

Below I will outline the components of our real estate team and share my knowledge and proficiency methods in the hopes that you as well can realize greater success in your real estate endeavors.

TEAM LEADER (THE QUARTERBACK)

The role of team leader is awarded to the agent forming the team and is multifaceted. This person sets an example, for this is where trust and confidence are born. It is crucial to know that one is capable and confident to fulfill the responsibilities of this vital role. As team leader your role might be that of teacher, crusader, confidant, leads supplier, babysitter, financial consult, marketing director, or community leader. But the most important role is that of a *money source*! It is imperative that your team have complete faith in your ability to "write the check."

The team leader must list and sell real estate. I believe the volume of real estate sales will vary among different teams based on the components of the team. The education of a team leader is critical. Having a broker's license will always enhance the safety net of your team.

While this leadership role can be challenging, the rewards are far greater. To witness your teammates grow and mature into a complete, unified entity is an accomplishment that cannot be acquired through monetary satisfaction. Only through sharing experience and knowledge does a true team leader bask in fulfillment. The challenge is accomplishing a "team" mentality. It sounds simple, but it is very difficult to achieve. However, with hard work, it can become reality. Once your team is established and you begin to reap the rewards of labor, the building part becomes only a memory. You are ready for Game Day (which, by the way, is every day).

LISTING PARTNER

This player has an extremely important role on the team: the responsibility of listing properties for your teammates to sell. The old adage of "list to last" will remain true until the end of time. If you own the market share of listings, you will increase total dollar volume and GCI. This teammate must be a person you trust, as ultimately they will be spending *your* money.

Duties include pricing the listing in market-value terms, substantiating the real estate fee, and staging the property. This person must be well educated in the market, a master in working systems (e.g., For Sale by Owner, expired listings, Tiger Leads, Vulcan7, RedX, R.A.T.E., Infusionsoft), a CDPE and CIAS graduate, and possess a strong sense of action.

We know that in all economies there will always be death, divorce and relocation clients in our market. We have been inundated with short sales and foreclosures, but as we evolve past these two categories, we will need to revert to our consistency of doing MAA (market absorption analysis, formerly referred to as CMA, BPO, BMA) and focus on our customer service.

The listing contact is where it begins. The amount of listing partners may vary in your individual market, but all have found this position on the team will be a strong influence on the success of your teammates. The perfect hire would be an experienced agent of three years or more, detail oriented with extremely competent people skills.

Keynote: *Train this mate like no other. It is vital.*

BUYER'S SPECIALIST

This player will represent your team as a whole but is responsible for working with all buyers, so the person must be very versatile in nature. The buyer's specialist is your matchmaker—matching people to houses.

This player must have a strong MLS background, be a master at Tiger Leads, and be able recite the team inventory from memory. Additional duties include ensuring daily car care, housewarming party planning, monitoring the supply of bottled water in your car for guests, and moving truck scheduling. The candidate should hold a CRS designation, be a graduate of a buyer specialist university, and Flex-Counselor. One of the most critical skills is possession of a strong sense of flexibility.

I believe that out of all my hires this role is one of the most fun. This position is a team player on steroids. People skills are impossible to train, so they must inherent. When you find someone who wakes up every day and says to themselves, "What am I going to sell today"—and mean it—you have the right mate.

While listing partners tend to be more scientific, the buyer's specialist position is not. Dealing with buyers that are about to make the largest investment of their lives seek competent, knowledgeable agents who can assist them. When deciding who will represent the team on the buyers' side, you must evaluate carefully. You must always be cognizant of the fact that this position presents your team to the buyer's agent.

The buyer's specialist also has duties at closings such as preparation of the closing bag and books for the housewarming party as well as presentation of the keys to the moving van and handwritten thank you notes with gift cards inside. It is all about creating a lasting impression that the buyer will take with them and if positive, will result in referrals. The perfect hire would be a very social and confident individual who has the capacity to work the room. Attention to detail is crucial and a person with no experience is preferred.

Keynote: *Maintaining focus with these mates can be a challenge.*

CLIENT RELATIONS MANAGER

This team player compliments the listing partners and is an administrative position handling the preliminary work in preparation for the listing appointments. The tasks may vary from agent to agent, as some may desire a particular way of presentation. Time sensitivity is key for this role and the candidate must possess a vast knowledge of the market area. This position on the team can be accomplished via a virtual assistant or in-house. I have tried both ways and prefer the virtual method. A complete listing package can be done and the agent out the door in less than an hour. This teammate also does all listing maintenance, such as team lists, team statistics, advertisements (print), MLS system maintenance, internet postings, marketing campaigns, housewarming party set up as well as numerous other administrative tasks. I do have a Director of First Impressions who works hand in hand with this teammate to accomplish all virtual and nonvirtual responsibilities.

A perfect hire for this position is a strong and detailed-oriented individual. The precision that is necessary in this role commands a higher level of accountability to the team. One must be completely task oriented and subject to quick change.

Keynote: *End-of-day reports from all administrative positions are a must have.*

TRANSACTION MANAGER

This teammate holds an administrative position paired with the buyer's specialist. This team effort processes files from executed contract to closing and it is the role of the transaction manager to ensure the client is extremely satisfied with the experience of working with the team.

This job description includes ordering all maps, surveys, title insurance, and coordinating distribution.

A strong knowledge of the Infusionsoft system, MLS system, and lead-generation system is a must as this player distributes leads. Closing coordinator is another function of this job with a tremendous amount of buyer interaction. Approximately 50 percent of each day will be spent in personal contact with clients. A perfect hire for this position is a nurturing person who is patient, precise, flexible and very street smart.

Keynote: *Time sensitivity must be a priority. If not observed, this will directly affect the bottom line.*

OPERATIONS MANAGER

This team player is an administrative position and requires an individual with a talent for multitasking. This person must be an IT master who is able to handle all internet, website, and coordination of all "outside" needs for the team. Duties include procurement of all photos, sign placement, install pending rider on signs, lockbox installation and accountability, and welcome-to-neighborhood sign placement. This is an important position as it requires major interaction with all facets of any transaction. The perfect hire: a flexible individual, computer savvy; excellent driving record, as they are in your vehicle wrapped in the team logo; a nurturer of life; a neat presence due to exterior exposure.

Keynote: *Buy a car and wrap it. Mileage will be a financial burden but worth the investment.*

CLIENT SERVICES ASSISTANT

This player is a licensed individual that assists the buyer's specialist with leads. They are assigned weekly to different teammates to assist consummation of the sale. They conduct open houses, manage the lead-generation system, and make arrangements for inspectors, tradesmen, etc. They do whatever necessary to assist the agent of the week. This is a commission-paid position per transaction upon closing. The client services assistant plays a vital role allowing the realtor time to negotiate, which is their strongest skill. This person must be on call sometimes seven days a week on select calendar months and possess the innate ability to be a background player in lieu of a front-line runner.

This is an entry-level position into the apprentice world of real estate. It offers the ability to make money while observing, gaining vital knowledge, and educating themselves in the pursuit of mastering the art of real estate. The perfect hire would possess a high energy level, be a self-motivator, have a flexible schedule, and be somewhat of a nurturer.

Keynote: *Hire the organized socializer.*

I have defined the duties of each teammate. Everyone becomes a specialist in their role to make the team cohesive. If you want to achieve double digit production, the golden years where one agent has the ability to do all of the tasks outlined above is long past.

For all the diverse aspects of a team, there is safety in numbers. Be mindful that there are personality types that do not embrace the idea of having teammates. It is my belief that these team principles should be embraced for the future of our real estate industry. Weekly team meeting are a priority, and no one is permitted to miss these sessions. The team should also participate in other activities, such as community and charity events, client appreciation days, and weekly education classes.

Since the mobile real estate agent is the wave of the future, we all must be diligent of the importance of staying connected. The team participates in audio and text groups, announcing accomplishments throughout each day. There are locker rooms to accommodate guests and we promote a child-friendly environment.

I strongly encourage the team set a "no gossip" policy. My rule has always been that one should be prepared to say it twice or don't speak it at all. Each member of the team must be mentally committed to a team mind-set and really grasp the "I've got your back" theory. There are definite boundaries and team rules that must be established, which work to the good of the team and eliminate unnecessary and nonproductive rhetoric.

Once the team is assembled and all the value of the team becomes evident, it eliminates a great deal of strife for the team leader. The team learns to benefit from each other, which will ultimately result in additional real estate closings—and produce the number-one team in the city, county, state, and *world*!

The other side of "Why a Team" is Mr. and Mrs. Consumer. The one goal that all superior agents strive for is service; it is all about the service we provide to our clients. A team is the ultimate service—the Ritz Carlton of real estate, the Nordstrom's of homes. A team that is all about the consumer is the only defined security we, as agents, possess. It is our future. If a robot can open doors with one click and there is absolute access to all our information (because of no MLS), then basic value of service is all we have left to equate fee structures.

I know that our team has a 15-year plan on how to survive the ever-changing real estate industry. My Real Estate 101 theory is not complicated; it is quite simple:

a) *Honesty and integrity:* even when you have to think about it.

b) *Work ethic:* will take your seller dollar volume higher than any other one ingredient in real estate sales.

c) *Technology:* will never replace an above average real estate agent. A computer, Mac or PC does not have the human-factor element. All successful agents with $5 million in annual volume consistently have one and only one common factor. All have perfected the art of negotiation. And the only way to get good at it is by doing so many offers a year. Even though you don't get paid, you are still getting educated.

d) *Gas theory:* This is the Butler favorite. We all use a lot of gas in a weekly allowance due to the nature of our profession. I have learned that no matter how full my tank is, if I don't drive the car in this real estate business, my GCI will never be good enough. We can apply it to so many things in life—*we must have drive.* Without it, we purely settle. For me, computers are like the gas theory. We must understand the dynamics of our business.

I would make a prediction that if all things are equal, this specialization team implemented properly would be preferred by the consumer. Choose a team; save a nightmare.

About Renee

Renee Butler first became a licensed realtor in 1978 after attending Polk Community College and Florida Southern College. In 1981, she established Brokers Realty of Central Florida Inc. and the full-service real estate firm has grown to include more than 18 agents with no signs of stopping expansion. She is Quality Service Certified, a Certified Residential Broker, a Certified Distressed Property Expert, a Board of Realtors Professional Standards Committee Chairman for Florida, on the Far-BAR Grievance Committee for the 10th District, and a relocation specialist. Because of her strong commitment to providing excellent service as well as her personal sales success, Renee has earned the Multi-Million-Dollar Producer designation for the past 28 years.

A Missouri native, Renee resides in Winter Haven, Florida and has one son, John, who is a listing partner in the firm. Her hobbies include cooking and selling real estate. Active in the Winter Haven community, Renee is a youth motivator through the Winter Haven Chamber of Commerce and has served two terms on the Florida Bar Grievance Committee, appointed by the governor. Her years of knowledge have afforded her the experience and wisdom to build a successful team and business.

CHAPTER 28

THE NEW SELLER'S MARKET: THE TOP 3 CHALLENGES HOME BUYERS AND SELLERS FACE AND HOW TO OVERCOME THEM

BY TIM MAJKA, ESQ.

After experiencing one of the worst housing market corrections in history, the U.S. housing market is now undergoing a complete 180 degree turn from being a buyer's market to a seller's market. The inventory of homes on the market in the U.S. is now declining and median home prices are increasing. According to the National Association of Realtors (NAR), the median price of a home in the U.S. increased 11.3 percent in September 2012 from the previous year. Home buyers are now seeing home prices going up in most of the country and are increasingly finding that they have to compete against multiple buyers. Home sellers, who up to recently had been seeing their home values decline, are now wondering if now is the right time to sell and how they can sell for maximum price. This chapter will discuss the current state of the housing market and the top three challenges home buyers and sellers are facing and how to overcome these challenges.

THE NEW SELLER'S MARKET

In February 2013, there was 4.2 months of residential homes in inventory for sale in the United States versus in September 2012 when there was 5.9 months and September 2011 when there was 8.1 months of inventory. A "buyer's market" is typically defined as a market where there is six months or more of active inventory on the market, and a "seller's market" is where there is less than six months of inventory. In some markets, the inventory levels are extremely low. For example, in my market, in Long Beach, California, for most of the latter half of 2012 we had less than two months of inventory. Realtors all across the country are reporting low inventory levels and are having a tough time finding homes for their buyers.

Change in inventory levels of homes on the market from June 2011 to June 2012:

Phoenix, AZ	- 48%
San Francisco, CA	- 44%
Minneapolis/St. Paul, MN	- 36%
Riverside, CA	- 36%
Los Angeles, CA	- 36%
Miami, FL	- 35%
Denver, CO	- 35%
Orlando, FL	- 33%
Sacramento, CA	- 32%
San Diego, CA	- 30%
Tampa, FL	- 27%
Seattle, WA	- 27%
Dallas / Ft. Worth, TX	- 26%
Atlanta, GA	- 25%

Source: Zillow

One reason for the decline in inventory is that many underwater homeowners who were previously unable to afford to keep their homes are now receiving relief in the form of reduced interest rates and principal reductions in the amount that they owe. According to NAR chief economist Lawrence Yun, the number of distressed sales in the U.S. is expected to go from 25 percent in 2012 to 8 percent in 2014. The decline in short sales affects the market in two ways. First, it decreases inventory, and second there are fewer distressed sellers willing to sell their home for less than market value.

Another reason for the decline in inventory is the recent interest of private equity firms that are earmarking hundreds of millions of dollars toward investing in residential real estate. These firms are purchasing properties directly from some of the largest lenders in the country via private auctions and bulk sales. The private equity firms are then holding onto the properties and turning them into rentals. Oftentimes, these sales are not listed on the Multiple Listing Service (MLS) and do not show up in the available inventory of homes for sale.

As supply has been dwindling, the result is that we are now seeing values increase. According to NAR, home values in the U.S. are expected to increase in 2013 by 5.1 percent with comparable gains in 2014.

CHALLENGES FACING HOME BUYERS

As the real estate market changes from a "buyer's market" to a "seller's market," home buyers and sellers are now facing new challenges. The top three challenges that home buyers are facing today are: 1) lack of inventory, 2) increasing prices, and 3) increased competition from other buyers.

Ways to Overcome Lack of Inventory

While most home buyers find their home with an agent using the MLS, agents now have to think outside the box to find inventory for their clients. One way that agents can do this is by contacting other local agents to find out if they have any "pocket listings," which are homes that are for sale but not on the MLS yet. In some cases, these are homes where the seller is getting the property ready to place on the market or perhaps they don't want the neighbors, or the tenants, to know that it's for sale.

Another way is that agents can contact homeowners who have previously tried selling their homes. These homes are now listed in the MLS as

"Expired," "Canceled" or "Withdrawn." They can also contact absentee owners who may be getting tired of renting their property to see if they want to sell. There are also websites that some agents have access to that list bank foreclosed homes before they are placed on the MLS. You can also have your agent contact homeowners who are trying to sell their home For Sale by Owner. Lastly, agents can pinpoint a specific building if the homebuyer is looking for a condo or a specific neighborhood of houses and send letters to the homeowners to see if they want to sell.

How to Deal With Rising Prices

The second biggest challenge for home buyers is dealing with increasing prices. In California the median price of single-family homes and condominiums increased 18.8 percent in October 2012 from the previous year. Phoenix, Arizona, saw the median single-family home price jump 34 percent in August 2012 from a year earlier.

To overcome this challenge, it is important for homebuyers to understand the reasons behind the price appreciation and to compare the cost of owning a home versus the cost of renting.

For example if you purchase a home for $400,000 and put 10 percent down at a 4 percent interest rate, your principal and interest payment would be $1,719 plus taxes, private mortgage insurance (PMI), and insurance on a 30-year amortized loan. Assuming taxes, PMI, and insurance are about $600 per month, the cost of owning would be about $2,319 per month plus the $40,000 down payment. In my market, a $400,000 home would typically rent for around $2,400 per month.

The comparison, however, does not end there. A homebuyer should also factor in their mortgage interest tax deduction, which may allow them to deduct the interest paid on their mortgage from their taxable income. Additionally, a home buyer should factor in that in 30 years they will no longer have to pay a mortgage and will own their home free and clear. Additionally, while a homeowner's mortgage payment is not going to go up with a fixed-rate mortgage, rents over the long term do go up as inflation goes up. Thus, that rent payment of $2,400 per month today, could potentially go up to $3,909 per month 10 years from now, if rents go up 5 percent per year.

How to Compete Against Multiple Offers

The third biggest challenge for home buyers is getting their offers accepted.

For example, I recently called the listing agent on a townhome that just came on the market in the neighboring city of Torrance, California, for $310,000, and they told me that they had over 20 offers, and the highest offer was an all-cash offer for $420,000. Home buyers who are not expecting such a tough time getting their offer accepted can get very frustrated and in some cases loose interest in buying if they keep getting outbid on homes. To overcome this challenge, a home buyer needs to examine the key factors that determine whether or not an offer is accepted.

The most important aspect of a buyer's offer is typically the offer price. When a buyer is trying to determine what price to offer on a property, it is not simply a matter of reviewing the last sales price of comparable properties, rather it is also important to look at the prices of homes that are currently in escrow and the direction that prices are going. A home buyer and their agent should review market data to see how prices in the market have changed since the date of the sold comparable properties. For example, if the most comparable homes closed escrow two months ago at $400,000, and the market is going up a rate of 12 percent per year, these properties would be increasing in value by 1 percent per month, which after two months would be $8,000. Thus, the relative change in the market can be used to evaluate expected values of homes.

Home sellers are also looking for the best financially qualified offer. If a buyer will be obtaining a loan to purchase the property, they should use a lender that is highly experienced with a strong reputation in the local market and ask them to call the listing agent directly to put a good word in for the buyer. If the buyer's lender can call the listing agent and explain how well qualified the buyer is and reassure the listing agent that they will be able to close without any delays in obtaining financing, this will help give the buyer an advantage over some of the other offers.

Lastly, a home buyer should choose an agent with a lot of experience, who has a strong reputation among other agents in the community for being honest, responsive, and for having a high success rate in helping buyers close escrow. If a seller is considering two similar offers, they are going to look to their agent to recommend which offer they think is most likely to close on time and with the least amount of hassles. That listing agent will oftentimes prefer to work with an agent on the other side whom they have worked with in the past or that they know has a strong reputation in the community. A highly experienced agent can also advise the home buyer on whether they should reduce certain time frames in the offer, such as the buyer's inspection period and the closing date, to make their offer look stronger. Thus, I recommend that home buyers choose their agent wisely by seeking referrals from people that they know and trust and that they review testimonials. Home buyers can save a lot of money and time by choosing the right agent.

CHALLENGES FACING HOME SELLERS

For home sellers, their top three challenges in today's market are: 1) how to market their home to take advantage of the new seller's market, 2) how to price their home for maximum value, and 3) how to know when it's the right time to sell.

How to Market Your Home to Take Advantage of the New Seller's Market

To market your home to take advantage of the new seller's market I recommend that you seek an agent who is a marketing expert with proven repeatable systems in place to ensure that they sell your home for maximum value. While it is not hard to sell a home in a market when there is no inventory and increasing prices, homeowners can sell their homes for significantly more if they hire the right agent.

The right agent will be able to identify the target market for the home and will be able to implement a strategy to most effectively market the home to that target market. For example, if the homeowner is selling a luxury home, they should hire an agent who knows how to market to luxury home buyers. One way to do this is by creating and promoting marketing "events," such as professionally catered open-house parties, to capture the attention of luxury home buyers and their agents.

The right agent will be an expert at online marketing and have systems in place to ensure that the home is featured prominently on the most highly visited websites. The homeowner should ask if the agent uses a professional photographer, to make sure the photos grab the attention of prospective buyers searching through photos online. I also recommend that a home seller consult with a professional home stager, as homes that are professionally staged sell on average 3 to 6 percent more than nonstaged homes.

How to Price Your Home for Maximum Value

To fully understand the market value of a property, the homeowner and their agent should not only look at the value of comparable homes that have sold recently but also look at the direction the market is going. Looking at the current national, state, and local markets to identify future trends in the market can accomplish this.

I recommend using the absorption rate to determine if the market is accelerating or decelerating. For example, if the local market is appreciating at 12 percent per year, but the inventory of homes per sale is dropping from four months to two months of inventory, this indicates that prices are starting to increase at a faster pace. Conversely, if inventory is increasing from two months of inventory to three months of inventory, then this indicates that the market is slowing and that the rate of price appreciation may start slowing down. Thus, by looking at the change in inventory levels, sellers and their agents can see not only where the market is currently but also where the market is going and factor that into their pricing.

How to Determine When It's the Right Time to Sell

Another challenge home sellers are having in today's market is determining when it's the right time to sell. If the owner's property is located in an appreciating market and they are considering purchasing a new home that costs more than their current home, it might be best for them to sell sooner rather than later and purchase the new home since the value of the new home will be going up even more than the value of the current home. For example, if you own a home that is worth $400,000 and you are looking to purchase a home that is currently worth $600,000 and the market is currently appreciating at 12 percent per year, your current home is appreciating at $4,000 per month while the new home you want to purchase is appreciating at $6,000 per month. Thus if you wait a year, the difference in value between your current home and future home will be $24,000 more than it is today.

It is important for homeowners thinking of possibly moving and purchasing a new home in the near future to talk to their lender to see what their interest rates and financing terms will be on the new home. While talking with their lender it is also important to compare the interest rate on their current home to the expected rate on the new home. With interest rates being very low right now, it is possible that if a homeowner has not refinanced lately, their interest rate on their new home may be less than their current interest rate. For example if you currently owe $500,000 on a home paying 5.5 percent interest, your principal and interest payment (assuming a 30-year amortized loan) is $2,839, while a $600,000 loan balance at 4 percent interest would give you a monthly payment of $2,864. Obviously, the homeowner should be looking to refinance their current mortgage in this situation if they decide not to buy right now, but if they are accustomed to paying $2,839 per month, they can actually afford a home worth $100,000 more without having to pay more than what they are currently paying as a monthly mortgage payment.

With the real estate market having recently changed from a buyer's market to a seller's market, home buyers and sellers are being faced with new challenges. With interest rates at historically low rates and with home prices now increasing, these challenges also present opportunities for home buyers to purchase the right home before prices and interest rates go up. This market is also providing them with new opportunities to own the right home and to position themselves to build equity as the market continues to improve.

About Tim

Tim Majka, Esq. has dedicated the past 10 years to immersing himself in the real estate market and developing systems to ensure that home buyers and sellers receive the best representation. As seen on The Learning Channel's TV show "Property Ladder," Tim Majka with The Tim Majka Home Selling Team has proven repeatable systems to help home buyers find the right home for the best price and for helping homeowners sell their home for up to 18 percent more than traditional real estate agents.

Tim is the founding principal of the Tim Majka Home Selling Team and broker-associate with Keller Williams Coastal Properties in Long Beach, California. The Tim Majka Home Selling Team has over 50 years combined experience in the real estate industry and is one of the top-selling real estate teams in the Long Beach, Los Angeles and Orange County markets.

Tim is a California licensed real estate broker and attorney. He is a graduate of The Ohio State University, *magna cum laude*, and The University of California Hastings College of the Law. Prior to becoming a real estate broker, Tim held senior legal positions with two fast-growing internet companies, one of which was ultimately acquired by Viacom and the other by VeriSign.

Tim has built a "who's who" list of some of the best real estate agents in the country. If you are thinking about buying or selling anywhere in the U.S., Tim would be happy to recommend a great real estate agent in your city. To receive a referral to a local agent, send a request to referral@calhomesearch.com.

Stay in touch with the changes in your local real estate market by visiting www.calhomesearch.com and clicking on "Market Update" to receive future updates on your local real estate market.

CHAPTER 29

WHEN YOU NEED MORE THAN JUST A REALTOR

BY JEREMY GANSE

"A customer is the most important visitor on our premises; he is not dependent on us. We are dependent on him. He is not an interruption in our work. He is the purpose of it. He is not an outsider in our business. He is part of it. We are not doing him a favor by serving him. He is doing us a favor by giving us an opportunity to do so."

~Mahatma Gandhi

Recently I met with a couple who was expecting their unexpected third child. They had purchased their home eight years prior intending to stay in the home for 15-plus years. As a result they invested money to remodel the kitchen, update bathrooms, replace flooring, and add an outdoor deck. While they were realistic with their price expectations, they were discouraged by several meetings with realtors…including the agent who sold them the property. The value these agents saw in their home was limited to the "CMA's," or comparable market analysis they prepared. After listening to their hopes, dreams, and goals, we were able to position their home in the market and sell it using our proven repeatable system within 14 days for 97 percent of their desired list price. Had they accepted the historical numbers prepared by multiple realtors they would have left $25,000 dollars on the table!

Realtors receive no formalized training on how to prepare these commonly used, but archaic, CMA reports and select comparable properties from historical sales data to determine what your home's current value *should be*. The problem is that two similar homes will never be identical. CMAs don't tell you if the home was professionally staged, if the sellers were getting a divorce, if the home was overpriced for months before being reduced, or if the neighbors dog barks 24/7. None of those factors play a role in the value of your home, and you should not position the price of your home in today's market to attract the highest offer based upon the unknown.

What is shocking to me is that even successful agents with good systems and technology still use CMAs. None of the agents who met with our expecting couple client took the time to listen or be open to the possibility that there was financial value in the home beyond the historical numbers. By including the customer in the process and believing there was an opportunity to serve them, we were able to apply our proven repeatable system backed by market research and help our seller get up to 18 percent more for their home in even the worst of markets. Our goal was the financial success of our seller. We knew that if they were happy with the job we were doing, we would reap the benefits and rewards once the job was done. Our focus remains on providing a world-class real estate transaction experience that our customers will want to tell their friends about.

The challenge for today's consumers is to find a trusted real estate advisor who has the education, training, systems, technology, and customer service focus. No one can dispute that the internet has changed the way we do business. Since the late 1990s consumers have become increasingly comfortable with online purchases. It started with small transactions, including books and music, and has transformed into major life investments, including automobiles, real estate and finances. The internet can also be credited with leveling the playing field for small business to compete in an increasingly global marketplace. Without a website and an internet marketing strategy, very few businesses and industries will be positioned for growth in the coming decades.

Many industries have already seen the dramatic impact that systems and technology can have on their business model. Take, for example, your local travel agency. Until the advent of online travel agencies like Expedia, Travelocity, Orbitz, and CheapTickets, your local travel agent held a secure job with exponential sales potential on commodities, including airfare, hotel rooms, and rental cars. Successful travel agents have adapted to the changing market, by adopting new systems and technology, and have found a niche as "travel consultants." They essentially act as advanced concierges assembling complex packaged travel and cruise vacations. Their primary point of differentiation is customer service. No longer do they sell a commodity and no longer can the average travel agent compete without technology and a focus on customer service.

The same is becoming true in the real estate industry. Websites like Zillow and Trulia provide buyers and sellers with property information, photos, and pricing that was once only available at your local real estate office. Realtors have continued to hold the "key" quite literally in terms of physical access to the majority of homes for sale. However, with the average realtor only selling eight homes per year, holding the "key" is not enough to justify their fee. The majority of the 1,200+ realtors in Lancaster, Pennsylvania, are part time and do not have the education, systems, technology, and negotiation skills necessary to represent their clients in the single largest financial transaction of their life.

Compounding these issues are the state licensing requirements. In Pennsylvania you need only be 18 years of age, have completed 60 hours of training, and pass the real estate salesperson licensing exam. Compare that to the 1,500-hour training requirement to become a licensed beautician, and you will begin to see the tip of the iceberg. In the coming years it will not be difficult for large corporations, including Zillow and Trulia, to transform the real estate industry and put the average realtor out of business.

With all of that being said, where does this leave today's real estate consumer? The last 10 years have been a nationwide rollercoaster in value explosion, contraction and stabilization. Facilitating all of the tasks that need to be done, from contract to closing and beyond, has become nearly impossible for one person, but a team working together allows for specific attention to individual clients needs. Here are seven questions you can ask to be certain you are hiring the right real estate advisor.

1. How often will I hear from you; how long have you been in the business; and do you work full time?

A: How frequently the agent normally communicates with his clients and what methods of communication the agent uses (phone, e-mail or fax) will help you determine if you are on the same wavelength. Ultimately the agent's communication strategy should take your needs into consideration. You are a critical part of the team and your first impression is likely to be repeated should you hire the agent. With a national average of eight homes sold per agent, you want to be certain this isn't your agent's first time at the rodeo. Be certain that they have the experience and transaction history necessary to represent you and your needs. Lastly, the days of the part time agent are long gone. You need a full-time agent who keeps up with the national/regional/local market, financing considerations and laws.

2. How do you get paid?

A: Real estate agents earn their commissions from sellers at the time of closing, which are split between the seller's and buyer's brokerages and then split again with the individual agents. As a buyer in Pennsylvania you will be asked to sign an agreement to exclusively rely upon a single agent. This exclusivity agreement is in exchange for the time and hard work that goes into communicating with buyers, keeping current with the market, preparing contracts, showing properties, and reviewing sellers' disclosures. It is important to understand how real estate agents get paid so that you don't accidentally engage multiple realtors, spend months working with them, and then have to inform them that another agent found you the home you want.

3. How do you handle "dual agency"?

A: Pennsylvania believes that realtors are schizophrenic enough to get the highest and fairest price for the seller while also obtaining the lowest and fairest price for the buyer. I have yet to meet a living human being that can equally represent both the buyer and the seller. As a consumer you need an agent who will maintain their agency relationship with you as being primary and who works in a team environment with other agents who can capture and separately represent prospective buyers for your home.

4. What is your negotiation strategy and how do you handle home inspections?

A: Real estate agents have an ethical and legal responsibility to put your financial interest first. You want to be certain you can trust that your realtor will negotiate from a position of strength and has the negotiation training necessary to help the cooperating agent acknowledge little victories, creating a mutual advantage so that negations on any larger future issues will be easier. If you are selling your home, it is important to understand that it will most likely be inspected by the buyer prior to settlement. Market research shows that a seller preinspection can save between 2 to 4 percent in repair costs vs. price. We believe preinspection is essential.

5. What is your cancellation, termination and expiration policy?

A: Hope for the best but plan for the worst. There should be no upfront fees, no cancellation fees, no termination fees, and no expiration fees for either buyers or sellers. You may find that the brokerage has a transaction fee for the internal processing of paperwork and cost of closing your transaction, but that should only be payable at the time of closing. There may also be other optional incentive programs that do have an upfront cost, but you should receive a service in return, and they should not be mandatory. If you are not quite ready to engage an agent in writing, be clear and upfront on where you stand.

6. What is your marketing plan, and how does the internet play a role in it?

A: Before you ask this question…Google the agent you are interviewing and "homes for sale in <insert your hometown>". If nothing is returned on the agent you are interviewing or you don't like what you see, you may be better off interviewing the agents who are returned in your search results. Ninety percent of buyers use the internet to search for homes, and 81 percent of internet searches are done on Google. If the agent doesn't have a strategy to promote themselves via the internet, it is unlikely they will adequately market your home on the internet.

7. *What do you do to ensure that the leads generated by my listing are followed up with in a timely manner so that we don't lose any qualified buyer inquiries?*

A: In today's fast-paced Internet society, people want instant information and are able to get it. Make sure you hire a realtor working in a team environment who has an immediate response system to get highly trained professionals responding within five minutes, 16 hours a day, seven days a week. No one individual can accommodate this requirement, and accordingly you need to be comfortable with the team that is in place to accomplish this crucial task for the marketing of your home. Remember, you are a part of the team.

About Jeremy

Jeremy Ganse is a licensed realtor, bestselling author, entrepreneur, education chairman of the Lancaster Young Professionals Network, and Certified Expert Advisor™. Over the course of his 15-year career, he has built several successful internet marketing and e-commerce websites that have produced sales of over $40 million in real estate and consumer storage products. His information systems and technical communications background gives him a unique insight into the application of technology in the facilitation of the residential consumer real estate experience.

He is CEO and founder of The Jeremy Ganse Home Selling Team, a dynamic customer-centric business dedicated to embracing technology to enhance their client's real estate experience. Jeremy helps his clients to understand, comprehend, and navigate today's real estate market. His systems and processes provide consumers education on avoiding common pitfalls while capitalizing on opportunities. Jeremy believes that knowledge is power and that his clients deserve access to information and coaching so that they can make informed choices and play an active role in one of the most significant transactions they will make in their life.

Jeremy represents a new breed of real estate agents. As a Certified Expert Advisor™ he has emerged as a leader in specialized knowledge, skills and advisory services in the real estate industry. He is the real estate agent of choice for professionals, business owners, community leaders, doctors and lawyers who understand that to run a real estate business you must have the highest level of specialized knowledge, a solid track record of success, and the systems and resources to execute a proven plan.

Jeremy holds a dual BS degree in information systems and technical communications from Clarkson University in Potsdam, New York. He resides in Lancaster, Pennsylvania, with his wife, Lisa, a graduate of York College, with her BS in nursing. Lisa is currently at home with their two children. To learn more about Jeremy Ganse and how you can receive the free special report *When You Need More Than Just a Realtor*, visit www.jeremyganse.com, or call toll-free (877) 271-5520.

CHAPTER 30

PERFORMANCE OUTSELLS PROMISES: PERFECTING PRICING TO GET A HOME SOLD

BY DENISE SWICK

In my 23-year career as a realtor listing and selling homes, one thing has not changed—the combination of price and a seller's motivation is the reason a home sells or doesn't sell. Many will debate that upgrades made or not made, location, time of year, and number of competing homes for sale, are the reasons a house does or does not sell. Actually, these are just contributors.

Pricing the property accurately for the market will attract the highest number of serious buyers to the door. The right market value also signals to a buyer that sellers are both serious and reasonable. Purchasers naturally buy by comparison. They know that a good value is still a good value, regardless of the market and regardless of the price point of the home. It is possible to have multiple offers in any type of market, buyer or seller, when the property is priced for the current market conditions. Most often realtors won't even show and truly motivated qualified buyers cannot waste their time looking at overpriced properties.

Several years ago, a national speaker, mentor, and coach shared the formula for measuring the price effectiveness in the market that works in almost every case and in every part of the country. If a property sells within the first 30 days, the market indicates the price was accurate for the market. If the property has not sold within 30 days, the listing agent and seller must look at the following data: When more than five qualified buyers take time to schedule a showing through an agent, walk through the home, and choose not to buy it, the market is indicating the property is 5 to 10 percent over the current market value. Similarly, in the same time frame, if less than five buyers come through the home, and no offers made, the market is indicating the property is at least 10 percent over market value. Buyers will not waste their time looking at it. While in some cases a seller will receive, what in their opinion and often to an untrained agent as well, an offer that is "low," it is important to negotiate that offer to its highest and its best. Historically the first offer received is typically the highest and best, once that negotiation process is complete.

Naturally, it just makes sense that the buyers, who are coming through a "new" property listing, have seen all the other homes on the market competing with this property and are not selling. Therefore, when a buyer and agent see a property that is new to the market and priced for the market conditions, condition of the property, and the other factors affecting the home, they know if it is a good value or not and will quickly want to make an offer!

Clearly, buyers buy by comparison. When the homes they are looking at meet their basic criteria, square footage, number of bedrooms and baths, and the other must haves, the comparison begins. If a property has more square footage, yet is in need of major updates compared to one with a little less square footage but is move-in ready, most buyers will choose the move-in ready, unless they get a significant discount to make up for the improvements necessary to bring the larger home to today's selling standards.

Buyers compare all the buzzwords: features, benefits, updates, amenities, and square footage, yet when they see a good value, they will purchase it quickly. Whether one is listing a home or shopping for one, these factors must be known that affect the sale.

MARKET FACTORS

So how should a real estate professional arrive at the right price? One works from the micro to the macro; begin with close to same type of home in the same area, as in within a quarter mile, same subdivision, same building etc., and then compare the details and amenities. Comparable homes are a good starting point; however, comparing two ranch-style homes with the same square footage will not give you the right price. The floor plan and square footage might be the same, yet the home with recent updates and with the amenities that the market demands will sell for more. A home might have been the top of the line with Corian countertops and brass fixtures and pickled-oak cabinets when constructed in 1998, but now a buyer would expect granite countertops, maple cabinets and pewter fixtures, all of which can be expensive cosmetic changes.

Current trends do affect the price of homes, even in a down market. If the market starts to rebound a little and new home contruction begins again in earnest, existing home prices for homes without updates may still take an even bigger hit, depending on the market. It is important to understand that real estate is really a supply and demand market.

Market factors that also affect your sale are the current inventory on the market and buyer interest. Existing homes will sell more slowly if they cannot compete with the current inventory. People purchase by comparison. Extras increase buyer interest because they feel they are getting more bang for the buck. Maintenance items such as a new hot water heater are not something to count as an "extra." The new carpet installed five years ago is not new anymore. It has five years worth of dirt on it. Updates and improvements will change the playing field, but keep the following as a guideline.

UPDATES

New roofs, windows, furnaces, and central air are all maintenance items. Compare them to oil changes and new tires for your car. These items, when new, might help your home sell more quickly, but they do not increase the value of your home to the market. After all, who would live in a house with a leaking roof? These items have to be replaced, but it is not a dollar-for-dollar recoupment of what the seller spent. The most cost-effective things one can do are give the home a perfect, neutral fresh coat of paint and really great new flooring, and a good first impression.

The rules I speak of are for the masses. Yet we all know occasionally there is an exception to every rule—with the operative word here being "occasionally." I had a client once who had "wallpapered" her kitchen a deep Ralph Lauren shade of red. Her dishes matched the wallpaper. The look suited her. I advised her that she may need to repaint the kitchen promptly before listing her home, yet the client decided to wait and see. Despite her loud red wallpaper, the client's house sold the next week when a buyer with the *exact same* dish pattern loved the kitchen. That client should have played the lottery that day, as her chances of finding a buyer such as this was one in a million.

Several factors will affect the price at which a home will sell. One cannot change the location or the bones of a home, but one can bring it in line with other homes on the market so that the home will be more competitive. The seller's goal is to make the home stand out from among all the other MLS listings. It may cost $10,000 to replace the flooring in the home before it is listed, but a potential buyer will surely ask for much more in allowances if they need to replace the flooring themselves. Think of model homes when making updates; neutral and normal are the standard. The masses want to blend in; they don't want their home to stand out. The longer a seller waits, the lower the price a property will bring. Homes do not gain value sitting on the market, unless market conditions dramatically change due something unforeseen, like a company such as Microsoft moving into your neighborhood and bringing 50,000 jobs.

"UNWANTED" HOMES

The saddest stories are those of clients—like several I have helped—whose homes were on the market for years because the client believed they should be able to get out of the home what they had paid for it. I have seen clients who desperately needed to sell unwisely use second mortgage equity lines and other credit devices to make payments for the first mortgage and other bills, rather than sell for less than what they originally paid for it. In the end, the client still had to do a short sale for nearly half of what they paid, due to the second mortgage and other debt creeping up like a cancer. Short sales are not "bad" homes; they are homes where a seller owes more than the current market value.

One of the most troubling things I hear from clients whose homes have been listed with another realtor but didn't sell are the stories of having gotten an offer and the *realtor* tells them not to accept because they can "get more" for the house. As mentioned before, once negotiated to the fullest, the majority of the time the first offer received on a home is the highest and the best offer. The longer a home is on the market, the more people can assume they will get a deal on the home. Laws of supply and demand affect sales prices too.

SUPPLY AND DEMAND: BUYER'S MARKET OR SELLER'S MARKET

In a seller's market, there is less supply than demand. People will pay over the asking price for a house with all the bells and whistles and sometimes without bells and whistles, depending on how low the supply is. However, people will not overpay just because you think your house is worth X amount of money. Realistically, there are only two things that will make a person's home sell quickly: the seller's motivation to sell (where the market is at now, not what they paid for the home or what they think it should be worth), and the asking price they arrive at with a professional realtor's help. Sellers will sometimes mention to me that their "friend" says their home is worth X amount of money, to which I reply, "Then let's ask your friend to buy it first before we price it right for the market. It is always my goal to get you the most money." For your information, the friends have never stepped up to the plate. A home's asking price needs to be computed using fact, not emotion, nor unqualified opinion. Its value is set by the market, not by how much you owe on your mortgage or by how much your taxes are. New construction affects resales, loss of jobs affects resales, increase of jobs affect resales and interest rates affect all sales.

The web has become bigger and bigger in the industry for generating information. Nothing is secret anymore. Buyers can go to the internet and see that the house they are looking at has been for sale 455 days. Human nature dictates that a person really does not want a home that no one else wants either. Buyers want to know what is wrong with a home that has been on the market a long time. Naturally, often they conclude that if there is something wrong with the house, the seller is unreasonable, or they really do not want to sell. After 20+ years of working with sellers who had previously hired other agents prior to me, that is not the case. They were sometimes only 5 to 10 percent over the actual market value.

Remember, home sales are strictly a matter of supply and demand, based on conditions; the market is either a buyer's market or a seller's market. Think of supply and demand with regard to large gas guzzler SUV sales. The sales go down as gas prices go up. Do you see an abundance of Hummer dealerships in your town? Housing markets vary in much the same way. Typically, a six-month supply of homes on the market compared with demand equals a neutral market. Fewer homes listed than there is demand for equals a seller's market. And a greater than six-month supply of homes compared with demand equals a buyer's market. Shadow inventory, houses that will probably enter the market as distressed sales in the future, also affect resale markets. If reading this is causing a minor feeling of dread about pricing a home for resale or purchasing one, know that a competent realtor can help. Knowing what to look for in your real estate agent is as important as knowing the factors that can affect your price.

CHECKLIST FOR HIRING A REALTOR

I became excellent at pricing by selling three to five home listings per week and studying the market daily. Most agents have at most zero to three listings at a time. When selecting a realtor, interview more than one real estate professional before hiring someone. In fact, interview two to four agents before hiring one. Automatically listing with the agent who reports the highest asking price for a home, without convincing proof, can cause your home to sit on the market unsold. Here are more points to keep in mind:

- Avoid listing for the highest price in area.
- Select a realtor who lists and sells at least 25 homes per year, otherwise, the realtor might not have the experience to manage the home sale properly. Realistically that is only two per month.
- Ask all realtors who you interview: "What is your average number of days on the market for your listings?"
- Make certain the agent understands economies of scale.
- Ask all the realtors what their communication is with you. How often and what kind?
- Ask if they have a proven system that is duplicatable,

predictable and measurable.

All realtors have the same tools in their toolbox, yet, clearly, the top agents use them more effectively and add their own solutions.

Just by putting a home on the MLS, the home will get a ton of exposure, yet it might not sell because the price is wrong. Companies that will list a home on the MLS charge anywhere from $500 or $1,000 up front to get the home exposure in the marketplace, but they do not help price it, and if the home doesn't sell, the seller loses that money. An experienced agent with knowledge and expertise will show why a home is going to sell and for how much it is going to sell. However, some agents will suggest an appraisal to determine the value of a home to help set a listing price. Appraisers are skilled in numbers not people. They do not work with hundreds of buyers like we do and understand the buyer mentality. Our team has sold four homes in the recent years owned by property appraisers that were expired listings. An expired listing means the home didn't sell at the asking price the appraiser probably determined the home was worth! It's funny, but it's true.

Any realtor can list a home, yet a seller doesn't want a listing, a seller wants a sale. Performance outsells promises. Locate an area realtor with proven results, and you'll find the realtor who prices homes accurately to transact the highest sale. Anything else in the realtor's presentation—how wonderful they or their company is, what clubs they belong to, or their tenure in the business is fluff. The right market price is what sells the home and an agent that can exemplify this is the right agent for the job of selling the home.

About Denise

Denise Swick, founder of Denise Swick & Company, has been a realtor in the Dayton, Ohio, area for over 20 years. Her philosophy is simple: Performance outsells Promises. Denise really enjoys actually assisting buyers buy and sellers sell. It is imperative that the buyers and sellers want to buy and sell as much as she and her team want to help.

In addition to earning her bachelor's degree in marketing in 1992 from Wright State University, Denise obtained her real estate sales license in 1989 and her broker's license in 1995. She received "Top Ten Teams" for Southern Ohio Remax region for 2004-2012 and is listed in the "40 under 40" by the *Dayton Business Journal*. Additionally, Denise qualifies annually for the highest levels of awards from the state and area board of realtors.

Denise has distinguished herself in her field by building winning relationships with her clients and ensuring that both sides feel they can work together to form a partnership. She believes that her clients must trust the process and her plan to sell and/or buy their home. Additionally, as part of a partnership, her clients are as committed to selling their homes as she is.

In her free time, Denise serves as president of the Dayton, Ohio, Habitat for Humanity, is a member of Rotary Club of Dayton #47, and serves on the board of advisors for the Dayton Racquet Club.

CHAPTER 31

INVESTING IN REAL ESTATE: 6 POWER POINTS FOR SUCCESS

BY GEORGE PAUL VLAHAKIS

Real estate isn't just about finding a home for your family to grow; it can also be about finding the right place for your *money* to grow. I happily learned that myself through my own investment experiences. Back in 1994, I bought my first property. I wasn't as knowledgeable about real estate as I am now, so I chose to invest in a commercial property, which is much harder to finance than the residential variety. Still, I raised the capital to use as a down payment and took a leap of faith. Nineteen years later, I'm very glad I took that leap. That single investment has grown by a staggering 473 percent—and the long-term success of that single property has allowed me to leverage it and invest more heavily in the residential sector, which is easier to finance and also a lot less costly.

To this day, I continue to be an active investor, while also heading up a full-service real estate agency team, The George Paul Team, that's committed to helping others who are also interested in investing in property. By helping, I mean guiding clients through the entire process. For example, a young couple in their mid-20s came to us because they were about $27,000 in debt and really needed help getting into a home.

We started them off with our credit counseling service, which we offer to help people just like them. Fourteen months later, they had fixed their credit and cleared their debt. Seven months after that, they had accumulated enough in their savings account for a down payment. We assisted them in buying a home: They rented out the basement to a tenant, lived in the upper portion of the house, and ended up realizing a 43 percent savings over what it cost them to live in their rental apartment!

That kind of success in real estate is attainable for almost anyone—provided you know the right steps to take to make it happen. In this chapter, I'll focus on six different "Power Points" regarding real estate investments so you can learn a little more about what it's all about, why it can offer a great long-term wealth-building strategy, and what you must do to ensure the best chances for success. After that, I'll share a story that demonstrates just how life-changing real estate investment can be—if you're willing to do your homework and make the commitment. But first, let's dig a little deeper into what real estate investment is all about.

POWER POINT #1: MONEY LOSES VALUE, REAL ESTATE GAINS VALUE

When you invest in real estate, it's not unheard of to transform $20,000 into $300,000 or even $500,000 over the long haul. And the sad fact is, there aren't many other ways to realize that kind of yield from your money. The stock market, of course, can always crash when volatile economic times hit, as they did in 2008. As far as just depositing your money into a savings account or CD, interest rates are so low that your bank account actually ends up costing you money over the long run, because of the cost of living continuing to go up.

Even if you decided to just put a thousand dollars in a shoebox under your bed, that money will actually *lose* value in five to 10 years. When you take it out and spend it, you won't be able to buy as much with it as you could have when you originally hid it away. Again, blame inflation—it hits virtually every currency because of the rising prices of food and energy.

Real estate, in contrast, tends to go up and stay up over the long term. There will be, of course, temporary fluctuations in the market, but the overall pattern of property is that it continues to increase in value.

POWER POINT #2: FEAR PREVENTS PEOPLE FROM PROFITING FROM REAL ESTATE

When you tackle something for the first time that seems like a big challenge, you naturally experience some anxiety. That's normal. Unfortunately, that anxiety prevents many people from doing things that would *benefit* them. This is a common human condition that applies not just to financial matters but to everything from relationships to trying a new type of food that you actually might end up thinking is delicious.

The fact is that buying a home merely for the purposes of a personal residence is the biggest investment most people will make in their lifetime, which, of course, means it's a transaction that's somewhat stressful. That makes most of us reluctant to buy property as an investment. It's initially a huge debt that you might feel you don't want to have on top of whatever other debt you might be carrying, such as student loans, credit cards, etc.

What you probably don't realize, however, is that when you work with the right professionals who help you take the right steps, this kind of debt ends up actually making you money. And the stress can be minimized: When you employ a reputable property manager to oversee your investment, the property manager will help you put a trustworthy tenant in the property to give you a constant cash flow and also deal with any maintenance issues. You don't have to lift a finger, except if a decision needs to be made that requires your input.

That's why real estate investment can actually bring you more security and peace of mind about your financial future, as well as the cash you need to make the mortgage payments (with extra money left over, when you do it right).

POWER POINT #3: PROCRASTINATION DELAYS PROFITS

You may study real estate investment, understand its benefits, lose your fear about putting your money in a property…and still never take action!

We know many people who have done just that—and, by the time they did invest, property values had risen, and they didn't make as much money as they could have. With the world economy gradually improving, more money will go into property and values will rise.

If you genuinely understand the opportunity in real estate investment, you should make the move as soon as you can to take full advantage of improving conditions. The second richest man in America, Warren Buffet, recently made a huge investment in real estate, so guess where he thinks the market is going?

POWER POINT #4: ALWAYS THINK LONG TERM

Maybe you want to spend a lot of your disposable income on leasing a BMW or another luxury car. In a few years, when that lease is up, the money from those big lease payments will be completely gone—and you'll have to start all over again with more payments that are just as big if you want another nice car. Why not, instead, put that disposable income into real estate—and, in a few years time, pay *cash* for a new BMW with the cash flow and/or potential profits from that investment?

Now, you may think you can't handle making the mortgage payments on that investment, but, as I noted earlier, if you do the math correctly (and we have formulas in place for our clients to use), you won't have to. You'll have a tenant paying you rent for living in the home you invest in, and those rent payments should more than take care of the mortgage. Meanwhile, the home will be appreciating in value, without you having to put any more money out yourself. Result? You realize a consistent cash flow, you end up owning the home, and finally cashing in on the increased value when you sell.

POWER POINT #5: CHOOSE THE RIGHT REAL ESTATE INVESTMENT ADVISOR

Everybody and their mother thinks they know what to do in real estate, even though their experience may be limited to just buying the home in which they live. The truth is you can't know how much they or anybody else you know really understands about investing in property. That's why you need to seek out a professional who has both the experience and the expertise to give you the valuable advice you need to make the *right* investment.

If you needed heart surgery, you wouldn't go to someone who looked up "Vital Organs" on the internet; you would go to a doctor, a professional who *knows* what he or she is doing. A large undertaking like property investment should be no different—you want not just a real estate expert but one who practices what they preach when it comes to investing.

POWER POINT #6: POSITIVE GOALS INSPIRE POSITIVE BEHAVIOR

When you seriously think about long-term financial goals and you decide something like real estate investment will help you achieve those goals, it creates an important level of commitment and motivation that benefits your life.

You end up dedicating yourself to saving money for the down payment in a property, which, in turn, causes you to think about holding on to your money, instead of spending it on frivolous things. You won't waste your money on a second wristwatch you don't need, more clothes when you have enough, or expensive drinks at a bar that end up running you a hefty tab. You'll be more careful but still enjoy your life.

While you're enjoying your life, you'll also be working toward a life-changing investment that can bring you big future benefits, and you'll avoid impulse purchases that waste your money and sidetrack your financial life goals. In short, real estate investment can help you create a level of discipline that will bring its own rewards down the line.

As I mentioned at the beginning of this chapter, I want to close with an outstanding success story in which we were proud to play a part. What this person accomplished demonstrates how, if you stick to a plan and work with a professional, you can literally change the direction of your life with real estate investments.

The person I'm talking about was a young man who was 22 years old when he first came to me. At that time, he had a full-time job in the auto industry, working on an assembly line, and, from his salary, he had managed to save enough for a down payment on a home. He wanted to buy a property strictly as an investment; he intended on continuing to live with his parents.

We helped him buy that home, and he rented out both floors of the house to two different tenants, giving him two monthly rental payments from the same property. Two years later, he was financially ready to purchase his second home. The tenants from his first home had provided a good cash flow, and he had saved enough for another down payment; only this time, he was ready to move out of his folks' home. However, he still viewed this next home as primarily an investment, so he finished the basement in his new home and moved into it, while renting out the remainder to a tenant. His cash flow improved, and a year later, we worked together to buy him a *third* home.

This was already much more than most people are willing to take on, so I was shocked when, two years later, at the age of 27, he called to let me know he was ready to buy his *fourth* home. But the surprise didn't stop there—he also informed me that after he made this purchase, he was going to quit his job.

Now, as you can tell from this chapter, I'm a pretty strong believer in the power of investing in real estate, but even *I* thought he was making a big mistake. I tried to talk him out of leaving his job at the auto plant, but he gave me a list of reasons why he thought it was a good idea for him at this point. I wished him well, and we found him that fourth property.

After that purchase, he did indeed quit his job and followed through on the rest of his plan. He bought a small van and had "Mr. Fix-It" painted on the side. He began cutting the lawns, doing the painting and performing other needed maintenance on all four of his properties, and put signs in the front of his homes advertising his services. Soon, he began to pick up enough side jobs until he became a full-time Mr. Fix-It but still well-off enough to turn down work he didn't want to do.

And today? Mr. Fix-It is in his mid-30s, and he now owns *nine* homes. I can only guess how many he'll have by the time he's 40!

This is what determination and smart investment planning can accomplish for anyone willing to make the commitment. But again, you should always work with a professional who can help you identify the right property, inspect it and make sure it will be attractive to a paying tenant. Your realtor should also help you run the numbers to make sure it's the right investment for you, your budget and your goals, and also help you work out your ultimate exit strategy with your investment, if one is necessary.

If you're interesting in knowing more about property investment, please feel free to contact me or any member of The George Paul Team for help. You can reach us at (416) 556 5656, or contact us through our website at www.georgepaulteam.com.

We wish you the best in all your property pursuits—and many happy returns.

About George Paul

George Paul Vlahakis bought his first investment property at 19 years of age, and has been passionate about everything real estate ever since.

With 20 years of sales and real estate experience, along with a background in architectural design, George Paul possesses a vast knowledge of all things real estate. This includes everything from spearheading development projects, real estate architecture and design, and trading both in residential and commercial properties.

Driven by his passion, George Paul continues to educate himself on all things real estate, including new technologies and systems that affect the real estate industry in Canada and internationally. He frequently attends and participates in cutting-edge seminars hosted by industry leaders.

In addition to George Paul's knowledge of the industry, his loyalty, dedication and strong negotiating skills have made a large impression on clients and industry professionals over the years. His understanding of clients' needs and requests prompt clients to constantly approach George Paul for his real estate advice and direction when it comes to investing, purchasing selling or developing.

Through modern-day technology, including web and social media, George Paul continues to expand his portfolio, increase his database and widen his network of contacts that includes clients and industry professionals. This network of contacts creates an opportunity to bring a client together with the right property and an investor with the appropriate development and needs to be met efficiently and cost effectively.

It is George Paul's passion for real estate as a whole that made him realize that there was a need for a full-service real estate boutique. By bringing together a group of real estate professionals who have the expertise to better service investors, builders and real estate clients, The George Paul Team was born. A one-stop shop for all things real estate.

The George Paul Team
(416) 556-5656
www.georgepaulteam.com
1119 O'Connor Dr.
Toronto, ONT, CAN M4B 2T5

CHAPTER 32

REFRIGERATOR AND DOG CONVEY: ELEVATING NEGOTIATION TO AN ART FORM

BY JUSTIN KILISZEK

A man once hired me to help him find a house. He did not want just any house. My client had been transferred far away from "home," and he desired a property that would make him feel a little less like a transplant. After learning there were many lakes where my client grew up and that he missed home, I took him to see a home on a lake that had was recently listed. The home was pristine. The furniture was exactly right for the house. While perusing the property, a mixed-breed dog began following the client room to room. When my client went out to the dock on the lake to consider the property further, the dog went too, and seating himself next to the buyer, waited patiently by his side. They watched the boats go by. They looked like a postcard picture. When the client finished thinking, he got up and returned to me, dog in tow. Inquiring as to how he liked the property, he told me, "I love it! I want everything." I asked, "Do you want the furniture? The dog?" He said, "Yeah, I love this guy" (referring to the dog). The client would only purchase the home if the dog came with the house. I laughed to myself. Then I realized my client was quite serious; he wanted the dog that made the house feel like a home.

Having nothing to lose but a significant real estate deal, we drew up an offer and asked for the dog in the deal. I knew I had to present this offer in person, as it would never fly over the phone. I arranged a meeting with the listing agent because I needed to figure out how to persuade the other side so it was a win-win for them. What I mean is people negotiate differently based on how they are wired; no two people have the same abilities in the way they handle things. Some are direct and do not want any fluff. They want the direct numbers, such as how much will they make off the property after commission, while some grasp charts and PowerPoint presentations. By the same token, others simply want to know that the buyer's family will be similar to them and that they will enjoy the home as much as the sellers did. Sometimes when dealing with a couple who are opposites, it becomes necessary to deal with both parties and give them both what they need before the couple will see the value in the deal. Meeting everyone's needs can be tricky.

I explained the story to the sellers to bring a genuine person to the situation and called my client by his name rather than the "buyer" to the seller. I asked about their occupations and could tell how they were wired. I explained how leaving the dog here would not only bring joy to the buyer, but it would also go to a great home and the dog would be comfortable in its older ages not being moved. To our surprise, the owners accepted! When asked how it was that they were so willing to give up their dog, they replied, "He wasn't our dog to begin with. He just showed up when we bought the house." I learned two things that day: Always listen to the client's wish list (no matter how odd it might seem), and *everything* is negotiable.

By meeting face-to-face where I could better guage the sellers' reactions, I was able to create a strategy of using names and telling my client's personal story, which ultimately enabled me to close the deal. In addition to willingness to meet clients' needs and asking for what the client desires, a superior realtor and his team will anticipate frequently overlooked items in a transaction and plan accordingly.

Perfect real estate deals "by accident" are as scarce as hens' teeth. The planets rarely align just for one individual's real estate transaction, so unless a person values increased stress, it behooves one to hire a realtor with not only experience but also a solid plan. Determining what sets one realtor apart from the rest can be a daunting task. As a professional with over a decade of transactions under my belt, I recognize that many hairdressers have done more licensing training than some realtors have. Hanging out a shingle on the door does not ensure smooth, effective transactions. A realtor must choose to become the best in his or her field by consciously creating an environment of success. The realtor with a full-time team who understands preparing for every element of the transaction, and who furthermore, has superior knowledge of the market in the area, will be the best choice to help a person buy or sell a home.

FULL-TIME TEAM

We work hard full-time for our clients while some realtors work a day job and only "do" real estate on evenings and weekends. Clients list and sell their homes 24 hours a day, seven days a week. Part-time agents might miss opportunities to sell a home or help a client purchase one because that agent is not available at the right time. Our team works for our clients fully and efficiently so we do not miss a thing. We can go "above and beyond" what an average agent might do, such as meeting an appraiser at a home to explain the merits of the property. An agent with another full-time job might not be able to meet appraisers and inspectors to do the best for their client.

Consider that an average real estate transaction can have as many as 40 people involved with making a deal happen: town officials, title companies, attorneys, surveyors, inspectors, bankers, paralegals, movers and contractors. A seller is paying the real estate team to work for them, to meet with all of the people involved in the deal, not just sit at a desk at their day job, waiting to collect a fat commission check.

PREPARATION MEETING OPPORTUNITY

Since my team does not merely dabble in real estate, we have extensive experience that has allowed us to anticipate what might go wrong during a deal. We always recommend to our clients ways to circumvent those little disasters, such as a wood-destroying insect inspection that finds evidence of damage. Preparing and planning ahead removes surprises from the equation, and surprises can sway a buyer out of the deal. When listing a home, we recommend that our clients have the following inspections before they list:

- wood-destroying insects

- wells and septic systems
- radon gas
- buried oil tanks
- mold
- electrical/wiring
- roof
- appliances
- HVAC system

There is a phrase that "It is easier to deal with the enemy you know." Knowing about a home's pitfalls enables both sides of the deal to make educated decisions before ink has dried on a contract. When a seller has inspections ahead of time and knows beforehand what issues may be present in his/her home, he/she can then decide whether to repair them or to simply inform buyers that there are known defects. We treat each property the way that jewelers do diamonds (and each of our listings is a diamond); by listing the known defects in our diamonds, we allow the purchaser to decide which elements are most important. One neutralizes potentially combustible situations by not hiding flaws that could detonate in the middle of the deal.

APPRAISAL 101:
SUPERIOR KNOWLEDGE OF THE MARKET

In today's real estate market, we defend our client's sales price and usually have to fight off comparables used by the appraiser that may not be the right ones to use. It is a good idea for a realtor to bring his own comparables to meet the appraiser for a home he is listing. Recently, for example, I had brought some comparables to an appraisal appointment for which the appraiser, of course, had his too. His comparables were unacceptable. He had a list of previously sold comparables that had sold for much less than the norm in the area, and he was not even very familiar with the area. The appraiser had selected comparables that sold for lower amounts, not realizing that of the "comparable homes" he had chosen, one reeked of pets, one was part of a messy divorce where the couple just wanted to sell quickly, or that one sold at this price because there were no other homes on the market at that time. He had comparables that were estate sales and even one that was a short sale. Because I had studied appraisals and I knew about adjustments for condition, and the amounts used for this priced home, I fought for the fair number. This appraisal could have gone horribly wrong for everyone involved. Everyone involved in the deal knew the price was fair and knew that if this appraiser did not feel the same way, the bank would not finance the home. Worst of all, the buyer would not be able to purchase the home nor would the sellers, who were already packed up and under contract on another home move.

NEGOTIATION TO GET THE LISTING

As important as negotiation can be in purchasing or selling a property, sometimes negotiation becomes a major element in the listing process as well. Two brothers called me up to list their mother's home after she had passed away. The brothers were in town from Colorado and Michigan, respectively, to figure out their mother's estate. As we toured their mother's property, they both told stories about various rooms, and I could tell by their voices that since they had grown up here this house had a lot of meaning to them both. The brothers had learned of my reputation as an agent who fights tooth and nail for his client, so they hired me immediately after my appointment with them. As excited as I was for the opportunity to help their family handle the estate, the home oozed originality. By originality I mean almost everything was original, as in never had been updated (yep, baby blue- and yellow-tiled bathrooms, shag carpeting, wood paneling, and I'm pretty sure the furniture might have been original too). In a situation such as this, the agent has two choices: List the house as an estate sale in "as-is" condition or provide the client with an attainable option to allow them to maximize their profit.

Should they choose to maximize their profits, which I explained would be in their best interest, the brothers had their work cut out for them. They had limited time and a limited budget, so I put my team to the challenge. As always, we recommended hiring our preferred stager to come in to evaluate and obtained his recommendation on how to maximize the buyers' experience when they tour the home. Next, we analyzed the brothers' budget for the project and helped them to obtain multiple bids for the renovations, and negotiate repairs with local vendors based on our stager's recommendations. The project included the removal of carpets, refinishing of the hardwood floors, painting, fixtures, and rental of furniture and accessories. To create a win for the seller, we even negotiated that the vendors receive their money at closing.

Our home inspector preinspected the property so we could repair any items that would come up at the dreaded home inspection and had an appraisal done to get an idea of how an appraiser would be viewing this home in the bank's eye. We even provided the inspection report and appraisal to all interesed buyers who were considering making an offer.

We elected to premarket the property as a "Coming Soon" home and started the buzz in the town with our buyers through our office's exclusive websites and with the buyer brokers who represented so many other buyers. Before the open house, we already had two verbal offers from buyers, but experience told us that if we just got more buyers in to see the home, we could really drive up the price. When all was said and done, we had seven offers on the table of well over the asking price. The winning buyer had two young boys who will be growing up in the same rooms as our clients did, which made everyone involved happy.

Despite the many books written on the art of negotiating, a vast number of realtors lack the expertise required to go the extra mile for their clients. It might be easy for an inexperienced agent to convince his client to accept a lower offer that comes in or to help him offer money back from home inspections, but the distinguished realtor takes it upon himself to provide his client with value that exceeds their expectations. The distinguished realtor will negotiate every aspect of the transaction to a win-win scenario, whether it means standing firm on the price and reiterating the value to the buyer or asking for the family dog in the deal.

About Justin

Moving is never easy, but working with a seasoned professional who has a proven track record can mean the difference between a smooth transition and a major disaster. Justin's track record of success proves that he never settles for business as usual. Committed to always providing the highest level of service, he will professionally and effectively guide you through all aspects of buying or selling a house. Justin loves what he does and it shows. He has received numerous awards recognizing his success and the outstanding level of service he provides his clients and is consistently ranked as one of the top RE/MAX New Jersey real estate agents.

He is a RE/MAX Hall of Fame member, closing over $200 million in sales volume and ranking in the top 1 percent of RE/MAX realtors worldwide. All of this is made evident by his numerous designations, including the (CLHMS) Certified Luxury Home Marketing Specialist, (CRS) Certified Residential Specialist, Accredited Buyer's Representative (ABR), and e-Pro certification. Justin has received top awards, such as RE/MAX Platinum Club, and the Realtor.com Online Marketing Award of Excellence.

As someone who thrives on hard work, attention to detail and professionalism, Justin will strive to make you more than happy with your Morris county real estate needs. Justin is committed to providing you with the highest level of customer service to make your real estate transaction as smooth as possible. His attention to detail and commitment to excellence is what makes his clients customers for life.

With years of professional experience under his belt, Justin is expertly qualified to produce top results in residential and investment real estate in the Morris, Sussex and Warren counties of New Jersey.

Working with Justin Kiliszek as your New Jersey realtor, you'll have the advantage of personal, one-on-one attention, alongside dynamic web and e-mail resources. With superior expertise, years of experience and great connections in the industry, he looks forward to eliminating any hassles and stress on your end and to help you discover all that New Jersey real estate has to offer.

Top Producer RE/MAX, #5 Agent in New Jersey, Closed Sales 2009

Top Producer RE/MAX, Consistently Top 10 REMAX Agent in New Jersey, Closed Sales 2006-2010

Helped Over 400 Families Move

Over $200,000,000 in Sales Volume

CHAPTER 33

SELLING WITHOUT STRESS: TAKING THE ANXIETY OUT OF REAL ESTATE

BY RYAN SMITH

Selling your home can be extremely stressful—and with good reason. Your home is likely the biggest investment you have; that means there's a lot at stake and you want to do everything you can to make sure you get the biggest return possible. Make even one small mistake, and it could cost you thousands of dollars (not to mention months of time spent trapped in your home waiting for it to sell).

Yes, real estate is complicated. And unless you're a real estate professional, the home-selling process can be hard to understand and get right.

That's where I come in.

My name is Ryan Smith, and I'm a real estate agent in Temple, Texas. I started selling real estate at the end of 2006, which was an interesting time to get into the business. My first full year was 2007, the year real estate bubble burst—home prices began to fall and the big economic downturn began. Luckily, I still managed to do fairly well, selling somewhere around 30 houses my first year. My second year was even better, and by 2009, I was regularly selling about 100 homes a year. That lasted until this year…when I'm on track to sell somewhere between 175 and 200 houses.

Now, unless you live in or around Central Texas, my track record probably won't do you much good, at least not directly. However, I can offer you the same professional advice I offer my clients to make their home-selling experience as stress-free—and profitable—as possible.

Here are my tips for stress-free home-selling, wherever your home happens to be.

TIP #1: GOOD EXPECTATIONS

The right agent is essential to making home-selling stress free. And the best real estate agents out there are the ones who set good expectations.

By "good," I'm not talking about the kind of expectations where an agent tells you to expect your home will sell in a month, or expect that it is worth 10 or $20,000 more than other agents say.

I'm talking about expectations that are based in *reality*. Which, I realize, may not be especially fun or exciting. But good expectations, those that are based on *real* facts about your home and your market, go a long way in making what is otherwise a stressful process a lot easier.

The right real estate agent will explain everything that's going to happen, step by step, so that you can make the best, most informed decisions to help your home sell as quickly and fairly as possible. That means being brutally honest about what your home is worth in the current market. There are a lot of agents out there who will tell you your home is worth 10 or $20,000 more than it actually is just to get you to list with them.

I'm not one of them. I don't want to be the agent who, six months into the listing, has to go to my clients and tell them that they need to cut their price by twenty grand.

I would rather be real with them up front. I know my market better than anyone, and I won't pretend a house is worth more than it is, even if that means I'm going to miss out on business. Believe me, I have. I've seen plenty of real estate agents come in right behind me and say they can sell a house for a lot more than my estimate.

But those clients haven't been happy with the results. And you probably won't be either.

Speaking of expectations, some agents also mislead clients about how *quickly* they can sell a house. If you meet with a real estate agent who tells you your house is going to sell in a month, you might feel great at that moment. But every month that goes by when your house doesn't sell is probably going to add to your stress level.

Stress can even come at the end of the home-selling process, in the form of surprise costs. For example, in our market, most sellers are expected to pay the buyers' closing costs. But there are plenty of real estate agents who don't share that important information ahead of time. So while the amount of money they expect to make when they sell their home might make that agent look great, it also doesn't reflect reality. And that reality is, after closing costs, the number will be lower, because the sellers will be expected to pay for something they never saw coming.

I like to say that surprises are your worst enemy in real estate. So I do everything in my power to eliminate them.

My goal is to set realistic expectations from the get-go. It starts with the listing appointment. I'll be the first to admit, my listing appointments normally take longer than most agents, but this time is well spent. I go into vivid detail up front about each aspect of the process, so my clients know exactly what's going to happen (within reason of course!), how often we'll be communicating with them (at least weekly), how long sales in the area are taking, and most important, how much money my clients can expect to make when they finally sell their home.

By the time I leave, my sellers know *exactly what to expect*—and they can relax and trust the process. And when the contract comes in and I sit down with my clients at closing, 99 percent of the time we're right where I told them we were going to be.

That eliminates a lot of stress. Good expectations lead to great results and a smooth process.

TIP #2: SET THE STAGE FOR SUCCESS

When I sit down with my clients for that first meeting, we always focus on staging their home for success. "Staging," if you've never heard the term, means decorating your home in a specific way to appeal to the majority of buyers, so they can picture themselves living in your home. You want your home to appeal to as many buyers as possible, and that means setting up rooms to reflect what they're meant for (i.e., putting a dining set in the dining room as opposed to your kids' playhouse), replacing worn carpet and fixtures, repainting walls in neutral colors, making sure any outside garden areas are neat (and any plants are alive and healthy), and, above all, any inside rooms are *clear of clutter*.

"Decluttering" is by far the biggest challenge people face. I don't know how many times I've gone to a house and advised the homeowner to declutter, only to be told, "But I already did!" It's easy to understand: In your normal everyday life, you're not even aware of how much "stuff" you leave around the house. So you don't necessarily notice it, but anyone looking at the house with an eye toward buying it, will.

So trust me, if your realtor says you haven't decluttered, then you haven't decluttered.

At this point, you may be wondering why I recommend staging as a stress-buster. After all, it sounds like I'm adding more to your workload and stress level. But I have a saying: "The short-term easy leads to the long-term difficult, while the short-term difficult leads to the long-term easy." Staging is a perfect example of this.

And frankly, television is a big culprit here. Today's home buyers have come to expect homes that are for sale to look a certain way. Blame it on HGTV and shows like "Designed to Sell," but sellers want to be able to walk into a house and picture themselves living there. So if you're competing with homes that are valued about the same as yours that have been staged, guess which house will probably sell first, and for more money?

That's how staging eliminates stress. It sets your home up for eventual success. You can be confident your home is going to show well and compare well with the competition in your area. For that reason, I advise my clients to meet with me and go through my staging process to get their homes ready to list.

Beyond the decluttering problem, staging also means proactively addressing issues now rather than let buyers address them later. If you know your home has issues needing to be addressed, it's better to fix it them yourself and control the cost, rather than have the buyer ask you to fix it later. By failing to address these things up front, you put the buyer in the driver's seat on the potential costs of repair.

Sure, you can offer a buyer a credit to repaint your daughter's hot pink bedroom, but you can also paint it yourself for less before you list *and* attract all those buyers who would have been put off by a home that didn't seem "move-in ready."

The goal is to stage your house to a point where, when a potential buyer steps into your house, they can imagine themselves living there. They don't have to see a bunch of repairs they have to make or unusual décor choices they would have to change to be comfortable in your home. Instead, they can imagine their furniture, their stuff, their style all fitting into your house.

And what could be a bigger stress-buster than that?

TIP #3: KEEP IT LOCAL

This stress-busting tip isn't just for sellers. However, chances are, if you're selling your home, you're going to be buying a new one. And that means you'll need financing. My advice to keep this part of the process stress-free is to make sure that you go to a reputable, *local* lender.

Why local? Generally speaking, when you go far out of town to one of those giant financial institutions, often times you're nothing but a number to them. The process becomes extremely inefficient. You send your paperwork to people in New York, who may use a processor in Charlotte, North Carolina, who's using an underwriter in Lynchburg... all your information is getting bounced around like crazy. And in the process, stuff gets lost, you experience delays, and the bottom line is... more stress.

Proven local lenders, on the other hand, many times may have their underwriters and their processors in-house, so everything gets done under one roof, by one group of people who are used to working together as a team. Even better, they may actually know your name and your face and care about you as a human being. And the rates are usually competitive too.

Financing is one of biggest stressors I see, but with a good local lender, one who does only mortgages and doesn't deal with car notes or things like that, the process can be much smoother.

TIP #4: YOU DESERVE GOOD SERVICE

Finally, your real estate agent is the key to understanding everything that goes on in the process of selling your house. He or she should communicate with you regularly and keep you informed of everything regarding the process and the timelines, including what to expect when you finally get out of your house and how much money you need to bring to the table when you buy a new one.

Some real estate agents do go the extra mile to provide a stress-free experience, and I'm proud to be one of them in my market. For example, I've got my own moving truck, so after selling a home, my clients can use it to move their household goods for free. I also have a huge list of helpful items available to my clients to help make the selling and staging process simple, including commercial grade carpet cleaners, paint sprayers, weed-eaters, lawn mowers, and plenty of staging materials in place...all to help this process be as stress-free as possible.

The bottom line is, when it comes to your home, you deserve the best. And that might mean shopping around for the best, most helpful (and yes, most brutally honest!) real estate agent in your market. So don't look for the person who promises you the highest price and the fastest closing. Instead, look for a real estate agent who can be honest enough to provide good and clear expectations, help you stage your house to sell in your market, and guide you to the right professionals to help with every aspect of the process, including any financing needs you might have.

Those are the best tips I can offer to make the selling process stress-free—unless you happen to live in Bell County, Texas. If that's the case, and you really want to sell your home without stress, all you need to do it pick up the phone and give me a call.

About Ryan

Ryan Smith has always possessed an innate interest in real estate. Ryan believes there is nothing better than the good fortune to be passionate about one's work. His top priority is helping his clients achieve their goals while taking the stress out of their home selling process.

Originally, from Indianapolis, Indiana, Ryan moved to Clearwater, Florida, to study and play basketball at Clearwater Christian College. Prompted by the 9/11 tragedy, he left college to join the U.S. Army where he served five years as a noncommissioned officer with two combat deployments to the Middle East. His military service and tours in Iraq, Ryan says, "put life and challenges into perspective." Ryan continued his college education in business management while in the Army, but when he returned to the United States in 2006, he chose to earn his real estate license instead. Although Ryan might modestly tell you that his business's growth and success are part luck and part skill, his formula for success obviously works because his real estate business is booming in the Temple-Belton, Texas, area near Austin.

Ryan's exceptional focus and drive have naturally led to his goal this year of $30 million in sales and 250 homes sold. He has also earned a reputation as a home-staging guru in the Temple-Belton, Texas, area for his use of home staging to help clients' homes sell faster.

Ryan is a member of the RE/MAX International Hall of Fame and the RE/MAX International Chairman's Club. He received the following distinctions for 2012 alone: Listed in "Top 100" Individual RE/MAX Agents in the United States (#83); RE/MAX of Texas Top 20 Individual Agents in the State of Texas, 2nd Qtr. (#5); RE/MAX Vanguard Council Top 20 Agents, 2nd Qtr. (#1); RE/MAX Vanguard Council Top 20 Agents, 1st Qtr. (#7); Temple Area Builders Association "Realtor of the Year;" and #1 Residential Real Estate Agent in Overall Sales Volume and Units Sold for the Temple-Belton MLS in 2012.

Ryan is a member of the Temple-Belton Board of Realtors, the National Association of Realtors and the Texas Association of Realtors. He has also volunteered for many local organizations and is an active member of the Temple Bible Church.

Ryan and his wife, Justine, have been married since May 2007. They have one daughter, Sloan, and are excited to announce they are expecting another child later this year. In his free time, Ryan is an avid college football fan who loves to watch games whenever he can.

Contact Ryan Smith at www.ryansmithhomes.com or www.ryansmithravingfans.com.

CHAPTER 34

7 CRITICAL MARKETING FACTORS FOR YOUR HOME SALE

BY ALEX SAENGER

So you're thinking about selling your home? Take a minute to think about what it takes from a marketing perspective to sell a home. It takes as many prospective buyers to see your home as possible. That translates into eyeballs that actually see your home. And that starts online for 93 percent of all home buyers in today's market.

As a professional realtor, my job can roughly be broken into four main categories, each taking about 25 percent of my time when selling your home. These include: marketing, negotiating, contingencies, and settlement. Finding a buyer is 100 percent contained in the marketing component. It is by far one of the most important parts of my work, and finding a buyer starts with great photos, gets you maximum online exposure, draws in prospective buyers from all sources, and gets eyeballs into the house so those prospective buyers can fall in love with your house and put in a great offer. While there are many factors to consider, seven critical factors jump out as the most important for you to consider when selling your home.

FACTOR #1: PROFESSIONAL PHOTOS

Have you searched for a home online lately? As a home seller, you are probably also a buyer. And chances are you have been poking around the internet looking at possible places you could move into. Have you ever noticed that some properties have horrible photos, or in some cases, none at all? What was your impression of those properties? Were you interested to find out more, or were you just happy to move on to find that really promising home that is worth your time to visit? Chances are, if you are like most home buyers, and even most real estate agents, you focused your time and attention on the homes that fit all your criteria (number of bedrooms, bathrooms, lot size, etc.) but that also looked great online. The houses that had professional photos with perfect lighting made you stop and take time to look through every photo. They made you stop long enough to add the house to your favorites, email your agent, or even pick up the phone, and tell that agent you want to see the house right away!

So if that was your experience, isn't that what you would want potential buyers to experience when looking for a home just like yours? Of course it is. And if you haven't been looking for a home, I bet this is what you want everyone who sees your house online to do—that is stop, look and make an appointment to see your home in person. If a buyer doesn't come to your home, they can't fall in love with it and make you a real offer to purchase, let alone multiple buyers to drive up the price in a bidding war.

So when selling your home, the number-one marketing factor you need is to have professional photos taken and use them in everything you do to market the home. From uploading to the MLS, virtual tour, print brochures, postcards, Facebook and more, professional photos are an absolute must!

FACTOR #2: INTERACTIVE VIRTUAL TOUR WITH STATISTICS REPORTING

Once you have professional photos, you are ready to have a professional virtual tour put together. What is a virtual tour? It is an interactive online presentation of your property that anyone looking for a home can use to experience your home online. It is a series of photos, images and even panoramic/moving photos/movie clips that tell the story of what it would be like to live in your home. It can have music or narration to set the mood, and give critical information about the agent you are working with so the buyer knows who to call to see the house in person. With full-screen high dynamic range (HDR) images that let the viewer see details, including views through windows, the virtual tour is essential in setting the right tone for your condo, townhouse, single-family house, vacation home or other property.

There are many solutions in the marketplace. Many are good, but the best one I have found is by Real Tour Vision. I use this solution on all my properties, for sale or for rent. I believe in this technology so much, I opened up my own virtual tour business based on using this technology and it has proved to be a successful marketing tool for over 3,500 properties personally and for those my company (BakerB Solutions) serves.

Additionally, this solution allows me to automatically update my clients every week with statistics, graphs and information that shows you how many people have visited the home online. It tells you what websites they are coming from and what pictures they spent the most time viewing. These statistics are very important to help us understand if we are getting the kind of traffic we expect online. Whether we have great traffic or little traffic, these numbers tell us something about what we need to do to get the home sold outside of marketing.

FACTOR #3: SINGLE-PROPERTY WEBSITE WITH SIGN RIDER

Now that we have great photos and an outstanding virtual tour, we are ready to transform that into something usable. After all, marketing is not something geeks do well. You don't want to have to enter some cryptic website to see images of a property, right? So why do that? Take that virtual tour and transform it into a single property website. One of the easiest ways to do this is to secure a web domain specific to the property (something like: www.14322NightHawk.com). Now this website can be used in all marketing, from print marketing (brochures, fliers, postcards, business cards, print/magazine advertisements, etc.) to online marketing (social media websites like Facebook and Twitter, blogs, online advertisements, websites, even Craigslist).

I take my single-property websites even further. I take that web domain and put it on a sign rider that hangs out in front of the house. But I don't stop there: I also add photos and a QR code to the sign. This allows people driving by the house to see the web domain and type it in their computer when they get home or at a stoplight. For those on foot, or who stop at the property without an agent, they can pull up the virtual tour by typing in the web domain or scanning the QR code with their phone or tablet. The virtual tour, photos and information are pulled right into their device as they are standing in front of the property or sitting in their car. How powerful is that? I can't tell you how many times I get calls from prospective buyers who are sitting in front of one of my listings looking at the photos on their iPad while they are talking to me on the phone. This is powerful stuff!

FACTOR #4: ACCURATE SUBMISSION TO REGIONAL MLS SYSTEM

This point goes almost without saying. But why is it so important other than the obvious? Accurate information from the start is critical. Visiting a home and getting information firsthand from the homeowner and actually seeing the home is paramount. Public tax records are filled with inaccurate information and without verifying everything about your house, you could make a costly mistake when marketing your home by misrepresenting what you are actually selling.

Once you have the information correct, and have your agent enter it into your local MLS, most of these systems will take that information and propagate it out to thousands of other websites, such as broker websites and the like. Other realtors who have buyers will use this system to pull homes they think are a good fit for their clients. I use this to set up automatic searches for my buyers so the system will automatically notify them when fresh properties hit the market or when prices drop to fit within their budget. These systems are super powerful, but if you have a four-bedroom house that is entered as a three bedroom, all those automated searches set up for a four bedroom will miss your listing, and the buyer most likely will too. Entering and marketing accurate information is critical.

FACTOR #5: SYNDICATION EXPOSURE ENGINE

Outside of your MLS systems and real estate broker websites, there are a number of third-party websites that are gaining increasing popularity among tech-savvy buyers. These real estate portal sites include Zillow, Trulia, Realtor.com, Homes.com, HomeSeeker, HotPads, and Oodle to name a few. These sites pull information from the MLS but can be augmented with additional photos, information and separate virtual tour submissions. You see, most of these sites will only pull basic information and just a few photos from the MLS. They typically do not pull virtual tours or additional photos.

In addition, they can lag in time to get this information from these other systems. So in some cases, it is actually prudent to manually enter this information days before it is pulled. This also gives you a head start over other properties that have not been pulled yet.

Proactively syndicating your property's information, photos and virtual tour is an added step you can make sure your agent does to maximize your potential to be the first property those prospective buyers see for your first weekend on the market.

FACTOR #6: SOCIAL MEDIA MARKETING

Oh, so you've heard of Facebook? Well, so have half of all Americans, each with their own Facebook account. And there is this little thing called Twitter, too. You've heard of that also? Have you considered these social media outlets as prime sources of getting the word out about your home that is for sale? If you haven't, you should.

How do you do this exactly? It all starts with thinking about who is most likely going to move into the house you live in and are trying to sell? It is most likely someone like you, your neighbors or your friends. And who do you have relationships with on Facebook? It's all these same types of people. Using your virtual tour link and your single-property website, you can share the fact that you are selling your house with everyone you are connected to on Facebook. After all, they have friends that may very well be looking to find a home in your neighborhood. So why not save them the extra step and just tell them about your house and invite them to contact your realtor for a showing? Or better yet, have them share the link with their friends and keep the cycle going. Eventually it will hit that buyer within 2 or 3 degrees of separation.

Another way to use Facebook is to take out a Facebook advertisement. They are very inexpensive, yet can be very specifically targeted so they don't cost a lot of money. I have used this technique very effectively with properties that had difficulty selling by the traditional means. That is what tuned me in on what a powerful tool this can be. In fact, my clients even appreciate how powerful this tool is. I have a video testimonial online at YouTube.com/AlexSaenger where you can see him stating that 7 percent of all hits on his virtual tour came from Facebook. Compare that with the fact that nationally only 4 percent of homes sell because of an open house, and you can see why this really matters.

FACTOR #7: OLD FASHIONED SNAIL MAIL DONE RIGHT

With all this great technology, one thing still stands true: If they don't know about it, they won't act on it. In this case, we are talking about the fact that your home is available. Most buyers that are actively looking are going to know about your house when it hits the internet, either from their agent or searching online on their own. But there are still quite a few people who wish they could move up into a house like yours or are maybe renting for a couple years before making the decision to buy. So what if we were to proactively approach these people with information to entice them to consider your home? That is when a postcard advertising your home makes a great presence.

By specifically targeting renters in your neighborhood, or move-up prospects (i.e., people in townhouses in your neighborhood who want single-family homes in the same neighborhood and school district, etc.), we can take the initiative to show them how much payments would be on your home (by working with a lender who can do the math given current market lending rates), and make 200 to 500 postcards specifically targeted work wonders. That is the way you make old fashioned snail mail work for you the smart way.

About Alex

Alex is a native to the Washington, DC, Metro Area and Montgomery County, Maryland, where he has resided for more than 40 years. He is a graduate of Walt Whitman High School in Bethesda, Maryland. After graduating high school, Alex received his Bachelor of Science from the Rochester Institute of Technology (RIT) in applied mathematics/statistics. Later, he obtained his Master's of Science in information management with a concentration in marketing from Marymount University. He spent time early in his career in the information technology industry, with telecommunications companies, and then participated as a founding member of a successful start-up. Recognizing his skills in marketing, Alex started a marketing firm called BakerB Solutions (www.BakerB.com) that eventually focused on real estate marketing. The company eventually became a strong provider of virtual tours and real estate marketing, offering unique services that other competitors did not.

In 2005, Alex obtained his Maryland real estate license and worked with leading realtors in the area. Since then, Alex has learned the industry from the roots up, becoming a top producer for his real estate broker, Avery Hess Realtors in Maryland. Combining a unique set of information technology and marketing skills makes Alex different than most realtors. He brings to the table a unique and successful combination of assets that his clients benefit from on every transaction. For more information on Alex, visit www.AlexSaenger.com, connect with him on www.facebook.com/AlexSaenger or visit his video channel at www.YouTube.com/AlexSaenger.